Joyce Lamont's

Favorite
Minnesota
Recipes

& Radio
Memories

WITH **Linda Larsen**
FOREWORD BY
Sue Zelickson, WCCO Radio

Voyageur Press

First published in 2008 by Voyageur Press, an imprint of MBI Publishing
Company, 400 First Avenue North, Suite 300, Minneapolis, MN 55401 USA

Voyageur Press titles are also available at discounts in bulk quantity for
industrial or sales-promotional use. For details write to Special Sales Manager
at MBI Publishing Company, 400 First Avenue North, Suite 300,
Minneapolis, MN 55401 USA.

To find out more about our books, join us online at www.voyageurpress.com.

ISBN-13: 978-0-7603-3291-7

Editor: Margret Aldrich
Designer: LeAnn Kuhlmann

Printed in China

Lamont, Joyce, 1916-
  Joyce Lamont's favorite Minnesota recipes & radio memories / by Joyce
Lamont and Linda Larsen ; with a foreword by Sue Zelickson.
    p. cm.
  ISBN-13: 978-0-7603-3291-7 (comb bound)
1. Lamont, Joyce, 1916- 2. Cookery, American—Midwestern style. 3.
Cookery—Minnesota. 4. WCCO (Radio station : Minneapolis, Minn.)—
History. 5. Radio broadcasters—Minnesota—Biography. I. Larsen, Linda,
1958- II. Title. III. Title: Favorite Minnesota recipes and radio memories.
TX715.2.M53L35 2008
641.59776—dc22
                                                2007039561

CONTENTS

FOREWORD

Her first time on air was an accident, she never had a speech lesson, and she didn't like microphones, but Joyce Lamont had a perfect voice for radio, and after writing copy and commercials it seemed only natural that she was pressed into service to read them on the air.

If you were a WCCO listener during the past sixty years, you will most likely remember *Dayton's Musical Chimes,* the Dayton's Reporter (with no name), *Special Events News,* and Farm-City Days—where Joyce Lamont was the first and only woman in the big boys' broadcasters club.

I remember them clearly, as well as her *Today's Best Buys,* where she reported on products and ingredients and shared listeners' recipes in a newsletter that she mailed out to twenty-five thousand subscribers at the end of each month.

For over forty years, Joyce arrived at the WCCO station at four o'clock in the morning and was the soothing voice that got us to the school bus on time, told us what was happening in the community, and shared her food knowledge with us . . . *and* made a mug of cocoa for Sid Hartman every morning when he arrived and said, "Where's my chocolate?"

Her Cocoa Syrup recipe for hot chocolate is included in this book, along with others you will want to make immediately. Some of the three hundred tried-and-true recipes that will bring back memories are Creamy Cole Slaw, Rumaki Spread, Guacamole Dip, Tomato Avocado Salad, and Cheese Crackers.

Joyce Lamont was honored by the Museum of Broadcasting Hall of Fame as a Pioneer Broadcaster, even though she says that so much of her career depended on luck. In 1989, Joyce moved to KLBB with her friends Howard Viken and Chuck Lilligren and kept the food lines open until 2003, when she retired from that station. She continues doing commercials and giving talks, however, so we can still hear that wonderful voice.

In looking back on her radio career, Joyce says she feels like she won the lottery, but in truth it was all of her listeners who were the winners.

—Sue Zelickson
Food Editor, WCCO Radio

Sue Zelickson is the host of WCCO Radio's Food for Thought *and writes the "Sue Z Says" column in* Minnesota Monthly *magazine.*

4

JOYCE LAMONT
WCCO

Joyce Lamont's first publicity photo. "I was kind of shy," she says.
"I never dreamed of speaking in front of a lot of people."
(Courtesy of the Pavek Museum)

PREFACE

I remember growing up in Chanhassen in the 1970s. The radio was always on when I got up in the morning, and it was always tuned to WCCO-AM. My sisters and I could hear the announcer chatting about something or another as we got ready for breakfast. We didn't have to get dressed before we ate, but we did have to comb our hair and put on robes and fuzzy slippers. When school was in session, on good days there were scrambled eggs or pancakes for breakfast; on bad days there was a pot of Roman Meal cereal burbling on the stove.

Every morning as we walked into the warm and bright kitchen, the richest, smoothest voice on the radio greeted us—it was Joyce Lamont. It didn't matter what she was talking about: I just loved listening. Joyce's voice was heard by thousands of listeners in the Twin Cities region for more than fifty years as she shared recipes and household hints. Many of those listeners, including my mother, subscribed to her monthly newsletter filled with the best of her offerings.

We all lined up at the breakfast bar to eat. My seat was against the wall, right where my mother kept newspaper clippings of recipes and missives from Joyce. I would stealthily read recipes as I ate, picturing how each might look when finished. (Yes, I know that reading at the table was impolite, but this rudeness turned into a career!)

I've always loved cooking and baking, so I stopped everything to listen to the recipes Joyce read on the air. (My husband didn't care about the recipes, but as a boy he would stop and listen too just because her voice was so soothing and beautiful.) I now temporarily have in my possession my mother's blue three-ring binder with all of Joyce's recipes inside, the dates typed on every sheet, starting with January 10, 1971. Most of the sheets are well worn and dog-eared, now preserved in vinyl covers, with notes and comments. None is less than "very good."

I had the idea for this book while watching a rerun of the *Mary Tyler Moore Show* on TV. I was working on another cookbook and suddenly thought of the 1970s, WCCO's heyday. Joyce Lamont, her gorgeous voice, and her wonderful recipes made an instant connection in my mind, and I contacted my agent, Barb Doyen, immediately. Barb agreed to call Joyce because I was too nervous, and I waited anxiously by the phone. Then Barb called back: Joyce was interested and would talk to me! It was my turn next, and I worked up my courage to call her. The phone rang twice, and then there was that rich, smooth voice! It took me a second to find mine, and I introduced myself.

The first time I met Joyce, my husband Doug and I took her to lunch at the Nicollet Island Inn in Minneapolis. We walked up to the hostess, and Joyce said, "Three for lunch please, under the name Lamont." The twenty-something waitress made a check in the big reservations book, then stopped and asked, "'Would that be *Joyce* Lamont?" Her appeal extends across generations, even years after she has been off the air. And for good reason.

When we dropped her off that first time, we drove away in silence. At a stop sign, we looked at each other and both screamed, "I can't believe it—that was Joyce Lamont!" "She just agreed to write a cookbook with me!" I exclaimed. And so we began, sifting through her thousands and thousands of recipes, selecting a good representation that embodies the 1960s and 1970s, and talking about her memories.

Joyce and I had an immediate connection. She loves animals, as do I, and we shared stories of our pets—hers of Rex, whom you'll read about in a bit, and mine of Schafee (my family's German shepherd) and Muffin (my first cat). We found that we both like to be early to appointments and that we really hate broadcasters who don't enunciate. She is the consummate lady, always dressed in a suit, with jewelry, heels, and a purse.

Working with Joyce has been a wonderful experience. I could listen to her talk all day, and I have been lucky enough to listen to her voice for hours as we've met to discuss this book over lunches and dinners. I have a few voice messages from her on my phone, and I don't think I'll ever erase them.

Until I started working on this book, I didn't realize that many of my favorite recipes came from Joyce. Treasure Chest Bars (page 169) were a staple at my house every Christmas, Cheese Crackers (page 25) were always served with chili, and Bean and Bacon Soup (page 58) is an inexpensive winner that tastes nothing like the canned variety. Try serving it with Wheat Germ Corn Bread (page 150). I love Joyce's method for cooking corn on the cob, and Beef–Cottage Cheese Pie (page 89) is still a soothing comfort on chilly fall evenings. And that's just a small sample of the treats in store for you!

You'll notice that the recipes don't skimp on butter, sugar, eggs, and red meats. This was the way we ate in the 1960s and 1970s. And I think it's notable that obesity rates in this country were much lower then than they are now, even with all of our low-fat, fake-fat, sugar-substitute, lean-meat eating. There's something in our food that's killing us. I think it's time to go back to the way we used to eat: whole foods, simply prepared, with no altered or artificial ingredients. I made a few changes in the recipes, mostly for changes in can sizes, cutting down the salt, and food safety reasons. If you're concerned about fat content, you can certainly substitute low-fat or nonfat ingredients for the cream, cheese, milk, and butter in these recipes. But I suggest you try these classic recipes the way they were written to truly savor the taste of home.

Enjoy this book: it's been a labor of love! And I've loved every minute of it.

—Linda Larsen

Linda Larsen is a cookbook author and home economist who has created and tested recipes for major food companies like Pillsbury and Malt-O-Meal since 1987. She is the Guide for Busy Cooks at About.com. Her books include The Everything Meals for a Month Cookbook *and* The Everything Quick and Easy, 30-Minute, 5-Ingredient Cookbook. *She lives in Minneapolis.*

INTRODUCTION

THE LIFE AND TIMES OF AN ACCIDENTAL RADIO STAR

"**N**o, I'm not doing that again!"

"Yes, Joyce, you are. We need a woman for this program, and you have the perfect voice for the radio."

That was part of the conversation I had with WCCO radio's station manager after my first experience speaking on the air. My first time on the air was an accident. I was hired by WCCO radio to do continuity work and write ads. But one day during lunch hour (I was too busy to eat lunch), one of the engineers came into my office and asked me to read something on the air. A client wanted a woman's voice for an ad, and I was the only female at the station. I said "NO, I don't have a good enough voice and probably wouldn't sound very good." But he persisted!

"Everybody's out to lunch, there's no one else around, and I have to have this done for a meeting at 1:30," he said. So, reluctantly, I went into the studio and read a line or two and went back to my desk.

After a few minutes, the station manager walked in and said, "I was listening to the monitor upstairs, and I heard you doing the commercial spot for Joe. It was good! You have a nice voice for the air. We'll be calling on you." I replied, "I don't like being on the air. I've never had a speech lesson! I don't like microphones. Please forget it."

He said, "But we *need* you. You are *writing* the copy. Why can't you *read* it?" And I said, "Because I don't want to." He just grinned at me and said, as he walked out, "We'll be calling on you." So I was reluctantly pressed into service, and the rest is history!

Several years ago, I was honored with the best award of my life: "Pioneer Broadcaster of the Year," given by the Minnesota Broadcasters Association. Only one thing bothered me a bit—that word "pioneer." It made me think of the famous Grant Wood painting, *American Gothic,* the man with the pitchfork and his wife whose face would sour milk. That's not exactly a flattering image! But I guess I was a pioneer of sorts.

I mentioned this nostalgia and dissatisfaction with forced change to a friend who said, "Look at it this way. Remember when you started at WCCO? Remember the theme then? Announcers (all MALE announcers) said it at every station break, and they all tried to sound like Edward R. Murrow: 'Good Neighbor to the Great Northwest!' Now, what is the theme at KLBB?" The theme at KLBB, just a few years ago, was "Cool, Baby!"

Radio was much more important in the 1940s and 1950s than now; it was the only connection to the outside world for a lot of people. We heard broadcasts and music with the family in the morning before going to school, soap operas during the day, and comedy shows at night after supper.

Yes, things have changed. I certainly don't regret the years. I'm thankful for them and the opportunity to work with dozens of talented people and thousands of great listeners.

WOMAN IN A MAN'S WORLD

From the start, I was the only woman in this big boys' club of 'CCO broadcasters. There were other women in the office, of course—secretaries and receptionists and so on—but I was the only one on the air.

I didn't get any special treatment—that's for sure. And because I wasn't trained in broadcasting, whenever something important was going on, a man would come along to oversee the technical end of things. Women were low on the totem pole in radio. It was tough to take because a job would open and you knew you wouldn't even be considered for it because you were a woman.

Here's a story to illustrate the status of women in radio in the early days. On the *Dayton's Musical Chimes* show, there would be a musical introduction, then Howard Viken would say, "Good Morning. This is *Dayton's Musical Chimes*. I'm Howard Viken, and here's your Dayton's Reporter." I never had a name. That was a deliberate ploy by the store's advertising department. They wanted the reporter's voice to sound the same, day after day, year after year. The program promoted records from Dayton's large record department. For one hour, we'd play snippets of the songs, and I'd talk about the singer and the songs. My first time, a bit of the tune was played, and the engineer said, "Now talk!"

Whenever I went outside the station, my gender wasn't really an issue. It was overshadowed by the fact that I was from WCCO, and 'CCO was a powerhouse. I ended up driving tractors and everything else you could imagine. Once they had me pose for a shot, pretending I was milking a cow. I pulled up the stool, and my goodness, that cow was big! I gave her a quick pat and told her, "Don't blame me." I posed for the shot, and then I got away from there as gracefully and as quickly as I could.

But I suppose my gender did influence my career. I'm best known for covering the more "female" areas: recipes, helpful hints, and such. Luckily, those were the topics I was good at, so it worked out fine.

EARLY YEARS

I was born in North Dakota. My father was a physician; the medical director in charge of San Haven, the state's tuberculosis sanitarium. In fact, he founded the hospital. My early years were spent helping my mother around the house and enjoying life on the bucolic grounds of the hospital.

One of the most important beings in my life was my dog Rex, who was a birthday present when I was five. Like most small children, I loved to pick up small animals—any little ball of fur I could find. The doorbell rang on my birthday, a cold February day, and there was Mr. MacDonald, a renter from one of my dad's farms, all bundled up in a buffalo coat and gloves, dressed like a policeman from Winnipeg. From his cavernous pocket, he pulled a tiny bundle of fluff. It was my birthday present, Rex! He had told my parents, "We have to get that child a dog."

He was a tiny little puppy—so adorable—a Spitz mix, with a black and white coat and those little ears that perk up and then hang over. He was so little that he fit in my hands! I was only five, and I was so overwhelmed that I just sobbed with joy. My parents were surprised and reassured me, "Don't cry dear, he's all yours," and things like that. Well, I loved him from the first moment. We grew up together, Rexie and I, and we were inseparable.

Dr. Lamont moved our family (my mother, my two sisters, and me) to Duluth when we reached high-school age. I graduated from Denfeld High School and attended Duluth Junior College, then went with the family to Minneapolis when Dad retired. I attended the University of Minnesota and graduated with a BA degree, majoring in English and Journalism.

I visited the family often during my college years, and Rex was always so glad to see me. When I graduated, I came home. Rex was eighteen by then, a very advanced age for a little dog. I asked my mother where he was, and she told me he was outside lying in the sun and mentioned that he wasn't feeling well. So I hurried to him.

I gathered him in my arms, said his name, and petted him. He put his head in my hand, heaved a big sigh, and then he died.

He had waited for me. He held on so he could see me one more time, and then he died happily. Oh, my, how I cried then too! To this day, whenever I tell that story, tears come to my eyes. Animals are so important to me; part of the proceeds of my second cookbook went to the organization Canine Companions for Independence. It's my fervent belief that animals should be treated well and taken care of, and adopted out to loving homes.

THE START

Fresh out of college, I got a job working for Batten Barton Durstine & Osborn, writing advertising copy for print media. I also wrote commercials for *Let's Pretend,* a radio show broadcast from CBS in New York City. Then I moved to McCann Ericson, where I wrote commercials for Pillsbury, Twin City Federal, Gluecks, and others.

One day a friend called and invited me to lunch. I met her, we sat down, and we started talking about our jobs. I mentioned that I liked writing for TV and radio much more than writing so-called "space copy" for newspapers and magazines. She said, "Hey, that reminds me. My cousin is leaving her job at WCCO. She just resigned yesterday and is going back to the university to get her master's degree. Why don't you go over there and apply for the job?"

"Okay, I will," I said. And I did. I when I walked out of the station that day in 1946, I was WCCO's Continuity Director. Talk about lucky! What if my friend hadn't asked me to lunch that day or if the line had been busy?

After that infamous time I recorded my first commercial, I filled in on another show. Dr. William A. O'Brien Sr. was the host for a health program at WCCO and had unexpectedly died a few days before. I was chatting informally with the announcer, talking about my memories of Dr. O'Brien and what he meant to me. That seemed to seal the deal—I was going to be on the air!

Soon after that experience, Dayton's needed a replacement for the woman on its *Musical Chimes* program—7:30 each morning, Mondays through Saturdays. The Dayton's Reporter at that time, the elegant Belle Winston, had contracted laryngitis, and I substituted for her. Belle was a buyer for Dayton's. There were a few women, called "Sound-Alikes," who took over the job when she was on vacation; no one knew the difference because their voices were all so similar. I joined their ranks.

When she resigned later in the year, I was asked to replace her. Hundreds of people had wanted that job, but the voice of Dayton's Reporter had to match hers, and mine resembled hers most closely. So much of our careers depend on luck! This program led to my other appearances on WCCO Radio—including *Special Events News* (which I originated), interviews, music programs, and food shows.

Special Events was a segment announcing events of general interest. They included things like church bazaars, pancake breakfasts, and turkey dinners. They were aired at 8:25, 8:45, 9:15, 9:45, and 10:10 each morning, Monday through Friday, on the *Howard Viken Show*, at the same times on Saturdays on the *Steve Cannon Show*, and between 7:30 and 10:00 a.m. Sundays. There was a long list of events we couldn't promote, which included sales at shopping centers, political rallies or fundraisers, biased talks, committee meetings, religious services, car auctions, teen dances, or paper, glass, or tin drives. The announcements had to be relevant and important to the community. This was an assignment I didn't like much at first; the items seemed unimportant.

Then one day I got a call from a man who said he was Minnesota's President of the Lions Club. He asked me to go that afternoon with a group of Lions Club members to the University of Minnesota.

I couldn't go because I was on the air, but I asked what the occasion was and why they wanted me there. He said, "We have a check to give to the University Hospital—a big check for the Children's Eye Bank—and you helped raise most of the money."

I asked, "How did I do that?" And he answered, "Remember all those pancake breakfasts you announced for us on WCCO? You got a lot of people to come to them, and all the dollars went to our fund. The check is made out for $100,000!"

From then on, I never thought of those little announcements as "trivial." Many great and inspiring projects are supported by these events, and all of them needed publicity. It's right they were aired on a regular basis.

Joyce on the air in 1950. "By this time, I was beginning to think that this accidental career just might work out after all," she reflects.

MUSICAL CHIMES

Dayton's Musical Chimes (later renamed *First Bank Notes* when the sponsorship changed) was considered one of the top jobs for women in radio at the time. It was not a demanding job—or at all creative. It was a matter of reading prepared copy and doing some interviews now and then. Of course, I was nervous at the beginning. But I found my stride and overcame it—I had to!

That show, which had an incredible 69 percent audience share at its most popular, had listeners from many states, including the Dakotas, Wisconsin, and Iowa. When it began, you first heard theme music, called "Good News." That was played by Ramona Gerhardt on the Wurlitzer. Yes, we had a big pipe organ right in the studio! Then Howard would give his intro.

Remember, my name wasn't used then—I was the "Dayton's Reporter." That anonymity had some interesting consequences. When I made a personal appearance, for instance at the Minnesota State Fair, this happened repeatedly. An elderly man would come up to me, all smiles, and say, "Know what? You put me on the school bus every morning when I was just a little shaver on the farm. When I heard you start that second song, I knew it was time to catch the bus." I tried many times to explain that the show was on the air for many years and that there were many "Dayton's Reporters!" They didn't believe me, so I stopped trying to explain. I thanked them, and I'm sure, as they walked away, they said, "She's quite well preserved. Must be at least one hundred!"

Eventually, I replaced Darragh Aldrich, WCCO's Women's Director, on her daily afternoon shows and held that position until 1989. I wrote the scripts for *Quiz of the Twin Cities*, *Sunday Prelude* (which highlighted music recorded by outstanding college and university choirs), *Red River Valley Gang*, and numerous commercials. In the 1980s, I started a show called *On the Air, Then and Now*, which included time for listeners' questions and answers.

There's an enormous amount of work being on the radio, because the job is highly competitive. I had to do lots of reading from all sources, because I had to know what was going on in the world.

THE LADY BEHIND THE VOICE

There's no rest for radio personalities! Every single day for more than forty years, I woke up at three o'clock in the morning and was at the station by four. Even before I went on the air, continuity work was very demanding. Continuity is another word for "scripts." In those days, everything was scripted and timed.

There was much preparation work to be done for each show; even station breaks were carefully written and timed with a stopwatch! You get used to such a rigorous schedule, and to this day I'm never late for an appointment. If you're late for a job on the radio, you're no longer employed on the radio!

I'm sometimes asked if I ever had to change my voice or way of speaking. I was told to change my voice range to a lower pitch and to raise the level. Also, when you're on the air, whether in television or radio, you must enunciate and be careful of certain sounds. So many times, the sibilants, or *s* sounds, lead to mistakes.

When I first went on the air at WCCO, I asked the head of the speech department at the University of Minnesota, Dr. E. W. Ziebarth (also known as "EZ"), how I sounded. I was such a neophyte, and I needed an expert opinion. He was kind (he always was!) and said, "You're doing very well, Joyce. Just watch your consonantal energy." I thanked him, promised that I would, and walked away saying to myself, "What in the world is the man talking about?"

Later on, I asked one of EZ's former speech students what consonantal energy means. She said, "Oh, that means pronouncing the final consonant of a word. A lot of people don't do that. They'll say 'northwess' instead of 'northwest' or 'doan' instead of 'don't'—not pronouncing the final *t*." That's how you learn as you go!

I never married. I dated Maynard Speece for a time. I came *very* close to the altar a couple of times, but it would have been a terrible mistake for me. I have no regrets and have enjoyed my life immensely.

FARM VISITS

For years, the WCCO team visited farms as part of our farm-reporting program. The program began in 1942 when Larry Haeg, who had worked in an agricultural extension office and later became General Manager of WCCO, hired specialized reporters who broadcasted live crop checks, weather information, and prices for beef, corn, and other commodities. Reporters included James Hilgendorf, or "Jim Hill," Maynard Speece, and later Chuck Lilligren and Roger Strom, who presented the morning farm report. And the *Noon Hour Ag Show* was a staple. Farming was an important and essential part of Minnesota life back in the 1950s and 1960s, and even those living in urban areas had connections with family farms and listened to the broadcasts.

Hourly agricultural reports were part of every weekday broadcast, starting at 5:00 a.m. Many farmers listened to WCCO around the clock from radios installed in their tractors, combines, and pickup trucks.

Several times a year we would coordinate Farm-City Days to spotlight and honor farmers. We visited one farm in the Upper Midwest, under the banner "'CCO—On the Go." In a live broadcast, I would interview the farm wives and talk about the food they prepared, as well as their various chores and duties around the farm. I remember visiting more than one root cellar!

The women would put on a fabulous spread of food for us. These hostesses took their reputations as good cooks very seriously and would make their best and most complicated recipes for us. You can find one of the recipes from these meetings, for Sour Cream Dessert Ring, in the Desserts chapter of this book. That was the specialty of Mrs. Harold Bremer of Lake City, Minnesota.

FLUFFS

When you're live on the air, it's inevitable that mistakes will happen. We always called them "fluffs." In the early days when I was hosting the Dayton's show, the copywriters from the store wrote all of the commercials for the show. They were accustomed to writing for newspaper ads, not for radio. So copy that might have been very effective when it was printed just didn't fly when it had to be read.

Nowadays, fluffs, or bloopers, are funny. Many announcers deliberately fluff words to get a laugh. But back then, fluffs were to be avoided at all costs! Fluffs were serious mistakes. The rule was that not a word of Dayton's copy was to be changed—ever! You had to read each sentence as written, or you would have to answer to Dayton's advertising department.

One day I was appalled when I read a sentence in a Dayton's commercial that was scheduled for the next morning: "Shop in the sixth-floor shirt shop for short-sleeved ship-and-shore sports shirts with elasticized sides." So I rehearsed that line a dozen times, and when I was on the air, I nailed it. I didn't fluff it, no sir! Feeling pleased with myself, I plunged into the next commercial, which advertised a sale on scissors and tweezers. Clear as a bell, I said, "twizzers and seezers."

One of our finest announcers once said on the air, "I remember coming on the scene of a bombing in London during World War II. It was dreadful—a mass of twisted girdles—I mean, twisted *girders!*" The sibilants sure got in the way!

And there was one that Roger Erickson told me about. He was on the air with Maynard Speece during the first flights of the astronauts.

Two astronauts landed in the ocean, and the aircraft carrier, the *Wasp*, was looking for them. For some time, nobody knew if they were safe. Maynard went into the 'CCO newsroom early one morning to pick up the latest news for their show, and he came running back into the studio, all excited, with the news headline that had just come over the wire.

He yelled, "Roger, great news about the astronauts! They're safe!" Roger turned on the mike and said, "Here's Maynard with news of the astronauts!" Maynard yelled, "Wonderful news. They're safe. Right now, they are on the desk of the *Wop*." A *long silence*. "Where?" asked Roger. Maynard, greatly subdued, said, "I mean, they're on the DECK of the *WASP*."

It happens to everyone on the air, sooner or later!

MY WCCO COLLEAGUES

I was lucky enough to work with some of the best broadcasters this nation has ever known. Has there ever been a better or more original local team than Boone and Erickson? Charlie Boone is the warm, affable man who never forgets a name and had a dozen voices to use in the talented Roger's skits. Many of them were based on the old soap operas. Everyone's favorite was "The Romance of Helen Trent," set in "Minnesota Hospital, proving that Minnesota is a good place to get sick in."

I spent a lot of time on the air with my good friend Howard Viken. He was just a teenaged tease! He loved to play that dreadful "stripper" music when he introduced me. Howard never listened to me when I objected to the musical introductions. Once he told me, "Don't knock it, kid—it made you famous!" But here's what is interesting: He never played that music on the Dayton's show, because they would not allow it—and *their* opinion mattered!

The stripper music provoked a lot of calls and letters of complaint from feminists. I got many of those calls myself. They insisted that the music degraded me and consequently all women. So eventually, management made Howard stop playing it. Howard and I always had a good time on the air together, but I tell you, I sure didn't miss hearing that music!

Bob DeHaven was a great emcee and writer, an intellectual, whom we called "The Star." To boost morale and get a laugh, he would scrawl "Approved—★" on the bottoms of inane memos posted on bulletin boards around the station. Once, after finishing a Northrup Seed corn commercial, he asked me what the yield was in my apartment flower box!

Sid Hartman, one of Minnesota's great sportscasters at WCCO, was a great gentleman with an infectious laugh. He always wanted his mug of cocoa when he arrived at the studio—and he wanted me to make it! Every morning, one of the first things he would say was, "Where's my chocolate?" He was wonderful with the athletes, and much kinder than his image made him seem. He is a great promoter of himself but a good man for all that!

And here's a name you'll recognize: Harry Reasoner. He was our news writer, who was quiet and unassuming with a subtle sense of humor. He went to New York and became one of the stars of the CBS show *Sixty Minutes*.

And there's one person with whom I worked who died too young: Cedric Adams. He had enormous talent. As a communicator, he couldn't

Joyce was part of a large WCCO on-air family in the 1960s. Bottom row: Paul Giel, Charlie Boone, Bob Allison, John Kundla, Dick Chapman, Franklin Hobbs. Second row: Ray Scott, Dr. E. W. Ziebarth, Jim Hill, Jergen Nash, Maynard Speece, Clarence Tolg. Third row: Dick Enroth, Joyce Lamont, Bob DeHaven, Roger Erickson, Paul Jay, Halsey Hall, Herb Carneal. Top row: Arv Johnson, Sid Hartman, Howard Viken, Randy Merriman, Jim Bormann, and Gary Bennyhoff.

be beat. He was a "Triple-Threat Man." He had a distinctive voice everyone recognized. He was a writer who knew how to appeal to people. And finally, his people skills were extraordinary. I was near him at the state fair one time when someone came up to him and started asking questions. He said, "I don't want to talk about me. I want to hear about YOU!"

Once, when I was new at WCCO, I had been out to lunch and stepped off the elevator on the second floor into the station's reception area. There were two farm women sitting there. They had the rough-textured hands that show hard work. They had shopping bags from Powers Department Store and wore little hats with veils, flowered dresses, and pearl necklaces. When I spoke to them, they said they were waiting for "SEEDRICK."

I told them he'd be along in a moment, because it was just a few minutes before his big 12:30 news broadcast. Just then the elevator door opened, and there he was. His eyes went right to the two women sitting there. He said, "Hello, girls!" They blushed and giggled. He went right over to them, sat down between them, took their hands, and asked their names, where they were from, and what they were doing.

As I walked away, I heard him say, "Tell me, how's your love life?" Now remember, this was decades ago! People just didn't talk like that, but Cedric did! And you know what? I bet they told him!

That's how he got material for his columns, all carefully edited. Some of his columns were reprinted in *The New Yorker* magazine, *the* classic *New Yorker* of E. B. White and James Thurber. And when Arthur Godfrey went on vacation, he would often call Cedric to substitute for him at CBS radio. Airline pilots used to tell us that when they were flying over the upper Midwest at night, they could tell when Cedric went off the air, because lights would go off simultaneously across the area.

BEST BUYS

In the 1960s, women's shows were going out of style, and one of WCCO's clients wanted to sponsor a food show. One day in 1965, I got a list from the newswires, detailing the best buys in the grocery store for every month. I thought, "That's useful information," and put it on the air with a recipe that used some of the ingredients. So I was asked to put a daily show together. Immediately, listeners started writing in, asking for more recipes—sometimes ten thousand letters a month. So I started collecting recipes, and it evolved into *Today's Best Buys*.

I typed them all out myself on a manual typewriter. At the end of the month, twenty-five thousand copies of those daily recipes were

161

The WCCO building in downtown Minneapolis advertises the station's slogan
"Good Neighbor to the Northwest" in this picture from the 1960s.

printed and were mailed out around the country to people in thirty states and several foreign countries. That meant I was distributing more than a quarter of a million recipes each year! Eventually, I published two cookbooks, one with WCCO and one with KLBB, which were best sellers at the Minnesota State Fair. The recipes in this book are from that huge collection.

It seemed to me that older people, even back then, were mesmerized by gooey desserts. Even as healthy, low-fat food became more important, people didn't lose their sweet tooth. Most of those requests were for desserts. Here's my philosophy: gourmet recipes are wonderful, but many of us are simply too busy for complicated recipes. We need nourishing recipes that can be made quickly and easily; that's where these recipes come in.

I enjoy cooking, but I never had much time to practice the art. I'm a journalist and a radio person, not a cook. My sister is an excellent cook and for years every Christmas made a turkey with Minnesota wild rice stuffing.

Here's the note that was sent out with each collection of recipes:

Joyce Lamont's BEST BUYS SHOW is aired Monday through Friday mornings at 10:15 on WCCO Radio, 8-3-0 on your dial.

The recipes on the show are printed the end of each month and are available free to those sending in a business-size, stamped, self-addressed envelope. Write the month of recipes you wish sent (March, April, etc.) on the inside of a flap of the enclosed enveloped. No more than 2 collections can be sent in each envelope.

While browsing through my collection, I picked out many favorites that really caught my eye. Over the years, my listeners supplied some wonderful recipes. Others came from old cookbooks, and some from family and friends. These recipes have been updated to include changes in can sizes and for some food safety reasons. But they are still a representative collection of the way people ate in the 1960s and 1970s.

KLBB

The "youth movement" finally caught up with WCCO. The station started changing things in the late 1980s and began cutting back on my on-air assignments. But the American Federation of Television and Radio Artists (AFTRA) came to my rescue, charging age discrimination. The "powers that be" at WCCO gave me a new office and treated me very nicely. But a few years later, my contract wasn't renewed.

In the end, with other WCCO personalities, including Howard Viken and Chuck Lilligren, I moved to radio station KLBB in the Twin Cities in 1989. Some media people called the station "'CCO 2" for a time. I left WCCO on July 14 of that year and started at KLBB on July 17. I didn't want to miss a beat!

My show was on from 6:00 to 9:00 a.m. I kept on with *Best Buys* and the monthly collection of recipes. And it seemed that listeners still wanted recipes—the more the better!

I spent many wonderful years at that station. It was such fun! I never realized how much stress I was under at WCCO every time I went on the air until I joined KLBB. I finally retired from the radio in 2003. I still work (old habits die hard!) and often will do voice-overs for commercials around town.

I'm kind of a shy person. I once canceled out of a speech course, scared at the thought of giving speeches in front of an audience. By accident, I ended up immersed in daily speeches to thousands of listeners on Twin Cities radio. I still can't believe it! When I look back on my career, it feels like I won a million dollars in the state lottery.

APPETIZERS

1

Appetizers can be a hostess's savior, occupying guests while she is still busy putting the finishing touches on a meal. They can even *be* the meal!

The next time you're entertaining a crowd, put out a diverse selection of appetizers, hot and cold, light and heavy, along with a selection of beverages. Provide plates, napkins, and lots of room around the table—then you can enjoy the party too.

Slow cookers and hot plates are good for keeping hot food hot, and double bowls filled with cracked ice, along with chilled serving plates, will keep cold food cold. All you have to do is replenish the food every once in a while.

CHEESE CRACKERS

Homemade crackers are so special, and they aren't difficult to make. Serve these with some hot homemade chili or beef stew that has been simmering for hours in your kitchen.

These crackers can be reheated in a toaster oven, for 4–5 minutes at 350 degrees F until they are sizzling.

$1^1/_3$ cups flour
$1/_2$ teaspoon salt
1 tablespoon minced chives

$1/_2$ cup butter, softened
2 cups grated sharp Cheddar cheese

Preheat oven to 350 degrees F. In a small bowl, combine flour, salt, and chives; set aside.

In medium bowl, cream butter until soft and fluffy. Add cheese and gradually work together with the back of a spoon. Add flour mixture and mix until a dough forms.

Roll dough into $3/_4$-inch balls. Place on ungreased cookie sheet and flatten with the bottom of a drinking glass to $1/_4$-inch thickness. Prick top of crackers with a fork to prevent puffing.

Bake for 12–15 minutes or until crackers are very light brown around the edges. Remove to wire rack to cool completely. *Yields 4–5 dozen crackers*

HERBED CREAM CHEESE SPREAD

This recipe is similar to the expensive flavored soft cheese you can buy at delis. Put it in a pretty bowl and surround it with crackers, toasted French bread slices, and carrot and celery sticks.

2 (8-ounce) packages cream cheese, softened
3 tablespoons heavy whipping cream
1/4 cup chopped fresh dill weed
2 tablespoons chopped fresh chives
1/8 teaspoon hot pepper sauce
1/4 teaspoon pepper
1/4 teaspoon garlic powder

Combine all ingredients in medium bowl, stirring until blended. Cover and refrigerate overnight. Let mixture stand at room temperature for about 15 minutes before serving with accompaniments. *Serves 8–10*

CHICKEN WINGS HAWAIIAN

Chicken wings are a good buy, especially during the fall. You can buy precut chicken "drummies," but they are more expensive. It's simple to just cut the wings in half, then cut off and discard the tips (or save them to make chicken stock). Serve this appetizer with lots of napkins!

3 pounds meaty chicken wings
3/4 cup low-sodium soy sauce
2 tablespoons hoisin sauce
3 cloves garlic, minced

3/4 cup minced green onion
1/4 cup sugar

1/4 cup honey
3/4 cup pineapple juice
1 teaspoon dry mustard
1/8 teaspoon crushed red pepper flakes
1/4 cup minced fresh ginger root
1/4 cup butter

Cut the tips off of the chicken wings and discard (or reserve for making chicken stock). Then cut the wings into two pieces. Arrange in a large glass baking dish.

In large saucepan, combine remaining ingredients and bring to a boil. Let cool for 20 minutes, then pour over chicken wings in dish. Cover and refrigerate for 4–8 hours.

Preheat oven to 350 degrees F. Place the chicken wings, marinade and all, in the oven and bake for 30 minutes. Turn chicken wings and bake for 15–20 minutes longer until chicken is thoroughly cooked (internal temperature registers 170 degrees F) and glazed.

Remove chicken from marinade and place on wire rack; cool for 10 minutes before serving. *Serves 8–10*

CALIFORNIA SNACK MIX

Most snack mixes use butter and seasonings, sometimes cheese. This one is unusual; barbecue sauce adds a crisp and flavorful glaze to cereal and nuts.

3 tablespoons butter	4 cups corn or wheat square crisp cereal
1/3 cup barbecue sauce	2 cups honey roasted peanuts
1 tablespoon honey	2 cups salted mini pretzel sticks
1/4 teaspoon hot pepper sauce	

Preheat oven to 300 degrees F. In medium saucepan, combine butter, barbecue sauce, honey, and hot pepper sauce and heat over medium heat until mixture just comes to a simmer.

Meanwhile, combine remaining ingredients in large bowl. Drizzle barbecue sauce mixture over ingredients in bowl, tossing until everything is evenly coated.

Spoon mixture onto a cookie sheet. Bake for 45–50 minutes, stirring three times during baking time, until mixture is toasted and crisp. Cool on paper towels, then store in air-tight container at room temperature. *Serves 16*

....

RHUBARB-LEMONADE PUNCH

This is a wonderful way to use rhubarb from your garden. The fruit adds a gorgeous pink color and delicious tartness to this refreshing punch.

3 cups sliced rhubarb	1 (6-ounce) can frozen lemonade concentrate
3 cups water	1 (16-ounce) bottle ginger ale
3/4 cup sugar	

In large saucepan, combine rhubarb with water and sugar. Bring to a boil, then cover pan and simmer for 10–15 minutes until rhubarb is tender.

Pour mixture through sieve into a large bowl, pressing rhubarb to remove as much juice as possible. Discard pulp. Add lemonade concentrate to liquid, then cover and chill until cold.

To serve, pour into a punch bowl and gradually stir in ginger ale. *Serves 12*

....

HERB-MARINATED CHERRY TOMATOES

An antipasto platter is simply an arrangement of vegetables, especially pickled and marinated vegetables, along with cured meats, served before an Italian dinner. These tomatoes are an excellent addition to that appetizer buffet, but are also delicious on their own. Serve with little crackers and a glass of white wine before a summer meal.

4 cups cherry tomatoes	1/2 teaspoon salt
1/2 cup vegetable oil	1/2 teaspoon dried oregano leaves
1/4 cup red wine vinegar	1/2 teaspoon dried basil leaves
1/4 teaspoon pepper	3 green onions, chopped

Bring a large pot of water to a boil. About a cup at a time, add the tomatoes to the boiling water; leave them there for 15 seconds. Immediately plunge the tomatoes into ice water.

When all the tomatoes are blanched, slip off the skins and gently place them into a large bowl.

In small bowl, combine all remaining ingredients and whisk to blend. Pour over the tomatoes, cover, and refrigerate overnight. Serve as an appetizer, as a relish with meat, or on lettuce as a salad. *Serves 6–8*

• •

CHEESE STICKS

This is a fun use for leftover bread, but it has to be unsliced bread. You can keep these sticks in the freezer up to one month; bake them as you need them! They are a great appetizer but also delicious served with soup.

1 (16-ounce) 9 x 5-inch loaf unsliced bread	1 (5-ounce) jar Old English cheese spread
1 egg white	1 cup grated Parmesan cheese
1/2 cup butter, softened	

Trim crust from bread. Cut loaf lengthwise into thirds, turn loaf one turn, then cut lengthwise into fourths, making twelve pieces. Then cut loaf crosswise into thirds, making 36 pieces total. Place on cookie sheet and freeze until solid, about 2 hours.

In medium bowl, beat egg white until frothy. Then add butter and cheese spread, beating until creamy.

Spread this mixture on all sides of bread pieces and roll in Parmesan cheese to coat. Return to cookie sheet and freeze until solid again. Place in hard-sided freezer containers, label, seal, and freeze up to two months.

To bake, place frozen sticks on cookie sheets. Bake in preheated 325-degree F oven for 14–19 minutes or until the sticks are light golden brown and crisp. Serve immediately. *Yields 36 sticks*

ROAST BEEF ROLL UPS

Appetizer recipes using deli roast beef are pretty common, but this one has a crunchy cucumber center that adds a great fresh taste. You can make these ahead of time; just don't slice them until you're ready to serve. I arrange these on a bed of flat-leaf parsley for a really pretty look.

1 (8-ounce) package cream cheese, softened
2 tablespoons prepared horseradish
1 tablespoon prepared mustard
1/2 teaspoon dill seed
12 thin slices deli roast beef
2 cucumbers

In small bowl, beat cream cheese until softened. Add horseradish, mustard, and dill seed and beat until smooth.

Arrange roast beef slices on work surface. Gently spread cream cheese mixture onto each slice.

Peel cucumbers and cut in half. Using a spoon, remove the seeds and discard. Cut cucumbers into thin strips about 3 inches long. Arrange cucumber strips on cheese mixture, then roll the beef around them. Cover and chill for 1–2 hours before serving.

To serve, cut rolls into 1-inch slices and arrange, cut side up, on platter. *Serves 6–8*

....

COCOA SYRUP (FOR HOT CHOCOLATE)

When you have this syrup in your fridge, you can make hot cocoa in a flash. Most cocoa recipes reconstitute the mixture with boiling water, but I think that using milk instead makes a richer cup.

2 cups cocoa powder
4 cups sugar
1/4 teaspoon salt
4 cups boiling water
6 teaspoons vanilla

Sift the cocoa powder to remove lumps. In large saucepan, combine the sifted cocoa with the sugar and salt. Gradually add the boiling water, stirring until smooth with a wire whisk.

Cook and stir the syrup over medium heat until it comes to a boil. Let the mixture boil, without stirring, for exactly 1 minute.

Remove from heat and let cool, then stir in vanilla. Pour syrup into a glass jar, cover, and refrigerate. Makes 5 cups of syrup.

To make hot chocolate, heat 1 cup of milk per serving until bubbles form around the edges, then stir in 2 tablespoons of the syrup. For chocolate milk, stir the same amount of syrup into cold milk. Store syrup in the refrigerator for up to 1 month. *Yields 40 servings*

HONEY WAFERS

These sweet crackers are delicious served with Chicken Salad with Green Grapes (page 39) or any other main-dish salad. Or they can be served with Creamy Fruit Dip (page 36) along with some fresh fruit. The tip at the end of the recipe for crisping crackers that have softened applies to every type of cracker!

$1/2$ cup butter, softened	$1/2$ teaspoon cinnamon
$1/2$ cup honey	$1/4$ teaspoon cloves
2 cups flour	$1/4$ teaspoon allspice
1 teaspoon baking soda	$1/4$ cup crushed bran flakes

In large bowl, combine butter and honey and mix well until combined. Stir in flour, baking soda, and spices and mix well. Then mix in the bran flakes.

Cover dough and chill for 1 hour. Preheat oven to 350 degrees F. Roll dough on lightly floured surface to $1/8$-inch thickness. Using a pastry wheel or sharp knife, cut into 2-inch squares.

Place squares on ungreased cookie sheet. Bake for 8–10 minutes or until light golden brown and crisp. Store, tightly covered, at room temperature. If crackers soften, heat them in a 200 degrees F oven for 5 minutes, then serve. *Yields about 48 crackers*

●●

CHICKEN LIVER PÂTÉ

Not many people make chicken liver pâté anymore, which I think is a shame. This spread is rich and delicious, perfect for a fancy party or a gathering before a ball game.

The original recipe used hard-cooked eggs, but simply scrambling eggs is much easier and, I think, tastes even better. You can use hard-cooked eggs if you'd like!

This pâté can be spooned or piped into a bowl and chilled or molded in a decorative mold. Serve it with water crackers and melba toast for a classic touch or with breadsticks and apple slices.

$1/2$ pound chicken livers	1 tablespoon chopped fresh tarragon
2 tablespoons butter	$1/8$ teaspoon pepper
2 eggs	$1/2$ teaspoon salt
2 (3-ounce) packages cream cheese, softened	1 tablespoon chopped flat-leaf parsley
	1 tablespoon brandy

Trim chicken livers and cut in half. In medium saucepan, melt butter until foamy, then add chicken livers and cook over medium heat for 7–10 minutes, stirring frequently, until livers are tender and thoroughly cooked. Remove livers from pan.

30

In small bowl, beat eggs until foamy. Add to skillet; cook eggs, stirring occasionally, until set but still moist.

In food processor, combine liver and eggs and pulse until finely chopped. Add remaining ingredients and process until mixture is smooth. Spoon into bowl or into a mold and chill for 2–3 hours before serving. *Serves 8–10*

....

TURKEY-PARSLEY ROLLS

This is another delicious make-ahead appetizer. You could use other types of meat and bread in this simple recipe as well. Slice the rolls into $1/2$-inch pieces just before serving and arrange them, cut side up, on a platter.

Flat-leaf parsley, also known as Italian parsley, has more flavor than the curly type, which is why it's called for in all my recipes.

2 (3-ounce) packages cream cheese, softened	$1/4$ cup chopped toasted almonds
3 tablespoons light cream	2 tablespoons chopped flat-leaf parsley
$1/2$ cup chopped cooked turkey	8 slices soft white bread
	1 cup chopped flat-leaf parsley

In small bowl, combine cream cheese with cream and beat until light and fluffy. Put $1/4$ cup of this mixture into another small bowl; set rest aside.

Combine $1/4$ cup of the cream cheese mixture with the turkey, almonds, and 2 tablespoons parsley and mix well.

Remove crusts from bread and flatten bread slightly with a rolling pin. Spread each bread slice with the turkey mixture, and roll up each slice like a jelly roll.

Spread the outside of each roll with the reserved plain cream cheese mixture and roll each in the chopped parsley. Wrap rolls separately in plastic wrap and secure tightly.

Cover and refrigerate until serving time. To serve, cut each roll into $1/2$-inch slices and arrange on a serving platter. *Serves 8–10*

Joyce poses in front of a microphone with colleague Ed Viehman in 1950.

31

Rumaki Spread

Rumaki is traditionally made by wrapping soy sauce–marinated water chestnuts with chicken livers in bacon, then broiling until the bacon is crisp. This recipe is easier to make and serve.

1 tablespoon soy sauce
$1/2$ pound cooked chicken livers
$1/2$ cup butter, softened
$1/2$ cup chopped red onion
$1/2$ teaspoon dry mustard
$1/4$ teaspoon nutmeg
$1/8$ teaspoon cayenne pepper
1 (5-ounce) can water chestnuts, drained and chopped
6 slices bacon, cooked and crumbled
$1/2$ cup sliced green onion
Water crackers and toasted baguette slices

In food processor, combine soy sauce, livers, butter, red onion, mustard, nutmeg, and cayenne pepper and blend until smooth. Spread onto serving dish.

Sprinkle with water chestnuts, bacon, and green onion. Cover and refrigerate for 2–3 hours before serving. Serve with crackers and baguette slices. *Serves 8*

....

Hot Apple Punch

When you're having company or an open house over the holidays, this fragrant punch is a great addition to a buffet. Serve it in a large slow cooker, turned to low to keep the punch hot.

$2 1/4$ cups sugar
4 cups water
2 cinnamon sticks, broken in half
8 whole allspice berries
10 whole cloves
4 cups orange juice
2 cups lemon juice
2 quarts apple juice or cider

In large saucepan, combine sugar with water and bring to a boil. Cover pan and let boil for 1 minute, then uncover pan and boil for 4 minutes longer until sugar is completely dissolved. In cheesecloth square or tea ball, combine cinnamon sticks, allspice, and cloves. Add spices to syrup and let stand for 1 hour, then remove and discard spices.

Just before serving, in large pot combine orange juice, lemon juice, and apple juice. Add the sugar syrup and bring to a boil, then pour half of this mixture into the slow cooker. Add the rest of the punch to the slow cooker as needed. Serve with cinnamon stick stirrers. *Yields 16 cups*

DILLED CARROTS

You can make this with carrots that have been peeled and cut into sticks, but baby carrots are so easy to use and so cute! This is a great addition to any appetizer tray, especially an antipasto platter.

1 pound baby carrots	$1/3$ cup sugar
$1/2$ cup vinegar	1 tablespoon mustard seed
$1/2$ cup water	$1/2$ teaspoon dried dill weed

In large saucepan, cover carrots with cold water. Bring to a boil over high heat; reduce heat to medium–low and simmer for 4–6 minutes or until carrots are crisp-tender; drain and set aside.

In medium saucepan, combine remaining ingredients and bring to a boil over high heat. Reduce heat to low and simmer, uncovered, for 10 minutes. Remove from heat, add carrots, and stir gently.

Let cool for 30 minutes, then cover and chill for at least 8 hours before serving. Stir and drain before serving. *Serves 8–10*

• •

SOYA CHICKEN DRUMMETTES

Drummettes are just the meaty part of the chicken wing, trimmed of the tip and less meaty section. You can find them packaged in the meat section of your grocery store. You can also trim chicken wings yourself. Remember to save the tips and thinner sections of the wings for chicken stock.

24 chicken drummettes	2 tablespoons olive oil
4 green onions, chopped	3 cloves garlic, minced
1 cup soy sauce	2 tablespoons minced ginger root
$1/3$ cup brown sugar	

The night before, place drummettes in plastic zip-top food storage bag. Add onions and remaining ingredients. Seal bag and knead to combine. Place bag in large bowl and refrigerate overnight.

When you want to serve the chicken, preheat oven to 350 degrees F. Remove drummettes from the marinade, reserving marinade. Place chicken in single layer in a shallow baking pan. Bake for 15 minutes, then turn drummettes over and spoon marinade over each piece.

Return to oven and bake 20–25 minutes longer or until chicken is thoroughly cooked and glazed. *Yields 24 appetizers*

• •

PEANUT SNACKS

This is an unusual treat. It starts with a corn muffin mix, and you end up with some crisp, buttery squares perfect to serve with a glass of wine before a company dinner.

1 (8-ounce) package corn muffin mix	1¹/₂ cups chopped salted peanuts
¹/₂ cup grated Parmesan cheese	1 teaspoon seasoned salt
1 egg	4 tablespoons butter, melted
¹/₃ cup milk	

Preheat oven to 375 degrees F. Spray a 15 x 10-inch jelly roll pan with nonstick baking spray containing flour and set aside.

In medium bowl, combine muffin mix, egg, and milk and mix until smooth. Spread evenly into a thin layer in the prepared pan.

Sprinkle peanuts, cheese, and seasoned salt over the batter. Then drizzle with melted butter.

Bake for 16–22 minutes or until bread is crisp and light brown. Immediately cut into squares, then let cool in pan for 5 minutes. Remove from pan and serve warm. *Yields 36 snacks*

• •

TOMATO RELISH COCKTAIL

This recipe is similar to gazpacho but is a bit thicker. It's delicious served as a first course for summer entertaining. And do serve it in cocktail or martini glasses for a beautiful presentation.

4 tomatoes	1 teaspoon salt
1 green bell pepper, diced	¹/₄ cup sugar
1 cup chopped celery	¹/₄ cup vinegar
1 cup chopped red onion	1 cup water
¹/₄ cup pickle relish	

Peel tomatoes and dice. Combine with green pepper, celery, and onion in medium bowl.

In small bowl, combine remaining ingredients and stir to dissolve sugar and salt. Pour over vegetables, stir gently, cover, and refrigerate overnight.

Serve in chilled cocktail glasses, garnished with parsley sprigs if desired. *Serves 6*

• •

GUACAMOLE DIP

Most guacamole is made with avocado and lemon juice along with some hot sauce. This recipe uses some dry onion soup mix instead for a kick of flavor. Serve it with tortilla chips.

2 ripe avocados	1/4 cup sour cream
2 tablespoons dry onion soup mix	1 ripe tomato, chopped

Peel avocado and cut into chunks. Sprinkle with onion soup mix and mash with fork. Stir in sour cream and tomato. Cover by placing plastic wrap directly on the surface of the dip; refrigerate for 3–4 hours to blend flavors. *Serves 4*

Over the years, Joyce worked with a large number of colleagues, whom she described as "dedicated, talented, and wonderful people." Here she poses with Gordon Eaton.

DILL-PICKLED ONION RINGS

These crisp and spicy onions make an excellent appetizer or sandwich topping. Try them on an antipasto platter. To sterilize the jar, you can submerge it in boiling water for a few minutes or run it through the dishwasher, then pack in the onions while the jar is still hot.

4 large onions	$1/2$ teaspoon dill weed
$1/2$ cup sugar	$1/2$ cup vinegar
2 teaspoons salt	$1/4$ cup water

Peel onions and cut into $1/4$-inch slices. Break slices apart into rings. Loosely pack the rings into a sterilized pint jar.

In small saucepan, combine remaining ingredients and bring to a simmer over medium-high heat. Stir until sugar and salt dissolve.

Immediately pour the hot liquid over the onion rings. Cover jar, refrigerate overnight, turning jar over several times, then serve. The onions can be stored in the refrigerator for up to one week. *Yields 1 pint*

• •

CREAMY FRUIT DIP

Every appetizer buffet needs something sweet. This easy dip is sweet and creamy, perfect to serve with all kinds of fresh fruit and some sweet crackers or cookies. Be sure to brush apples and pears with lemon juice so they don't turn brown while waiting on the serving tray.

1 (3-ounce) package cream cheese, softened	Pinch salt
2 tablespoons powdered sugar	$1/4$ cup currant jelly
2 tablespoons heavy whipping cream	$3/4$ cup heavy whipping cream
1 tablespoon lemon juice	1 tablespoon powdered sugar
	1 teaspoon vanilla

In small bowl, beat cream cheese with 2 tablespoons powdered sugar, 2 tablespoons cream, lemon juice, and salt until fluffy. Stir in currant jelly and mix well.

In another small bowl, combine $3/4$ cup cream, 1 tablespoon powdered sugar, and vanilla and beat until stiff peaks form. Fold into cream cheese mixture.

Cover and chill until serving time. *Yields about 2 cups*

• •

SALMON SPREAD

Appetizer spreads like this one can be turned into a dip, if you'd like, simply by adding more wine or lemon juice. Serve it with breadsticks, toasted and buttered baguette slices, and lots of crackers.

1 (15-ounce) can salmon, drained	1/4 cup chopped green onions
1 (8-ounce) package	1 cucumber
cream cheese, softened	1 tablespoon chopped fresh dill weed
1/3 cup white wine or apple juice	1/4 teaspoon salt
1 tablespoon lemon juice	1/8 teaspoon white pepper

Remove skin and bones from salmon and discard; flake salmon and set aside. In medium bowl, beat cream cheese until fluffy. Gradually beat in wine and lemon juice.

Stir in green onions. Peel cucumber, cut in half, and scoop out seeds. Grate cucumber and add to cream cheese mixture along with dill weed, salt, pepper, and the salmon; mix well.

Chill until spread is firm. Serve with small knives and plates along with bread and crackers. *Serves 6–8*

• •

SESAME BEEF CUBES

These richly marinated bits of beef are easy to make and delicious. I love the crunch of sesame seeds combined with the silky texture of the meat and the sweet-sour flavor of the marinade. Yum!

1 1/2 pounds beef sirloin	1/2 teaspoon Tabasco sauce
1/2 cup soy sauce	1 onion, chopped
1/2 cup red wine vinegar	Vegetable oil
2 cloves garlic, minced	Sesame seeds
2 tablespoons minced fresh ginger root	

The steak should be 1-inch thick. Cut it into 1-inch cubes. Place in a large, heavy-duty zip-top food storage bag.

Add remaining ingredients except for vegetable oil and sesame seeds to the bag with the meat. Seal the bag and knead to combine marinade with the meat.

Place in large bowl or baking dish and refrigerate overnight. When ready to serve, pour vegetable oil into a heavy skillet to 1/4-inch depth and heat until temperature reaches 350 degrees F.

Remove beef from marinade; discard marinade. Cook the beef in small batches in the hot oil, turning frequently, until browned on all sides, about 3–5 minutes total.

Place sesame seeds on a platter. As the beef cubes are done, toss the hot cubes in the sesame seeds. Serve immediately. *Serves 6–8*

CHRISTMAS PARTY PUNCH

Did you know that you can make ice cubes from fruit juices? Just freeze the juice as you would water in ice cube trays. Then you can float those cubes in punch, and as they melt, the punch just gets better instead of diluting.

1 (6-ounce) can frozen orange juice concentrate, thawed
1 (6-ounce) can frozen lemonade concentrate, thawed
3 cups pineapple juice
6 cups cranberry juice
6 juice cans cold water

Combine all ingredients in a large punch bowl. Add ice cubes or frozen juice cubes and serve immediately. *Serves 30*

••

FRENCH ONION DIP

Unlike the ubiquitous dip made with sour cream, this one uses yogurt and cottage cheese for more tang. Serve it with chips and Cheese Crackers (page 25) for a delicious appetizer.

1 (8-ounce) container plain yogurt   1 envelope dry onion soup mix
1 cup cottage cheese $1/8$ teaspoon Tabasco sauce

In food processor or blender, combine yogurt with cottage cheese. Process or blend until smooth and creamy. Spoon into a small bowl and stir in soup mix and Tabasco sauce. Cover and chill for at least 3 hours before serving. *Serves 8*

••

SALADS

If you're tired of serving the same old mixed green salad with bottled dressing, turn to these recipes to shake up your repertoire. Salads don't have to be cold either. A hot mixture served over cold crisp greens or pasta is a fabulous taste and texture sensation.

··

CHICKEN SALAD WITH GREEN GRAPES

Old fashioned chicken salad, with its creamy dressing, crunchy celery, and sweet grapes, is a classic. It was served at ladies' luncheons in the 1950s and 1960s usually with homemade fluffy rolls. This excellent recipe has the perfect blend of textures and flavors.

3 cups diced cooked chicken
1 cup finely chopped celery
1 cup green grapes
1 cup red grapes
1 cup chopped pecans
$1/2$ cup heavy whipping cream
$1/4$ cup mayonnaise

$3/4$ cup lemon yogurt
$1/2$ cup mango chutney
1 teaspoon minced onion
1 tablespoon lemon juice
$1/2$ teaspoon salt
Salad greens

Combine chicken, celery, grapes, and pecans in large bowl and toss to combine. Beat cream until stiff peaks form and stir in mayonnaise, yogurt, chutney, onion, lemon juice, and salt. Fold dressing into the chicken mixture, cover, and chill for 2–3 hours before serving on salad greens. *Serves 6*

··

FROSTED CRANBERRY SALAD

This colorful salad is perfect for the holidays. One of the best things about molded salads is they have to be made ahead of time, so that's one less thing to think about when you're entertaining. This salad is particularly beautiful, with a deep crimson color and pink frosting.

1 (6-ounce) package raspberry
    gelatin
1 (7-ounce) can crushed pineapple
1/2 cup cranberry juice
1 (16-ounce) can whole-berry
    cranberry sauce
1 1/2 cups ginger ale
1 cup chopped walnuts

2 cups peeled, chopped apples
2 teaspoons grated orange zest
1 cup heavy whipping cream
1 (3-ounce) package cream
    cheese, softened
1/3 cup powdered sugar
2 tablespoons cranberry juice

Place gelatin in large bowl. Drain pineapple, reserving juice. Add enough water to juice to make one cup. Combine this mixture with 1/2 cup cranberry juice in microwave-safe glass measuring cup and microwave on high until mixture boils. Stir into gelatin; stir until completely dissolved.

Add cranberry sauce and ginger ale; cover bowl and refrigerate until mixture starts to thicken, about 45 minutes.

Fold in pineapple, walnuts, apples, and orange zest. Pour into 8-inch square glass baking dish and chill until set, about 2 hours.

In medium bowl, combine cream with cream cheese and half of the powdered sugar; beat until thick. Add remaining powdered sugar and 2 tablespoons cranberry juice; beat until combined. Spread this mixture over the set gelatin salad; cover and chill for 2–3 hours until set. *Serves 9*

• •

TOMATO–AVOCADO SALAD

To ripen avocados, place them together in a brown paper bag and let stand for a day or two. Avocados are ripe when they yield to gentle pressure. This delicious and unique salad is perfect for a light lunch on the porch.

4 ripe tomatoes
1/2 teaspoon salt
1 avocado
1 cup small-curd cottage cheese
1/4 cup sour cream

1 tablespoon lemon juice
Dash white pepper
1 tablespoon chopped fresh chives
Butter lettuce leaves

Place the tomatoes on cutting board, stem end down. Cut each tomato into 6 wedges, cutting just to the base of the tomato. Spread wedges apart slightly and sprinkle with salt. Chill for 1 hour.

When ready to serve, peel, seed, and dice the avocado and combine with cottage cheese, sour cream, lemon juice, and pepper. Fill each tomato with about 1/3 cup of the avocado mixture. Sprinkle with chives and serve on lettuce leaves. *Serves 4*

COTTAGE CHEESE MOLDED SALAD

The combination of cottage cheese and French salad dressing is a classic, if slightly offbeat, snack or treat. This recipe takes those flavors to the extreme, in a smooth and crunchy molded salad that pairs perfectly with grilled fish or chicken.

2 (0.25-ounce) envelopes unflavored gelatin	1/2 teaspoon seasoned salt
1 cup whole milk	1 tablespoon prepared horseradish
2 cups small-curd cottage cheese	1 cup chopped celery
1 cup mayonnaise	1 green bell pepper, chopped
1/4 cup apple cider vinegar	1/2 red bell pepper, chopped

In medium microwave-safe bowl, combine gelatin and milk. Let stand for 5 minutes. Microwave for 1–2 minutes on high, stirring once during cooking time, until gelatin is completely dissolved.

Stir in cottage cheese, mayonnaise, vinegar, salt, and horseradish. Chill until the mixture begins to set, 45–60 minutes.

Fold remaining ingredients into gelatin mixture. Rinse a 5-cup mold with cold water and drain; do not wipe out. Add gelatin mixture to mold. Cover and chill for 4–6 hours or until firm. Unmold and serve. *Serves 8–10*

CREAMY COLE SLAW

Cream cheese is a surprisingly good ingredient in many recipes, from lasagna filling to salad dressings. Be sure that you soften it thoroughly before combining it with the light cream for the smoothest dressing.

The salad mixes available in the produce department of the grocery store certainly have made making salads and slaws easier. Be sure to watch the "best by" dates on these packages and keep them refrigerated so they last longer.

1 (3-ounce) package cream cheese, softened	$1/2$ teaspoon dried tarragon leaves
$1/2$ cup light cream	1 (16-ounce) package coleslaw mix
$1/4$ cup tarragon vinegar	1 cup minced celery
$1/2$ teaspoon salt	1 orange bell pepper, chopped
$1/8$ teaspoon white pepper	$1/4$ cup chopped green onions

In small bowl, beat cream cheese until smooth and fluffy. Very gradually add the cream, beating constantly, until mixture is smooth. Add vinegar, salt, pepper, and tarragon leaves and mix well. Cover and refrigerate.

In large serving bowl, combine remaining ingredients. Add dressing and toss gently to coat. Serve immediately or cover and chill for 2–4 hours before serving. *Serves 6–8*

• •

CRANBERRY WALDORF SALAD

Waldorf salad was created at the Waldorf-Astoria Hotel in New York City in the late 1800s. It's traditionally made of apples and walnuts in a mayonnaise mixture. Cranberries, marshmallows, and heavy whipping cream give this salad a nice, fresh twist.

2 cups fresh cranberries	1 cup chopped walnuts
3 cups miniature marshmallows	$1/4$ teaspoon salt
$1/4$ cup sugar	1 cup heavy whipping cream
2 cups unpeeled, diced apples	1 tablespoon powdered sugar
1 cup green grapes	1 teaspoon vanilla

Grind cranberries in a food processor or food mill and combine in a bowl with the marshmallows and sugar. Cover and refrigerate 6 hours or overnight.

Two hours before serving time, stir in the apples, grapes, walnuts, and salt. In small bowl, combine cream, powdered sugar, and vanilla and beat until stiff peaks form.

Fold into the salad, cover, and chill for 2 hours. *Serves 8*

ORIENTAL SEAFOOD SALAD

Try some shrimp and crab in this delectable salad. I like to make this salad and keep it in the refrigerator, so whenever someone is hungry, they can have a snack!

1 (16-ounce) package frozen
  baby peas, thawed
1 (10-ounce) package frozen
  pearl onions
1 cup sliced celery
1 red bell pepper, chopped
1 pint grape tomatoes
1/2 pound frozen lump crab
  meat, thawed

1/2 pound frozen cooked
  medium shrimp, thawed
2 tablespoons lime juice
1/2 cup mayonnaise
1/2 cup plain yogurt
1 teaspoon curry powder
2 teaspoons soy sauce
1/8 teaspoon pepper
1 (10-ounce) bag mixed salad greens

Thaw the peas and drain well on paper towels. Cook onions as directed on package, rinse with cold water, and drain well on paper towels. Combine in large bowl with celery, bell pepper, and grape tomatoes; cover and refrigerate.

In medium bowl, combine crab meat and shrimp. Sprinkle with lime juice and refrigerate for 30 minutes. Add to pea mixture and set aside.

In small bowl, combine mayonnaise, yogurt, curry powder, soy sauce, and pepper and mix well. Pour over salad and toss gently to coat. Serve immediately on salad greens or cover and chill for 4 hours before serving. *Serves 6*

• •

MOLDED APPLE-PECAN SALAD

Molded salads have a bad reputation, but I don't know why! Once you understand how to work with gelatin, they are very easy to make and are so versatile.

For perfect results with unflavored gelatin, first soften it in water, then heat the mixture, either in a microwave oven or on the stovetop or by pouring more boiling liquid over it, and stir until the gelatin is completely dissolved. Pick up a bit in a stainless-steel spoon; if you can't see any tiny grains of gelatin, it's properly dissolved.

This salad is excellent made with some of Minnesota's crisp and tart apples. Serve it with a drop of mayonnaise or sour cream to finish.

2 (0.25-ounce) envelopes
  unflavored gelatin
1/2 cup water
1/2 cup sugar
11/2 cups apple juice

3/4 cup apple cider
1/4 cup lemon juice
1 cup chopped pecans
1 cup sliced celery
2 cups peeled, chopped apples

43

In large bowl, combine gelatin with the water. Meanwhile, in large saucepan, combine sugar, apple juice, apple cider, and lemon juice. Heat over medium-high heat, stirring occasionally, until mixture just comes to a boil and sugar is dissolved.

Immediately pour over gelatin and stir until the gelatin dissolves completely. Cover bowl and chill mixture in refrigerator until it begins to thicken, about 30–40 minutes.

Fold remaining ingredients into gelatin mixture. Rinse a 5-cup mold with cold water, then drain; do not dry. Pour gelatin mixture into mold. Cover and chill until firm, at least 4 hours.

When ready to serve, rinse a kitchen towel in hot water, then squeeze until damp. Turn the mold over onto a serving plate and cover with the hot towel for 30–40 seconds. Remove the towel, hold the mold and plate firmly, and shake vigorously. Then lift the mold; the salad should drop right out. *Serves 6–8*

· ·

CRANBERRY–MANDARIN SALAD

This gorgeous salad has the most incredible color, flavor, and texture. It's great for the holidays or for a warm summer day, served with homemade muffins and tea sandwiches.

3 tablespoons sugar	1 (11-ounce) can mandarin oranges
1/2 teaspoon cinnamon	1 (16-ounce) can whole-berry
1/8 teaspoon cardamom	cranberry sauce
1/4 teaspoon salt	1/2 cup diced celery
1 (0.25-ounce) envelope	1/2 cup chopped pecans
unflavored gelatin	2 tablespoons lemon juice

In large microwave-safe bowl, combine sugar, cinnamon, cardamom, salt, and unflavored gelatin and mix well.

Drain oranges, reserving juice. Add juice to gelatin mixture and let stand for 4 minutes. Microwave gelatin mixture on 50-percent power for 1 minute, then remove and stir. Continue microwaving on 50-percent power for 30-second intervals, stirring after each interval, until gelatin and sugar are completely dissolved. Add cranberry sauce, celery, pecans, and lemon juice and mix gently to combine.

Rinse a $1^1/_2$-quart ring mold with cold water and drain; do not dry. Arrange drained orange segments in the bottom of the mold and pour cranberry mixture over all. Refrigerate for 4–6 hours until firm. Unmold to serve. *Serves 8*

· ·

CHICKEN SALAD IN CRANBERRY RING

If you're hosting a ladies' luncheon, this is the recipe for you. Do ladies still have luncheons? I know there are still showers for weddings and babies, along with Bunko parties and birthday parties. Make this old-fashioned recipe for your next get-together.

1 cup orange juice	2 tablespoons orange juice
1 tablespoon lime juice	1 tablespoon lemon juice
1 cup water	2 cups chopped cooked chicken
1 (6-ounce) package lemon gelatin	1 cup chopped celery
1 cup orange juice	1 cup grapes
1 (16-ounce) can whole-berry	1/2 cup chopped toasted hazelnuts
cranberry sauce	2 tablespoons chopped flat-leaf
1/2 cup mayonnaise	parsley
1/4 cup vanilla yogurt	

In microwave-safe glass measuring cup, combine 1 cup orange juice, lime juice, and water; bring to a boil on high power.

Meanwhile, place gelatin in large mixing bowl. Pour boiling liquid over and stir until gelatin dissolves. Add remaining 1 cup orange juice and cranberry sauce; stir until combined. Chill mixture in refrigerator until partially set, about 1 hour.

Stir and pour mixture into 6^1/2-cup ring mold. Chill for at least 8 hours or overnight until set.

For Chicken Salad, in large bowl, combine mayonnaise, yogurt, 2 tablespoons orange juice, and lemon juice and mix well. Stir in remaining ingredients except parsley to coat. Cover and chill.

When ready to serve, unmold the cranberry mixture onto a chilled serving plate. Pile the chicken salad in the center; garnish with chopped parsley and serve immediately. *Serves 6*

MASHED POTATO SALAD

This is a fun way to serve potato salad. The seasonings are added while the potatoes are still hot so they can absorb them. Serve this delicious salad with grilled hamburgers and a simple fruit salad.

To hard-cook eggs, place them in a medium saucepan and cover with cold water. Bring to a boil over high heat. When water boils furiously, cover the pan, remove it from the heat, and let stand for 15 minutes for large eggs. Then run cold water into the pan until the eggs feel cold to the touch. Crack them under the water for easier peeling; peel and refrigerate promptly.

4 pounds russet potatoes
1/2 teaspoon salt
1/4 teaspoon white pepper
1/4 cup apple cider vinegar
2 tablespoons prepared mustard
11/4 cups mayonnaise

6 hard-cooked eggs, chopped
1/2 cup chopped green onion
1 green bell pepper, chopped
1 cup chopped celery
2 tomatoes

Peel potatoes and cut into cubes. Place in boiling lightly salted water and simmer until tender, about 10–15 minutes. Drain potatoes and return to the pot; shake over low heat for about 30 seconds to remove excess water.

Turn potatoes into a large bowl and mash. Add salt, pepper, vinegar, mustard, and mayonnaise and mix well.

Fold chopped eggs, green onion, bell pepper, and celery into the potatoes. Cover and refrigerate until cold. Garnish with tomato wedges and serve. *Serves 8–10*

PINEAPPLE MOLDED SALAD

For the holidays, this creamy and sweet-tart salad is a good choice. Molded salads, because they're make-ahead, are a great boon for the hostess. I like this recipe because it uses unflavored gelatin rather than flavored.

2 (0.25-ounce) envelopes unflavored gelatin
21/2 cups pineapple juice, divided
2 cups miniature marshmallows
1 (14-ounce) can sweetened condensed milk
1 (20-ounce) can crushed pineapple
1 cup chopped celery
1 cup shredded carrots
1/2 cup chopped dried cherries
4 cups mixed salad greens

In small microwave-safe bowl, combine gelatin with 1/2 cup of the pineapple juice. Let stand for 5 minutes to soften. Then microwave mixture on 50-percent power for 1 minute, stir, and microwave for 1 minute longer or until gelatin dissolves completely.

Stir in remaining pineapple juice. Chill in the refrigerator until mixture is syrupy, about 45 minutes. Then stir in marshmallows, milk, pineapple (including juice), celery, carrots, and dried cherries.

Rinse a 2-quart mold or bundt pan with cold water and drain; do not dry. Pour pineapple mixture into mold. Cover and chill for at least 6 hours or until salad is set. Unmold and serve on salad greens. *Serves 8*

CRISPY TART COLE SLAW

Cole slaw can be used in so many ways. It's an obvious picnic favorite and perfect for a cookout. But did you know that it also makes an excellent sandwich topping? Use it to top ham sandwiches or slices of leftover meat loaf.

1 large head cabbage	1 cup sugar
1 onion, chopped	1 cup apple cider vinegar
1 green bell pepper, chopped	1 tablespoon celery seed
1 red bell pepper, chopped	1 teaspoon mustard seed
1 teaspoon salt	2 tablespoons minced flat-leaf
1 cup boiling water	parsley

Shred cabbage and combine in a large bowl with onion and bell peppers. Sprinkle salt over all and pour boiling water over that. Stir, then let stand at room temperature for 1 hour.

Drain mixture in a colander, then return to bowl. In small bowl, combine sugar, vinegar, celery seed, and mustard seed and whisk to combine. Let stand for 5 minutes, then whisk again.

Pour dressing over the cabbage mixture. Cover and refrigerate until very cold, about 4–5 hours. Sprinkle with parsley and serve. *Serves 10–12*

HOLIDAY GRAPE SALAD

This is a salad for grown-ups only. The wine isn't heated, so the alcohol content will remain in the finished product. It's a gorgeous salad with a beautiful color and texture.

$2/3$ cup sugar	1 cup rose wine
$1/4$ teaspoon salt	$1^1/2$ cups green grapes
2 (0.25-ounce) envelopes	$1^1/2$ cups red grapes
unflavored gelatin	$1/3$ cup heavy whipping cream
$2/3$ cup lemon juice	1 tablespoon powdered sugar
2 cups boiling water	$1/4$ cup sour cream

In large mixing bowl, combine sugar, salt, and the gelatin. Stir in lemon juice and let stand for 5 minutes. Then add the boiling water and stir until sugar and gelatin completely dissolve.

Add the wine and refrigerate mixture until it begins to thicken. While the mixture chills, cut the grapes in half lengthwise. Add grapes to the gelatin mixture, then spoon into a $5^1/2$-cup mold.

Cover salad and chill for at least 6 hours until firm. Unmold onto a serving plate and return to refrigerator.

In small bowl, combine cream with powdered sugar and beat until soft peaks form. Beat in sour cream. Serve this mixture with the salad. *Serves 6–8*

"Rise 'n' shine with Jack Huston and Joyce Lamont,"
encourages this WCCO advertisement from the May 9,
1956 *Minneapolis Tribune.*

AVOCADO–CREAM CHEESE SALAD DRESSING

You don't ever have to serve a plain green salad again with this recipe in your repertoire. It's creamy, flavorful, and the most gorgeous light green color. It doesn't keep long in the fridge, though—just about two days.

1 cup cottage cheese	1/2 cup mayonnaise
1 avocado, peeled and cubed	1/2 teaspoon seasoned salt
1/2 teaspoon grated lemon zest	1/4 teaspoon chili powder
1 tablespoon lemon juice	Dash white pepper

Combine all ingredients in food processor or blender; cover and process until mixture is thick and smooth. Transfer mixture to a small bowl. Cover by placing plastic wrap directly on the surface of the dressing and refrigerate. *Yields 2 cups dressing*

. . . .

TUNA–CARROT SALAD

Shoestring potatoes add crunch and nice flavor to this simple salad. Serve it on lettuce greens or use it as a sandwich filling. Did you know that you can now find preshredded carrots in the grocery store? That saves so much time!

1/2 cup mayonnaise	1 1/2 cups shredded carrots
1/3 cup milk	1 cup chopped celery
1 tablespoon prepared mustard	1/2 cup chopped red onion
1/8 teaspoon white pepper	1 cup shoestring potato sticks
1 (6-ounce) can light chunk tuna, drained	

In large bowl, combine mayonnaise, milk, mustard, and pepper and mix well. Add tuna, carrots, celery, and red onion and mix well. Cover and refrigerate for 3–4 hours to blend flavors.

Just before serving, stir in the potato sticks. Serve on lettuce leaves or as a sandwich filling. *Serves 6*

. . . .

CREAMY FRUIT SALAD

Canned fruits make a delicious salad with a few convenience foods. Cottage cheese and frozen whipped topping may sound strange, but the combination is delicious.

1 (11-ounce) can mandarin oranges, drained
1 (20-ounce) can crushed pineapple, drained
1 (15-ounce) can cherries, drained
2 cups small-curd cottage cheese
1 (8-ounce) container frozen whipped topping, thawed
1 (3-ounce) package orange gelatin

Combine fruits in large bowl. In medium bowl, fold together cottage cheese and whipped topping. Fold into fruit mixture. Sprinkle the dry gelatin over the salad and fold in gently.

Cover and refrigerate for 4–6 hours or until chilled. *Serves 6*

••

SOUR CREAM CABBAGE SALAD

Despite all the commercials about Wisconsin and California's dairy industry, Minnesota's dairy industry is a big deal too. Our state is fifth nationwide in dairy production. Milk, sour cream, heavy whipping cream, yogurt, and ice cream are all Minnesota products. You can use low-fat or full-fat sour cream in this delicious salad.

4 cups shredded cabbage
1 cup sour cream
2 tablespoons vinegar
2 tablespoons lemon juice
1/2 teaspoon salt
1 teaspoon sugar
1 teaspoon paprika
1/4 cup minced green onion
1/4 cup minced flat-leaf parsley
1/2 cup grated cucumber

Place cabbage in a large bowl and cover with ice water; let stand while preparing dressing.

In small bowl, combine remaining ingredients and mix well with wire whisk. Drain cabbage thoroughly. Add dressing and stir gently to coat. Serve immediately or cover and refrigerate for 2–3 hours before serving. *Serves 6*

••

TURKEY AND POTATO SALAD

This inventive salad uses frozen potatoes to cut preparation time. With this quick method, you'll be making potato salad with ease all summer long!

1 tablespoon olive oil	1 cup mayonnaise
1 onion, chopped	2 tablespoons prepared mustard
1 (16-ounce) package	$1/4$ cup milk
frozen potato wedges	4 green onions, chopped
$1/2$ teaspoon salt	1 red bell pepper, chopped
$1/8$ teaspoon pepper	2 cups diced cooked turkey
$1/2$ cup water	

In large skillet, heat olive oil over medium heat. Add onion; cook and stir until crisp-tender, about 5 minutes. Add potato wedges, salt, and pepper; cook and stir for 2 minutes. Add water and bring to a boil.

Turn down heat, cover pan, and simmer for 5–8 minutes or until potatoes are tender. Drain off any remaining liquid and let stand for 10 minutes.

In large bowl, combine mayonnaise, mustard, and milk and mix until smooth. Stir in potato mixture to coat. Then fold in green onions, bell pepper, and turkey. Cover and chill for 2–4 hours to blend flavors. *Serves 6*

• •

FROZEN WALDORF SALAD

Frozen salads are wonderful for entertaining. In fact, they're also great to have on hand if you have hungry teenagers in the house. Just point them to the cupboard with the plates and tell them there's a salad in the freezer!

1 (8-ounce) can crushed pineapple	2 apples, chopped
2 eggs	$2/3$ cup diced celery
$1/2$ cup sugar	$1/2$ cup chopped pecans
$1/4$ cup lemon juice	$1/2$ cup heavy whipping cream
$1/8$ teaspoon salt	1 tablespoon powdered sugar
$1/4$ cup mayonnaise	

Drain pineapple, reserving juice. In heavy medium saucepan, combine reserved juice, eggs, sugar, lemon juice, and salt. Cook and stir over medium heat until mixture thickens and just comes to a boil.

Remove mixture from heat and cool for 30 minutes. Chill for 1 hour. Then add pineapple, mayonnaise, apples, celery, and pecans.

In small bowl, combine cream with powdered sugar and beat until stiff peaks form. Fold into salad. Spoon into 9-inch square pan, cover, and freeze until firm. To serve, cut into squares. *Serves 9*

Refrigerator Carrot Salad

This combination will sound unusual, but it is very delicious. Tomato soup has lots of spice and tang, and when combined with seasonings, it makes a nice salad dressing.

2 pounds sliced carrots	1/2 cup vinegar
1 (10 3/4-ounce) can	1/2 teaspoon salt
condensed tomato soup	1/4 teaspoon pepper
1/2 cup sugar	1 onion, sliced
1/3 cup vegetable oil	1 green bell pepper, sliced

In large saucepan, place carrots and cover with cold water. Bring to a boil over high heat, then reduce heat to medium-low and simmer until tender, about 4–6 minutes. Drain carrots well.

Meanwhile, in large bowl, combine soup, sugar, oil, vinegar, salt, and pepper and mix well. When carrots are cooked and still hot, stir them into the soup mixture along with the onion and bell pepper.

Cover salad and refrigerate at least 4 hours before serving. *Serves 8*

• •

Fruit Salad with Creamy Dressing

Marshmallows melt into plain yogurt to form a sweet and tart dressing in this easy recipe. Use the fruits that look the best in the market, depending on the season. The fruits in this recipe are best in the winter months.

1 cup plain yogurt	3 oranges, peeled and chopped
1 cup miniature marshmallows	1 (13-ounce) can pineapple chunks,
1 1/2 cups green grapes	drained
1 banana	Mixed lettuces

In small bowl, combine yogurt with marshmallows. Cover and refrigerate overnight.

The next day, about 2 hours before you're ready to serve, combine fruit in serving bowl and toss to mix. Cover and refrigerate until cold, about 1–2 hours.

Beat yogurt mixture until smooth and fluffy. Place fruit mixture onto lettuce and top with the yogurt mixture. *Serves 6*

• •

BOB DeHAVEN and
JOYCE LAMONT

Bob DeHaven and Joyce Lamont started the day happily for listeners
with the program *First Bank Notes*, which came on the air at 7:30 in the
morning, Monday through Saturday.

CAULIFLOWER SALAD

Fresh cauliflower is delicious: It's crisp and mild with a slightly peppery taste. In this salad it's combined with more fresh vegetables for wonderful flavor and crunch. You could transform this recipe into a main-dish salad by adding chicken, turkey, or ham.

1 head cauliflower	3/4 cup mayonnaise
3/4 cup peeled, diced cucumber	1/4 cup plain yogurt
1/2 cup chopped green onion	1/8 teaspoon pepper
1/2 cup sliced radishes	2 teaspoons curry powder
1/2 cup sliced celery	

Break cauliflower into small florets. Combine in large bowl with cucumber, green onion, radishes, and celery and toss to mix.

In small bowl, combine remaining ingredients and mix well. Pour over vegetables and stir to coat. Serve immediately or cover and chill for 4 hours to blend flavors. *Serves 6*

SOUPS AND SANDWICHES

3

Sandwiches are the perfect choice for lunch on the run, lunchboxes, and even fancy get-togethers. You're only limited by your imagination! With all the wonderful artisan breads, unusual cheeses, herbs, vegetables, and fruits available today, you can have a sandwich every day for a year and never repeat once.

One easy way to update a classic sandwich recipe is to think about a new way to contain the filling. Pita breads, tortillas, and even lettuce leaves make great bread substitutes.

And soups are the perfect choice when the weather is cold . . . or hot! They can simmer on the stove for hours, or try using a slow cooker. Reduce the liquid in the recipe by one-third and let it cook all day on low. If you want to serve a chilled soup, make sure it's really cold and serve it in chilled bowls.

CARROT CHEESE SOUP

This simple creamy soup has such a beautiful color. You could make it a vegetarian soup by using vegetable broth instead of chicken stock. The new stocks you can buy in boxes are usually of better quality than canned soups. And with these products, you can store the leftovers in the fridge.

Top this soup with some crunchy croutons and serve it with a light fruit salad for lunch.

2$1/2$ cups chicken stock	$1/2$ teaspoon dried dill weed
1 cup shredded carrots	$1/3$ cup flour
1 cup thinly sliced celery	3 cups whole milk
1 onion, thinly sliced	2 cups shredded sharp Cheddar cheese
$1/2$ teaspoon salt	1 cup shredded Muenster cheese
$1/8$ teaspoon white pepper	

In large saucepan, heat chicken stock and add carrots, celery, and onion. Simmer vegetables in the broth for 10–12 minutes or until tender. Sprinkle with salt, pepper, and dill weed.

In small bowl, combine flour with 1 cup milk and stir with wire whisk until blended. Add to soup along with the rest of the milk; cook and stir over medium heat until soup thickens slightly.

Stir in cheeses; cook and stir until cheeses melt and soup is hot. Serve immediately. *Serves 6*

POTATO-BACON SOUP

This simple soup has a lot of flavor, and it's inexpensive too. Buy bacon when it's on sale and freeze it up to three months; you can put it in a skillet while still frozen and cook until crisp, turning it frequently.

1 (8-ounce) package bacon
1 onion, chopped
6 potatoes, peeled and cubed
1/2 cup chopped celery
1 teaspoon salt

1/4 teaspoon white pepper
11/2 cups water
4 cups milk
1/3 cup chopped green onion

Cook bacon in large skillet until crisp. Drain bacon, reserving 1 tablespoon drippings. Crumble bacon and set aside.

In large saucepan, combine reserved bacon drippings and onion; cook and stir for 3 minutes. Add potatoes, celery, salt, and pepper and stir. Add water, bring to a boil, then reduce heat, cover, and simmer for 15–20 minutes until potatoes are tender.

Mash potato mixture using a potato masher or large fork. Add the milk and bacon and heat through, but do not boil. Garnish with green onions and serve. *Serves 6*

• •

CREAM OF AVOCADO SOUP

A chilled soup is a nice change of pace, especially during the hot summer months. This soup is a gorgeous lime green color and has the perfect velvety texture. Serve it with a fruit salad and muffins for a satisfying lunch on a hot day.

3 ripe avocados, divided
1 tablespoon lemon juice
1/4 cup plain yogurt
1/2 cup chicken stock
1 tablespoon minced onion
1 clove garlic

2 cups light cream
1/8 teaspoon cayenne pepper
1/2 teaspoon salt
1/8 teaspoon white pepper
1 teaspoon lemon juice

Peel and chop two of the avocados and combine in a food processor or blender with lemon juice, yogurt, chicken stock, onion, and garlic. Process or blend until smooth.

Pour avocado mixture into a medium bowl and stir in remaining ingredients, except 1 teaspoon lemon juice and remaining avocado. Cover by placing plastic wrap directly onto the surface of the soup; chill for 3–4 hours.

When ready to serve, peel and dice remaining avocado and sprinkle with 1 teaspoon lemon juice. Ladle soup into individual bowls and top with avocado. *Serves 4*

NEW ENGLAND CLAM CHOWDER

Salt pork is an ingredient you don't see much anymore. Your butcher may have it. If he doesn't, use chopped bacon instead. This old-fashioned recipe is rich, thick, and creamy. Serve it with oyster crackers and a spinach salad tossed with red bell peppers and strawberries.

1/4 cup finely chopped salt pork or bacon	1/8 teaspoon white pepper
2 tablespoons butter	3 (7-ounce) cans whole baby clams
2 onions, chopped	3 cups light cream or evaporated milk
3 cloves garlic, minced	2 tablespoons flour
2 cups peeled, diced potatoes	1/4 cup whole milk
1/2 teaspoon salt	1/2 cup chopped flat-leaf parsley

In large saucepan, cook salt pork or bacon over medium heat until crisp and browned. Remove salt pork or bacon and drain on paper towels. Add butter to fat remaining in pan and add onion and garlic. Cook and stir until crisp-tender, 4–5 minutes.

Add potatoes, salt, and pepper and stir. Drain clams, reserving juice. Set clams aside. Add clam juice to saucepan and, if necessary, add water so potatoes are covered. Bring to a boil, then reduce heat and simmer until potatoes are tender, 8–12 minutes.

Add cream to saucepan and stir. In small bowl, combine flour with whole milk and stir until smooth. Add to saucepan and cook slowly over low heat until soup begins to thicken. Add clams and heat through. Garnish each serving with reserved salt pork or bacon and parsley. *Serves 6–8*

....

FRESH VEGETABLE BEEF SOUP

Make this delicious soup when you're at home on a snow day. The simmering soup will add the most fabulous aroma to your house. In fact, while you're at it, choose a bread from this book and make that too, then treat your family to a hearty, old-fashioned, soul-warming meal.

3 pounds beef bones	1 cup shredded cabbage
3 quarts cold water	1 green bell pepper, chopped
3 tablespoons butter	1 (14.5-ounce) can diced tomatoes, undrained
1 onion, chopped	1 teaspoon salt
3 cloves garlic, minced	1/8 teaspoon pepper
2 carrots, diced	1 cup frozen baby peas
3 celery stalks, diced	1/4 cup chopped flat-leaf parsley

In large stockpot, combine beef bones and water. Bring to a boil over high heat, then skim surface, reduce heat to low, and simmer, covered, for 3–4 hours until stock tastes meaty. Remove bones, strain broth, and simmer over medium heat until stock is reduced to 6 cups.

In large skillet, melt butter and cook onion, garlic, and carrots until crisp-tender, about 5 minutes. Add celery, cabbage, and green bell pepper; cook and stir for 5 minutes.

Add vegetables to beef stock along with tomatoes, salt, and pepper. Bring to a simmer, then add peas and cook for 5–8 minutes longer until hot. Sprinkle with parsley and serve. *Serves 8–10*

• •

BEAN AND BACON SOUP

If the only Bean and Bacon soup you've ever had is out of a can, you're in for a treat. This is the real thing—made with dried navy beans, bacon, and tomatoes. Serve it with some toasted garlic bread and a fruit salad. And for dessert? A classic chocolate cake is perfect.

1 pound dried navy beans	2 cups sliced carrots
3 quarts water	1 bay leaf
10 bacon slices	1 (8-ounce) can tomato sauce
4 onions, chopped	4 cups tomato juice
3 cloves garlic, chopped	1 teaspoon salt
3 cups peeled, diced potatoes	1/4 teaspoon pepper

Sort over the dried beans and rinse them, then drain. Place in large stockpot with the water. Bring to a boil and boil for 2 minutes. Remove from heat, cover, and let stand for 1 hour.

Meanwhile, cook the bacon in large skillet until crisp; remove bacon, crumble, and set aside. Cook onions and garlic in the bacon fat for 4–5 minutes. Add bacon, onions, garlic, and the bacon fat to the beans and water.

Bring to a boil, reduce heat to low, and simmer soup, covered, for 1 hour. Add the potatoes, carrots, and bay leaf; simmer for 20 minutes until potatoes are tender.

Then add tomato sauce, juice, salt, and pepper and bring to a simmer. Simmer for 15–20 minutes longer or until beans are tender. Remove bay leaf and serve immediately. *Serves 6–8*

• •

Italian Vegetable Beef Soup

This hearty soup is a meal in one. The combination of kidney beans and macaroni, along with tender beef, is really delicious and very satisfying.

1 pound beef sirloin tip	1 (14.5-ounce) can diced tomatoes,
1/2 teaspoon salt	undrained
1/4 teaspoon pepper	1 teaspoon dried Italian seasoning
2 tablespoons flour	1 (10-ounce) package frozen green beans
2 tablespoons olive oil	1 (15-ounce) can kidney beans, drained
2 onions, chopped	1 1/2 cups sliced carrots
3 cloves garlic, minced	1 cup chopped celery
2 cups water	1 cup shell macaroni
3 cups beef stock	Grated Parmesan cheese

Cut beef into 1-inch cubes; sprinkle with salt, pepper, and flour. Heat olive oil in large stockpot; brown beef, stirring frequently, for 5–8 minutes. Add onions and garlic; cook and stir until onions are translucent, about 5 minutes longer.

Add water, beef stock, tomatoes, and Italian seasoning. Bring to a boil, then reduce heat to low and simmer, covered, for 1 1/2 hours.

Add green beans, kidney beans, carrots, and celery and bring back to a boil. Reduce heat and simmer for 15 minutes. Then add macaroni; simmer for 12–16 minutes or until macaroni is tender. Serve with Parmesan cheese. *Serves 8–10*

. . . .

Hamburger Soup

This simple soup is easy to make and tastes so much better than any canned variety. Your kids will love it too, because it uses all of their favorite ingredients!

1 pound lean ground beef	3 cups beef broth
1 onion, chopped	1/2 teaspoon salt
1 (14.5-ounce) can diced	1/8 teaspoon pepper
tomatoes, undrained	1/2 teaspoon dried oregano leaves
3 carrots, sliced	1 cup frozen green beans
1/2 cup chopped celery	

In large saucepan, brown beef with onion; drain thoroughly. Add remaining ingredients except green beans. Bring to a simmer over medium heat, then reduce heat, cover, and let soup simmer for 15 minutes.

Remove the cover, add the green beans, bring to a simmer, and cook 8–10 minutes longer until beans are hot and tender. Serve immediately. *Serves 6*

U.S. SENATE BEAN SOUP

A version of this soup is served in the Senate building in Washington, D.C. It is hearty and filling with a subtle, rich flavor. Be sure to carefully sort the beans before soaking them to remove any extraneous material. If you don't have leftover mashed potatoes, make some using dried potato flakes, following the directions on the package.

2 cups dry navy beans	2 cloves garlic, minced
3 quarts water	$1/4$ cup flat-leaf parsley, minced
1 meaty ham bone	$1/2$ cup leftover mashed potatoes
3 onions, chopped	1 teaspoon salt
6 stalks celery, chopped	$1/4$ teaspoon pepper

Pick over the beans and rinse thoroughly; drain. Place in large soup pot and cover with water. Cover pot and let soak overnight.

The next day, drain the beans and add 3 quarts fresh water. Add ham bone and bring to a simmer over high heat. Cover pan, reduce heat, and let simmer for 1 hour.

Prepare vegetables and add to soup. Cover and simmer for 1 hour longer until beans are soft.

Remove ham bone and cut off the meat. Dice meat and return to soup; discard the bone. Season soup with salt and pepper to taste and serve immediately. *Serves 10–12*

• •

MEATBALL STEW

If you'd like, you could substitute a package of frozen precooked meatballs for the homemade meatballs in this hearty recipe. Serve this delicious stew with some crisp breadsticks and a fruit pie for dessert.

1 cup soft bread crumbs	3 cloves garlic, minced
1 egg	1 ($10^3/4$-ounce) can condensed
$1/2$ teaspoon salt	beef broth
$1/8$ teaspoon pepper	1 ($10^3/4$-ounce) can condensed
$1/2$ teaspoon dried marjoram	tomato soup
leaves	1 cup water
$1/2$ teaspoon dried thyme leaves	4 potatoes, peeled and chopped
$1^1/2$ pounds lean ground beef	4 carrots, peeled and sliced
2 tablespoons olive oil	2 tablespoons chopped
1 onion, chopped	flat-leaf parsley

In large bowl, combine bread crumbs, egg, salt, pepper, marjoram, and thyme and mix well. Add beef and mix gently but thoroughly until combined. Form into 24 meatballs.

Heat oil in large soup pot over medium heat. Add meatballs and sauté, turning frequently, until browned, about 5–7 minutes. Remove meatballs from pan with slotted spoon and drain on paper towels.

Add onion to drippings remaining in pan and cook for 5 minutes. Then add beef broth, tomato soup, water, potatoes, carrots, and the meatballs. Bring to a simmer, reduce heat, cover, and simmer for 20–30 minutes or until meatballs are thoroughly cooked and vegetables are tender. Sprinkle with parsley and serve. *Serves 6–8*

CHEESE-BROCCOLI SOUP

American cheese may be scorned by gourmets, but not me! It is delicious, easy to use, and full of calcium. This soup is rich and creamy with a wonderful flavor.

2 tablespoons butter	2 cups milk
1 onion, chopped	1 cup grated processed
2 cloves garlic, minced	American cheese
3 tablespoons flour	1^1/$_2$ cups chicken broth
^{1}/$_4$ teaspoon salt	1 (10-ounce) package frozen
^{1}/$_8$ teaspoon pepper	chopped broccoli

In large saucepan, melt butter over medium heat. Add onion and garlic; cook and stir until onion is translucent, about 8 minutes. Add flour, salt, and pepper; cook and stir until bubbly.

Add milk; cook and stir until soup begins to thicken, 5–8 minutes. Stir in grated cheese and cook and stir until cheese melts and soup thickens. Remove from heat and set aside.

In small saucepan, combine chicken broth with broccoli. Bring to a simmer over medium heat, then cover pan and cook until broccoli is tender according to package directions.

Add broccoli and cooking liquid to cheese mixture and heat over low heat until hot, stirring constantly. Serve immediately. *Serves 5*

SPANISH GAZPACHO

Gazpacho is a cold soup made with tomatoes and other vegetables. It makes a refreshing lunch on a hot day, served with some grilled cheese bread and fresh fruit.

To easily peel tomatoes, bring a large pot of water to a boil. Cut an X into the peel and drop tomatoes into the water. Boil for 30 seconds, then remove and place in ice water. The peel will come off easily.

1$1/2$ cups peeled, finely chopped tomato	1 clove garlic, minced
1 cup peeled, finely chopped cucumber	3 tablespoons white wine vinegar
	2 tablespoons olive oil
1 cup finely chopped green pepper	$1/2$ teaspoon salt
	$1/8$ teaspoon pepper
$1/2$ cup finely chopped celery	$1/2$ teaspoon Worcestershire sauce
1 tablespoon minced flat-leaf parsley	2$1/2$ cups tomato juice
	1 cup garlic croutons

Combine all ingredients, except croutons, in a large glass bowl. Cover bowl and chill in refrigerator for 4–6 hours.

Serve in chilled bowls, garnished with croutons. *Serves 6*

BEEF-TOMATO-RICE SOUP

Quick soups are a boon to busy mothers. And it's nice to serve a soup that didn't just come out of a can. If you have time, Cheese Crackers (page 25) are a great accompaniment.

1 pound ground beef	$1/3$ cup uncooked rice
1 large onion, chopped	1 teaspoon chili powder
4 stalks celery, chopped	3 cups beef broth
1 (14.5-ounce) can diced tomatoes, undrained	

In large soup pot, combine beef, onion, and celery over medium heat. Cook, stirring to break up beef, until meat is browned and vegetables are tender. Drain thoroughly.

Add remaining ingredients and bring to a simmer. Reduce heat, cover pot, and simmer for 15–25 minutes or until rice is tender. Serve immediately. *Serves 6*

CHILLED CUCUMBER-TOMATO SOUP

You can serve this cold, elegant soup immediately if you keep the canned soup in the refrigerator so it's already cold. Top this soup with thin slices of cucumber and some chopped fresh tomato.

1 (10$3/4$-ounce) can condensed
    tomato soup
1 $1/4$ cups whole milk
1 cucumber
2 tablespoons diced green onions

$1/4$ teaspoon seasoned salt
Dash pepper
$1/2$ teaspoon Worcestershire sauce
$1/4$ cup chopped flat-leaf parsley
$1/4$ cup sour cream

Combine soup and milk in medium bowl; stir with wire whisk to blend. Peel cucumber, remove seeds, and grate the cucumber. Stir into soup mixture along with remaining ingredients except parsley and sour cream.

Cover and chill soup for at least 2 hours. Serve garnished with parsley and sour cream. *Serves 4*

. . . .

FAMOUS CLAM CHOWDER

I don't know why this chowder is famous, but it certainly is good! The secret is the bacon and the large amount of cream. Yes, that's a lot of cream, but for a splurge—especially during the holidays—this soup fits the bill.

8 slices bacon
2 onions, chopped
3 cloves garlic, minced
1 cup chopped celery
2 cups peeled, finely chopped
    potatoes
3 (6-ounce) cans minced clams

$3/4$ cup butter
$3/4$ cup flour
4 cups light cream
1 teaspoon salt
$1/8$ teaspoon pepper
2 tablespoons white wine vinegar

In large soup pot, cook bacon until crisp. Remove bacon, drain on paper towels, crumble, and set aside.

Remove all but 2 tablespoons drippings from pot. Add onion, garlic, and celery to pot; cook and stir until crisp-tender, about 5 minutes.

Drain clams, reserving liquid. Add liquid to pot along with enough water to cover vegetables. Bring to a boil, reduce heat to low, and simmer, covered, until vegetables are tender, 8–10 minutes.

Meanwhile, in large saucepan, melt butter over medium heat. Add flour; cook and stir until bubbly, 5–6 minutes. Add light cream along with salt and pepper; bring to a simmer and cook, stirring frequently, until sauce starts to thicken.

Stir this sauce into the vegetables with the clams, reserved bacon, and vinegar. Cook and stir until chowder is steaming, then serve. *Serves 8*

CREAM OF CARROT SOUP

Now this is a soup you won't find in the canned-soup aisle! It's delicious served warm or cold. If you serve it cold, top it with sour cream and some chopped fresh dill weed.

2 tablespoons butter
1 onion, chopped
3 cups finely chopped carrots
4 cups chicken broth
2 tablespoons uncooked
   long-grain rice

1/2 teaspoon salt
1/8 teaspoon pepper
1/2 cup light cream
2 tablespoons chopped flat-leaf
   parsley

Melt butter over medium heat in large saucepan. Add onion; cook and stir until tender, about 5 minutes. Add carrots, chicken broth, rice, salt, and pepper.

Bring to a boil, then reduce heat and simmer for 25–30 minutes or until carrots are very tender.

Puree soup using an immersion blender or in batches in a food processor. Return to saucepan and add light cream. Heat until the soup almost comes to a simmer, then serve garnished with parsley.

Soup may be chilled and served cold; you may need to thin it with a bit more light cream. *Serves 6*

FAVORITE BEEF STEW

There's just nothing like a beef stew simmering on the back of the stove. It makes any house feel like home. This one reminds me of my mother's recipe. Stews are thicker than soups and can be a whole meal, served with some nice bread.

2 pounds beef stew meat
1/2 cup flour
1/2 teaspoon salt
1/4 teaspoon pepper
3 tablespoons vegetable oil
1 onion, sliced
3 cloves garlic, mashed
2 bay leaves
1/2 teaspoon salt

1 teaspoon sugar
1 teaspoon paprika
1/8 teaspoon allspice
1 teaspoon lemon juice
1 teaspoon Worcestershire sauce
4 cups boiling water
5 carrots, sliced
6 stalks celery, sliced
2 potatoes, peeled and diced

Toss together beef, flour, 1/2 teaspoon salt, and pepper. Heat vegetable oil in soup pot or Dutch oven. Brown meat on all sides, 5–8 minutes. Then add onion, garlic, bay leaves, another 1/2 teaspoon salt, sugar, paprika, allspice, lemon juice, and Worcestershire sauce.

Add boiling water, then cover pot tightly and simmer over low heat for 1^1/2–2 hours, until meat is tender.

Add carrots, celery, and potatoes; bring back to a simmer, then cook 15–25 minutes longer until vegetables are tender. Remove bay leaves before serving. *Serves 6*

· ·

BAKED CHEESE SANDWICHES

This recipe transforms a plain cheese sandwich into a brunch dish worthy of company. The end result is like Monte Cristo sandwiches, with an eggy, crisp crust and melted cheese filling, but is much easier to make.

Use your favorite bread and deli cheese in this simple recipe. One of my favorites is whole-grain bread and Havarti cheese with dill.

8 pieces whole-grain bread
4 thin slices Havarti cheese
4 thin slices processed American
   cheese
1 tablespoon minced fresh
   dill weed
3 eggs

2 cups whole milk
2 tablespoons prepared mustard
1/2 teaspoon salt
1/8 teaspoon pepper
1/2 cup grated Romano cheese
1/2 teaspoon paprika

Butter a 9-inch square glass baking dish and set aside. Cut crusts off bread and place 4 slices of the trimmed bread into prepared dish.

Top each slice with a slice of Havarti, then a slice of American cheese. Sprinkle evenly with the dill weed. Top with remaining bread slices.

In medium bowl, combine eggs, milk, mustard, salt, and pepper and beat until smooth Pour over sandwiches in the baking dish. Cover and refrigerate overnight, carefully turning sandwiches with a spatula several times.

The next day, preheat oven to 350 degrees F. Sprinkle sandwiches with Romano cheese and paprika. Bake for 50–60 minutes or until sandwiches are golden brown and puffed. Serve immediately. *Serves 4*

· ·

HOT CHICKEN SANDWICHES

When you make a roasted chicken for Sunday dinner, save some for these sandwiches on Monday or Tuesday. The blue cheese adds a nice snap of flavor, but you could use 1 cup of any other type of shredded cheese.

1/4 cup butter	1 cup chicken stock
1 onion, chopped	2 cups diced cooked chicken
1/4 cup flour	1/3 cup grated Parmesan cheese
1/2 teaspoon salt	4 slices toasted whole-grain bread
1/8 teaspoon pepper	1/2 cup crumbled blue cheese
1 cup whole milk	

Preheat broiler. In large saucepan, melt butter over medium heat. Add onion; cook and stir until crisp-tender, about 4 minutes. Add flour, salt, and pepper; cook until bubbly.

Add milk and chicken stock; cook and stir until mixture thickens and comes to a boil. Add the chicken and heat through. Stir in Parmesan cheese and remove from heat.

Sprinkle the hot toast with blue cheese and top with chicken mixture. Broil until chicken mixture bubbles and starts to brown on top, 5–6 minutes. Serve immediately. *Serves 4*

• •

CRUNCHY TURKEY SANDWICHES

These are a variation on Monte Cristo sandwiches, which are usually dipped in a batter and deep fried. This recipe is much easier and lower in calories too. Use your favorite cheeses and meats in this sandwich.

4 cups crisp rice cereal	12 large fresh basil leaves
12 slices whole-wheat bread	6 slices deli Muenster cheese
1/4 cup grainy prepared mustard	2 eggs
6 (1/4-inch thick) slices deli turkey	1/2 cup milk
6 slices deli Swiss cheese	3 tablespoons butter

Preheat oven to 450 degrees F. Crush the cereal very finely so you have 2 cups of crumbs; place on large plate.

Spread mustard on one side of each slice of bread. Layer turkey, Swiss cheese, basil leaves, and Muenster cheese on half of bread slices. Cover with remaining bread slices, mustard side down.

In shallow bowl, combine eggs and milk and beat until well blended. Place butter in jelly roll pan and place in oven just until butter melts. Remove pan from oven and spread butter evenly over pan surface.

One at a time, dip the sandwiches into the egg mixture, then into the crushed cereal to coat. As you work, place the coated sandwiches into the hot butter in the pan.

Bake sandwiches for 10–15 minutes, turning once with a large spatula during baking time, until they are lightly browned and crisp. Cut in half diagonally and serve immediately. *Serves 6–8*

••

PIZZA BURGERS

This classic recipe stretches a pound of ground beef to feed six hungry appetites. You can flavor it any way you'd like; substitute dried Italian seasoning or dried basil leaves for the oregano, or add hot sauce for a kick.

1 pound lean ground beef	1 teaspoon crushed dried oregano leaves
2 onions, chopped	1/4 teaspoon garlic powder
1 green bell pepper, chopped	6 hamburger buns
1 (6-ounce) can tomato paste	6 slices processed Mozzarella cheese
1/3 cup tomato juice	6 thin red onion slices

In large skillet, cook ground beef until most of the fat is rendered. Drain thoroughly. Add onions and green bell pepper to beef; continue cooking over medium heat until beef is browned and vegetables are crisp-tender.

Add tomato paste, tomato juice, oregano, and garlic powder. Bring to a boil, reduce heat, and simmer for 10–15 minutes until mixture thickens slightly.

Cut hamburger buns in half and toast. Place cheese and onion slices on 6 bun halves and ladle hot hamburger mixture over. Top with bun tops and serve immediately. *Serves 6*

"I find that many listeners remember me paired with Howard Viken on the *Morning Program*," Joyce says. "We made a good team. Oh, he could make me laugh!"

67

BAKED TUNA SANDWICHES

This unusual recipe is a good way to make sure that both sides of a baked sandwich stay crisp—place the sandwiches on a layer of chopped nuts! You could use any canned meat in this elegant recipe.

1 (10^3/$_4$-ounce) can condensed
   cream of onion soup
^{1}/$_4$ cup finely chopped onion
2 cloves garlic
2 tablespoons chopped pimento
2 (6-ounce) cans tuna, drained
3 tablespoons flour
^{1}/$_8$ teaspoon white pepper

^{3}/$_4$ cup milk, divided
^{1}/$_3$ cup grated Parmesan cheese
10 slices whole-wheat bread
^{3}/$_4$ cup chopped pecans
2 eggs
3 tablespoons milk
2 cups potato-chip crumbs

In heavy saucepan, combine soup, onion, garlic, pimento, and drained tuna. In small bowl, combine flour and white pepper with ^{1}/$_4$ cup of the milk and mix well. Gradually stir in remaining ^{1}/$_2$ cup milk and add to the tuna mixture.

Cook and stir over medium heat until mixture thickens and just begins to boil. Remove from heat, stir in the cheese, then place the tuna mixture in medium bowl, cover, and chill in the refrigerator until cold.

Place half of the bread in shallow baking pan, spread with the tuna mixture, and top with remaining bread slices. Cover and chill for at least 4 hours or overnight.

When you're ready to eat, preheat oven to 350 degrees F. Sprinkle pecans on a baking sheet. In shallow bowl, beat eggs with 3 tablespoons milk. Place potato-chip crumbs on plate.

Cut each sandwich in half diagonally. Dip sandwiches in egg mixture, then in the crumbs to coat. Place on pecans on baking sheet.

Bake for 25–35 minutes or until sandwiches are hot and crust is golden brown. Serve immediately. *Serves 6*

• •

BEEF-STUFFED BREAD

This is an unusual way to make hot sandwiches; it's great for feeding a crowd. You could use cooked chicken or chopped ham in the filling instead of the ground beef if you prefer.

1 pound unsliced French or
   Italian bread loaf
1 pound lean ground beef
1 green bell pepper, chopped
1 onion, chopped
^{1}/$_2$ cup chopped celery

^{1}/$_8$ teaspoon pepper
1 tablespoon Worcestershire sauce
1 (10^3/$_4$-ounce) can condensed
   Cheddar cheese soup
3 (1-ounce) slices Cheddar cheese

Preheat oven to 350 degrees F. Cut the top off of the bread. Pull bread out of center of loaf, leaving a $3/4$-inch shell. Tear the bread into pieces to make 2 cups; set aside.

In large skillet, brown beef with green pepper and onion; drain if necessary. Add celery, pepper, and Worcestershire sauce; cook and stir for 2–3 minutes longer. Add condensed soup and bring to a simmer. Simmer for 5 minutes, stirring frequently.

Stir bread pieces into beef mixture. Spoon mixture into the bread shell. Place slices of cheese on top and place top of bread back onto loaf. Bake for 30–40 minutes or until thoroughly heated.

Let loaf stand for 15 minutes, then cut into slices to serve. *Serves 6*

BAKED CHEESEBURGERS

You can make cheeseburgers for a crowd very easily with this recipe. It can also be made with a pound of pork sausage instead of the ground beef if you'd like.

8 slices bread	$1/4$ teaspoon salt
3 tablespoons butter, softened	$1/8$ teaspoon pepper
1 pound lean ground beef	1 egg
1 onion, chopped	$3/4$ cup whole milk
2 stalks celery, chopped	$1/4$ teaspoon salt
1 tablespoon prepared mustard	1 cup shredded sharp processed
2 tablespoons ketchup	American cheese

Preheat oven to 350 degrees F. Toast the bread until golden, then spread both sides of the toast lightly with butter. Cut each piece into 3 pieces lengthwise and set aside.

In large skillet, cook beef with onion and celery until browned; drain thoroughly. Add mustard, ketchup, $1/4$ teaspoon salt, and pepper and mix well.

In small bowl, combine egg, milk, and $1/4$ teaspoon salt and beat well.

Butter 9-inch square glass baking dish. Place half of the toast slices in the pan. Spoon half of the meat mixture over the toast and sprinkle with half of the cheese. Repeat layers using remaining ingredients. Pour egg mixture evenly over the layers in the dish.

Bake for 30–40 minutes or until casserole is puffed and golden brown. Cut into squares to serve. *Serves 6*

TASTY TUNA BURGERS

These savory burgers make a nice change from ground beef. The pickle relish adds a flavorful tang. Serve them on toasted onion buns with tomato, mustard, and mayonnaise.

1 (6-ounce) can tuna, drained	2 tablespoons minced onion
1 egg	2 tablespoons sweet pickle relish
1/2 cup mayonnaise	2 tablespoons butter
1/2 cup dry bread crumbs	4 toasted onion buns

In small bowl, mix tuna, egg, mayonnaise, bread crumbs, onion, and pickle relish. Form into 4 patties.

Heat butter in heavy skillet over medium heat. Brown patties until golden brown, turning once, 5–8 minutes. Serve immediately on toasted buns. *Serves 4*

CHICKEN AND TURKEY

Chicken and turkey are such popular meats because they are delicious and almost everyone likes them (including kids!). These foods are fairly inexpensive, easy to use, and adapt to just about any cuisine or seasonings.

Be sure to follow food safety rules when working with raw poultry. Keep raw and cooked foods separate; wash your hands, utensils, and the counter after handling the meat; cook until well done; and refrigerate foods promptly after serving.

Then enjoy these recipes!

∙∙

"LITTLE RED HEN" BAKED CHICKEN

This excellent recipe with the fun name was really popular with my newsletter subscribers. Try it, and you'll see why! When baked in this flavorful wine sauce, the chicken becomes meltingly tender. You could add small potatoes to round out the dish; add them along with the wine sauce before baking.

1 (3-pound) broiler/fryer chicken	2 teaspoons fresh thyme leaves
1 tablespoon butter, melted	1 teaspoon salt
4 whole cloves garlic, crushed	1/8 teaspoon white pepper
1 lemon, cut in half	1/2 pound frozen pearl onions
1 cup dry red wine	1 (8-ounce) package whole
1/4 cup port wine	mushrooms, wiped clean
3 tablespoons tomato paste	1 (9-ounce) package carrot chips
1 bay leaf	1 tablespoon cornstarch
1 teaspoon minced fresh rosemary	2 tablespoons water

Preheat oven to 450 degrees F. Place the chicken in large Dutch oven or deep baking pan that can be used on the stovetop. Brush with melted butter. Stuff chicken with garlic and lemon. Brown in the oven for 15 minutes. Remove chicken from oven.

71

In small saucepan, combine red wine, port wine, tomato paste, bay leaf, rosemary, thyme, salt, and pepper and heat to boiling, stirring until combined. Pour this mixture over chicken.

Cover pan tightly with foil. Reduce oven temperature to 350 degrees F and bake chicken for 30 minutes. Remove chicken from oven, carefully uncover, and add onions, mushrooms, and carrots. Recover with foil and bake 30 minutes longer or until chicken and vegetables are tender. An instant-read meat thermometer should register 180 degrees F when inserted into the thigh.

Remove chicken and vegetables from pan, place on serving platter, and cover with foil to keep warm. In small bowl, mix cornstarch with water and stir into sauce in pan. Place over medium heat and stir with wire whisk until sauce boils and thickens. Remove bay leaf. Pour sauce over chicken and vegetables. *Serves 4*

BAKED ALMOND CHICKEN

This delectable dish is rich and delicious, perfect for company. Since the chicken bakes surrounded by cream, it stays very moist. Serve it with a tomato salad and a fruit pie for dessert.

3$1/2$ pounds chicken pieces	6 tablespoons butter, melted
$1/2$ cup flour	1 cup sliced almonds
1 teaspoon celery salt	1$1/2$ cups light cream
1 teaspoon paprika	$1/2$ cup sour cream
$1/2$ teaspoon dried oregano leaves	$1/3$ cup dry bread crumbs
$1/4$ teaspoon pepper	2 tablespoons butter, melted

Preheat oven to 350 degrees F. Coat chicken pieces in flour. In shallow dish, combine celery salt, paprika, oregano, pepper, and 6 tablespoons melted butter. Roll floured chicken pieces in the butter mixture and place in 13 x 9-inch baking dish. Sprinkle with almonds.

Pour cream between pieces of chicken. Cover with foil and bake for 45 minutes. Meanwhile, place sour cream in small bowl. Combine bread crumbs with 2 tablespoons melted butter in another small bowl.

Carefully remove $1/2$ cup of the sauce that has formed in the pan and place into bowl with sour cream. Mix well with wire whisk and pour back over chicken. Sprinkle with the bread-crumb mixture and return to oven.

Bake uncovered for 15–20 minutes longer or until chicken is tender and thoroughly cooked, and bread-crumb mixture is browned. *Serves 6–8*

SWEET AND SOUR TURKEY MEATBALLS

Sweet and sour is a classic Asian flavoring that is delicious paired with tender meatballs, pineapple, and green pepper. Serve with hot buttered rice to soak up the sauce; try the aromatic varieties, like Basmati and Texmati, for a nice change.

1 egg
1 tablespoon cornstarch
1 teaspoon salt
3 tablespoons minced onion
1 pound lean ground turkey
1 tablespoon olive oil
1 tablespoon butter
1 onion, chopped
2 cloves garlic, minced
1 (15-ounce) can pineapple
   chunks, drained, reserving juice

1 cup reserved pineapple juice
1/3 cup sugar
3 tablespoons cornstarch
1/3 cup apple cider vinegar
1 tablespoon soy sauce
1/3 cup ketchup
6 tablespoons water
1 green bell pepper, thinly sliced
1 yellow bell pepper, thinly sliced

In large bowl, combine egg, cornstarch, salt, and 3 tablespoons minced onion and mix well. Add turkey and mix gently. Form into 1-inch meatballs. In heavy skillet, heat oil and butter and cook meatballs, turning occasionally, until browned on all sides, about 5 minutes. As they brown, remove to paper towel to drain.

Add chopped onion and garlic to pan drippings; cook and stir for 5 minutes until crisp-tender.

Stir in pineapple juice and sugar. In small bowl, combine cornstarch, vinegar, soy sauce, ketchup, and water and mix well; add to skillet. Cook and stir until the sauce begins to thicken.

Return the meatballs to the sauce along with the pineapple chunks and bell pepper strips. Bring to a simmer and cook for 10–15 minutes until meatballs are thoroughly cooked (internal temperature 165 degrees F) and peppers are tender. Serve over hot cooked rice. *Serves 6*

CHEESE FRIED CHICKEN

First frying, then baking chicken yields a crisp crust and juicy, tender meat. You can leave the skin on or remove it in this excellent recipe. You could also make this recipe using just boneless, skinless chicken breasts; reduce baking time to about 8–10 minutes.

Think about serving any fried chicken with a dip made of sour cream, fresh herbs, and some chopped vegetables like tomatoes and mushrooms.

3 pounds chicken pieces	1/4 teaspoon pepper
1 cup corn-flake crumbs	2 eggs
1 cup grated Parmesan cheese	1/4 cup milk
1/2 cup chopped flat-leaf parsley	1/4 cup butter
2 cloves garlic, minced	1/4 cup olive oil
1 teaspoon salt	

Wipe chicken pieces to dry. On shallow plate, combine crumbs, cheese, parsley, garlic, salt, and pepper. In shallow bowl, beat eggs with milk.

Dip chicken pieces into egg mixture, then into crumb mixture to coat. Let stand on wire rack for 20 minutes.

When ready to cook, preheat oven to 325 degrees F. Combine butter and olive oil in large heavy skillet over medium-high heat until drop of water sizzles when dropped into pan.

Fry coated chicken pieces on all sides, 6–8 minutes total, until browned. As chicken browns, remove it from skillet and drain briefly on paper towels. Place browned chicken in single layer on baking sheet. Bake for 25–35 minutes or until chicken is thoroughly cooked and tender. *Serves 6*

"'CCO's success brought big-name visitors to the station," Joyce says. "You can tell by the smile on my face that I was just thrilled to meet Mitch Miller!"

CHICKEN AND CRABMEAT CASSEROLE
WITH AVOCADO

Now this is a casserole worthy of a special occasion. The only trick is finding ripe avocados. If you plan ahead of time, buy hard avocados at the grocery store, then place them in a paper bag and keep on the counter for 1–3 days. The avocados are ready to use when they yield to gentle pressure.

Panko is Japanese bread crumbs that are lighter and crisper than regular bread crumbs. Do try to find them because they add wonderful texture to this rich casserole. You can substitute regular soft bread crumbs if you'd like.

$1/3$ cup butter	$1^1/_2$ cups sour cream
1 onion, chopped	3 cups cubed cooked chicken
1 cup sliced mushrooms	1 (1-pound) container lump
7 tablespoons flour	crabmeat, picked over
$1/2$ teaspoon salt	2 avocados
$1/8$ teaspoon white pepper	2 tablespoons lemon juice
$1/2$ teaspoon dried marjoram leaves	1 cup panko bread crumbs
$1/2$ teaspoon paprika	2 tablespoons butter, melted
$1^1/_2$ cups chicken broth	

Preheat oven to 350 degrees F. In large saucepan, melt $1/3$ cup butter over medium heat. Add onion and mushrooms; cook and stir until crisp-tender, about 5 minutes.

Add flour, salt, pepper, marjoram, and paprika to onion mixture; cook and stir until bubbly. Add chicken broth; cook and stir with wire whisk until mixture is smooth and thickened and begins to boil. Remove from heat.

Stir in sour cream, chicken, and crabmeat and set aside.

Peel avocados and cut into chunks; sprinkle with lemon juice as you work. Carefully fold the avocado into the chicken mixture. Pour into greased 2-quart baking dish.

In small bowl, combine panko bread crumbs with melted butter and mix well. Sprinkle over casserole. Bake for 25–35 minutes or until casserole is bubbly and bread crumbs are browned. *Serves 8*

CHICKEN AND WILD RICE CASSEROLE

Wild rice is a Minnesota staple. It is the official state grain even though it is technically not a grain but a grass seed. The grass grows naturally in the shallow lakes and streams so prevalent in this state.

If you've never tried wild rice, you're in for a treat! It's tender and nutty with a wonderful, slightly sweet flavor.

1/2 cup butter	2 teaspoons chopped fresh rosemary
1 (8-ounce) package sliced mushrooms	1 1/2 cups chicken broth
	3/4 cup light cream
1/4 cup flour	1 cup wild rice
1/2 teaspoon salt	8 boneless, skinless chicken breasts
1/8 teaspoon pepper	1/2 teaspoon paprika

Preheat oven to 350 degrees F. Butter 3-quart casserole dish and set aside.

In large saucepan over medium heat, melt butter and sauté mushrooms until they are tender, 5–6 minutes. Sprinkle flour, salt, pepper, and rosemary over the mushrooms; cook and stir until bubbly.

Add chicken broth and cream; cook and stir until sauce thickens.

Pour wild rice into casserole and top with the chicken breasts; sprinkle with paprika. Pour sauce into casserole and cover tightly with foil. Bake for 30 minutes, then uncover and bake 30–40 minutes longer or until chicken is thoroughly cooked and wild rice is tender. *Serves 8*

• •

TURKEY CLUB CASSEROLE

Club sandwiches combine tender, sliced meat with crisp bacon, creamy mayonnaise, lettuce, and tomato on toasted bread. This casserole makes serving a crowd a breeze—with the same flavors. Feed guests this wonderful meal during the holidays using leftover Thanksgiving turkey.

6 slices bacon	1 (10-ounce) package frozen chopped spinach, thawed and drained
1 onion, chopped	
3 cups chopped cooked turkey	1 cup cottage cheese
1 (10-ounce) container refrigerated Alfredo sauce	1/2 cup sour cream
	1 egg, beaten
1/4 teaspoon garlic salt	1/2 cup grated Parmesan cheese
1 tablespoon minced fresh rosemary	1 cup chopped tomatoes
	2 cups uncooked egg noodles
	1 cup shredded Mozzarella cheese

Preheat oven to 350 degrees F. Bring large pot of water to a boil. In large skillet, cook bacon until crisp. Remove bacon, drain on paper towels, crumble, and set aside. Remove all but 1 tablespoon drippings from skillet. Cook onion in bacon drippings until tender, about 5 minutes.

Stir in turkey, Alfredo sauce, garlic salt, and rosemary and set aside.

In medium bowl, combine drained spinach, cottage cheese, sour cream, egg, and Parmesan cheese and mix well. Stir in chopped tomatoes.

Cook egg noodles in water until almost al dente according to package directions. Drain and add to spinach mixture.

Spray 2-quart casserole with nonstick cooking spray. Layer half the turkey mixture, half the noodle mixture, and half the Mozzarella cheese in prepared casserole. Repeat layers. Sprinkle top with reserved bacon. Bake for 30–40 minutes or until casserole is bubbling and top is browned. *Serves 6–8*

• •

BAKED CHICKEN PECAN

When coated in a pecan and sesame-seed mixture, these flavorful chicken breasts turn into a gourmet treat. Serve them with mashed potatoes and cooked green beans, with a crisp green salad on the side.

8 boneless, skinless chicken breast halves	1 tablespoon paprika
1/2 cup buttermilk	1 teaspoon salt
1 egg	1/8 teaspoon pepper
1/2 cup flour	1/3 cup sesame seeds
1 cup ground pecans	1/4 cup butter

Preheat oven to 400 degrees F. Pat chicken breasts dry with paper towel. In shallow bowl, combine buttermilk and egg and mix until smooth.

On plate, combine remaining ingredients, except butter, and mix well. Dip chicken breasts into the buttermilk mixture, then into pecan mixture, pressing to coat. Place on wire rack.

Place butter in 13 x 9-inch pan and bake in oven for 4–6 minutes until butter is melted and hot. Carefully remove from oven and place coated chicken pieces in hot butter.

Bake chicken for 20–30 minutes or until juices run clear when pricked with fork and chicken is thoroughly cooked. *Serves 8*

• •

TURKEY POTATO PANCAKES

This is a fabulous recipe to make the day after Thanksgiving when everybody has lots of leftover turkey. And with cranberry sauce as the topping, there goes another Thanksgiving leftover!

3 eggs	$1/2$ teaspoon salt
3 cups refrigerated hash brown	$1/8$ teaspoon pepper
potatoes, drained	$1/2$ teaspoon dried thyme leaves
$1^1/2$ cups chopped cooked turkey	3 tablespoons butter
$1/4$ cup grated onion	3 tablespoons olive oil
2 tablespoons flour	1 cup cranberry sauce

In large bowl, combine eggs, potatoes, turkey, and onion and mix well. Stir in flour, salt, pepper, and thyme and mix again.

Heat large griddle over medium heat. Add some of the butter and olive oil to coat griddle. Drop turkey mixture by $1/4$ cup measures onto hot griddle, spreading to about 4 inches in diameter.

Cook over medium heat for 3–5 minutes on each side until pancakes are golden brown and crisp, turning once. Serve with cranberry sauce. *Serves 4–6*

. . . .

CHICKEN AND RICE *EN PAPILLOTE*

En papillote is a French cooking term that means "cooked in paper." Food that is cooked, baked, or grilled in paper (or foil) turns out very tender and moist. The presentation is also fun; each diner gets a package to open up at the table. Warn your guests to be careful of the steam that will billow out of the packages!

1 cup long-grain rice	8 boneless, skinless chicken breasts
1 tablespoon soy sauce	$1/2$ cup heavy whipping cream
3 cups chicken broth	$1/2$ cup butter, softened
1 cup shredded carrot	1 envelope dry onion soup mix

Preheat oven to 300 degrees F. In $1^1/2$-quart casserole, combine rice, soy sauce, and chicken broth. Cover and bake for 1 hour until rice is partially cooked and chicken broth is almost absorbed.

Cut eight 12-inch-square pieces of heavy-duty aluminum foil and place on work surface. Stir shredded carrot into rice mixture and divide among the foil squares. Top with chicken breasts. Drizzle each chicken breast with 1 tablespoon cream and top with a tablespoon of butter. Divide contents of onion soup mix among the chicken breasts.

Fold foil to form packages, leaving some room for heat expansion. Turn oven temperature to 350 degrees F. Place foil packets on cookie sheets. Bake for 60–70 minutes or until chicken is thoroughly cooked and rice is tender. *Serves 8*

TURKEY TETRAZZINI

Here's another fabulous recipe for using leftover Thanksgiving or Christmas turkey. This casserole can be made ahead of time and refrigerated; just increase the baking time to 45–55 minutes or until casserole is bubbly and browned.

1/4 cup butter	2 cups chicken stock or turkey stock
1/4 cup olive oil	2 cups cubed cooked turkey
1/2 cup flour	1 (16-ounce) package spaghetti
1/2 teaspoon salt	pasta
1/8 teaspoon white pepper	2 (8-ounce) cans whole mushrooms,
1 teaspoon dried thyme	drained
leaves	1/2 cup grated Parmesan cheese
2 cups whole milk	2 tablespoons butter, softened

Preheat oven to 350 degrees F. Grease 4-quart casserole dish and set aside. Bring large pot of salted water to a boil.

In large saucepan, combine butter and olive oil over medium heat. Blend in flour, salt, pepper, and thyme leaves; cook and stir until bubbly. Add milk and chicken stock. Bring to a boil, then cook, stirring constantly, until sauce thickens. Divide sauce into two equal parts.

Add turkey to one part of the sauce and set aside. Cook spaghetti in boiling water for 8–9 minutes or until almost fully cooked. Drain spaghetti, but do not rinse it.

Stir spaghetti and mushrooms into the second part of the sauce.

Make a "nest" of the spaghetti mixture around the edges of prepared casserole dish. Pour turkey mixture into the center. Sprinkle Parmesan cheese over all and top with bits of the softened butter.

Bake for 25–35 minutes or until casserole is hot, bubbly, and lightly browned on top. *Serves 6–8*

• •

CRISPY BAKED CHICKEN

This delicious recipe results in moist chicken with a crisp coating. Because the skin is removed, you can bite right into the crunchy crust with no qualms about your fat intake.

2 pounds skinless chicken pieces
1 (10³/4-ounce) can cream of chicken soup
1/4 cup water
1/2 teaspoon dried basil leaves

1/2 cup flour
2 cups finely crushed potato-chip crumbs
1/4 cup wheat germ

Preheat oven to 375 degrees F. Place a rack in large roasting pan big enough to hold all the chicken pieces in a single layer.

In pie plate, combine the soup, water, and basil; mix well to blend. On a plate, place the flour, and on another plate, combine the potato-chip crumbs and wheat germ.

Dip the chicken first in the flour, shaking off excess. Then dip into the soup mixture to coat and finally in the crumb mixture. Place the pieces on the rack in pan as you work.

Bake for 45–55 minutes until chicken is thoroughly cooked and tender and the crust is golden brown and crisp. *Serves 4–6*

INDIVIDUAL BAKED TURKEY SALADS

If you don't have leftover turkey on hand, you can buy some at your local deli. This recipe can be doubled to serve more people. And you can make it ahead of time, refrigerate, then bake as needed, just adding about 10 minutes to the time the salads spend in the oven.

1¹/2 cups diced cooked turkey
1 cup diced celery
1/2 cup chopped walnuts
1/4 cup chopped flat-leaf parsley
1 red bell pepper, chopped
2 tablespoons lemon juice
1 tablespoon grated onion

1/8 teaspoon white pepper
1/2 teaspoon dried tarragon leaves
1/2 cup mayonnaise
1/2 cup milk
3 tablespoons grated Parmesan cheese

Preheat oven to 450 degrees F. Combine all ingredients except cheese in a large mixing bowl and stir until well mixed.

Spoon mixture into 4 individual Pyrex baking dishes and sprinkle with cheese. Place dishes on cookie sheet and bake for 15–20 minutes or until food is hot and top is beginning to brown. *Serves 4*

CHICKEN AND WILD RICE RING

This unusual method of serving rice will work with long-grain white or brown rice, as well. It's very pretty and tastes great too!

8 ounces wild rice	1 tablespoon minced flat-leaf parsley
1/2 teaspoon salt	1 (10 3/4-ounce) can cream
1/2 cup chopped green	of mushroom soup
bell pepper	3/4 cup milk
1/2 cup diced onion	1 egg yolk
2 cloves garlic, minced	2 cups diced cooked chicken
2 tablespoons butter	2 tablespoons diced pimento
1 (4-ounce) jar sliced	1/4 cup slivered almonds, toasted
mushrooms, undrained	

Preheat oven to 325 degrees F. Rinse wild rice thoroughly, drain, then place in heavy saucepan and cover with water; add salt. Bring to a boil, then reduce heat, cover, and simmer for 40–45 minutes or until rice is tender.

Drain rice, if necessary. Butter a 6-cup ovenproof ring mold. Press hot rice firmly into the mold. Then set mold in a shallow pan of hot water. Bake for 30–35 minutes until firm to the touch.

Meanwhile, in large saucepan, cook bell pepper, onion, and garlic in butter until tender, about 5 minutes. Add mushrooms and parsley; remove from heat.

In small bowl, combine soup, milk, and egg yolk and mix well. Stir into vegetable mixture along with the chicken and pimento. Heat mixture over low heat, stirring frequently until hot, but do not let it boil.

When rice ring is done, carefully invert onto a heated serving platter, lift off the mold, then fill the center with the chicken mixture. Sprinkle with almonds and serve immediately. *Serves 6*

••

BAKED CHICKEN AND ASPARAGUS

Delis in grocery stores have some wonderful convenience foods that taste almost homemade. Rotisserie chickens, bought whole and fully cooked, are a great buy. You can cut the chicken apart and use some of it, then freeze the rest for another use.

This is an elegant casserole perfect for a dinner party. You can make it ahead of time and refrigerate until serving time; add about 20 minutes of additional baking time.

5 tablespoons butter	4 cooked chicken breasts, sliced
1 onion, chopped	2 (10-ounce) packages frozen
5 tablespoons flour	asparagus, thawed
1/2 teaspoon salt	1/4 cup dry bread crumbs
1/8 teaspoon pepper	2 tablespoons butter, melted

1/2 teaspoon dried tarragon leaves   2 tablespoons flat-leaf parsley
1 (6-ounce) can sliced mushrooms   2 tablespoons slivered almonds
1 1/2 cups chicken broth

Preheat oven to 375 degrees F. In large saucepan, heat butter over medium heat. Add onion; cook and stir until tender, about 5 minutes. Add flour, salt, pepper, and tarragon leaves; cook and stir until bubbly.

Drain mushrooms, reserving liquid. Add mushroom liquid and chicken broth to the flour mixture in saucepan. Cook and stir until mixture bubbles and thickens. Stir in mushrooms.

Butter a 1 1/2-quart baking dish. Arrange chicken slices in bottom of dish. Spoon half of mushroom sauce over the meat. Arrange asparagus spears on top, then top with remaining sauce.

In small bowl, combine bread crumbs, butter, parsley, and almonds and toss to coat. Sprinkle over casserole. Bake for 25–35 minutes or until food is hot and casserole is bubbling. Serve immediately. *Serves 4–6*

OVEN-BARBECUED CHICKEN

When you get a craving for barbecued chicken in the winter (which is fierce and long lasting in Minnesota and the Upper Midwest), pull out this recipe and make it in your oven.

1/2 cup flour   1/3 cup water
1 teaspoon salt   1/4 cup lemon juice
1/4 teaspoon pepper   1/2 cup minced onion
6 large pieces frying chicken   1 tablespoon Worcestershire sauce
3 tablespoons vegetable oil   2 tablespoons brown sugar
3 tablespoons butter   1 teaspoon paprika
1/4 cup butter   1 teaspoon dry mustard
1 cup chili sauce

Preheat oven to 350 degrees F. On plate, mix flour with salt and pepper. Roll chicken in this mixture. In large ovenproof skillet, combine vegetable oil with 3 tablespoons butter and heat over medium heat. Sauté chicken on both sides until golden brown, 9–12 minutes. Remove chicken from skillet and place on wire rack. Drain fat from skillet; do not wipe out. Set skillet aside.

In small saucepan, combine 1/4 cup butter, chili sauce, water, lemon juice, onion, Worcestershire sauce, brown sugar, paprika, and mustard and bring to a boil. Reduce heat and simmer for 5 minutes.

Return chicken to skillet and pour chili sauce mixture over all. Cover skillet and bake for 55–65 minutes or until chicken is tender, basting occasionally with the sauce. *Serves 6*

Deluxe Chicken Casserole

Rich casseroles with biscuits baked on top started appearing in cookbooks in the 1950s. These are the ultimate one-dish meals. All you need to add is a simple green or spinach salad, along with dessert, of course!

4 slices bacon	3 cups cubed cooked chicken
1 onion, chopped	2 teaspoons Worcestershire sauce
3 stalks celery, chopped	1/8 teaspoon pepper
1 green bell pepper, chopped	2 tablespoons milk
1 (4-ounce) can sliced mushrooms, drained	2 cups biscuit mix
	2 eggs
1 (10 3/4-ounce) can condensed cream of chicken soup	1/2 cup milk
	1 cup shredded Cheddar cheese
1 cup sour cream	1 tablespoon chopped pimiento

Preheat oven to 350 degrees F. In large skillet, cook bacon until crisp. Drain bacon on paper towels, crumble, and set aside.

Drain all but 1 tablespoon drippings from skillet. Add onion, celery, and bell pepper; cook and stir until crisp-tender, 4–5 minutes. Add mushrooms, soup, and sour cream and bring to a simmer.

Stir in chicken, Worcestershire sauce, pepper, and 2 tablespoons milk. Turn off heat.

In medium bowl, place biscuit mix. In glass measuring cup, combine eggs with 1/2 cup milk and beat well. Add to biscuit mix along with cheese and pimiento and mix just until combined.

Pour hot chicken mixture into a 2-quart casserole. Drop biscuit mixture by large spoonfuls over the chicken mixture. Bake for 45–55 minutes or until casserole is bubbly and biscuits are golden brown. *Serves 6–8*

• •

Turkey Loaf with Wheat Germ

In the 1970s, everybody started using whole grains and less processed foods as a backlash to the 1960s' prevalence of mixes, white bread, and prepared products. Wheat germ was used in a lot of recipes; this is one of the best.

1/3 cup butter	3 cups diced cooked turkey
1 cup minced onion	2 cups soft bread crumbs
1 1/2 cups chopped celery	5 eggs, beaten
3 tablespoons flour	3/4 cup wheat germ
1/2 teaspoon seasoned salt	2 tablespoons lemon juice
1/8 teaspoon pepper	1/2 cup cranberry sauce
2 cups milk	3 tablespoons prepared mustard

Preheat oven to 350 degrees F. Spray 9 x 5-inch loaf pan with nonstick cooking spray; set aside.

Melt butter in heavy saucepan over medium heat. Add onion and celery; cook and stir until tender, about 5–6 minutes. Then add flour, seasoned salt, and pepper; cook and stir until bubbly.

Add milk; cook and stir until mixture boils and thickens. Remove from heat and add diced turkey, bread crumbs, eggs, wheat germ, and lemon juice; mix well.

Pour into prepared pan. Bake for 30 minutes, then remove from oven. Combine cranberry sauce and mustard in small bowl and spoon over the loaf. Return to oven and bake for 30–40 minutes longer or until loaf is set and glazed.

Let stand for 10 minutes, then slice to serve. Garnish with parsley and serve with more cranberry sauce, if desired. *Serves 8*

••

OVEN-FRIED CHICKEN PARMESAN

When the oven is hot enough, chicken cooks quickly, and any coating stays very crisp. This classic recipe is delicious for a family dinner; serve it with mashed potatoes, an asparagus casserole, and cookies for dessert.

8 pieces frying chicken	2 eggs
1 cup flour	3 tablespoons milk
1/4 teaspoon pepper	1/2 cup fine dry bread crumbs
2 teaspoons salt	2/3 cup grated Parmesan cheese
2 teaspoons paprika	3 tablespoons butter

Preheat oven to 400 degrees F. Pat chicken dry with paper towels. In shallow bowl, combine flour, pepper, salt, and paprika and mix well. In another bowl, combine eggs and milk and beat until smooth. On plate, combine bread crumbs and Parmesan cheese and mix well.

One at a time, dip chicken into flour mixture, then into egg mixture, and finally in the bread crumb mixture. Place on wire rack and let stand for 10 minutes.

Melt butter in large roasting pan in the oven; when melted, place chicken in butter, skin side down. Bake for 30 minutes, then turn chicken over and bake for 30–40 minutes longer or until coating is crisp and chicken is thoroughly cooked. *Serves 6*

••

TARRAGON CHICKEN

Tarragon has a slight licorice flavor and complements the chicken and sauce beautifully in this easy recipe. Use bone-in, skin-on chicken for best results. To reduce calories, just don't eat the skin!

3-pound broiler/fryer chicken, cut up	1/2 teaspoon salt
2 onions, chopped	1/4 teaspoon pepper
2 cloves garlic, minced	1 (10-ounce) container refrigerated Alfredo sauce
1 teaspoon dried tarragon leaves	1 cup milk
1/4 teaspoon poultry seasoning	1/2 cup sliced almonds

Preheat oven to 350 degrees F. Arrange chicken in a single layer in large roasting pan, skin side up. Sprinkle with onions, garlic, tarragon, poultry seasoning, salt, and pepper.

In small bowl, combine Alfredo sauce and milk and mix well. Pour evenly over the chicken. Cover pan tightly with foil and bake for 1 hour.

Uncover pan and sprinkle with almonds. Bake, uncovered, for 10–15 minutes longer or until chicken is tender and thoroughly cooked. *Serves 6*

• •

CHICKEN LOAF

If you don't have leftover chicken available to make this old-fashioned recipe, buy a rotisserie chicken from the deli. Save the bones to make stock to get the most for your money!

2 eggs	1 tablespoon grated onion
1/2 cup chicken broth	1/2 cup finely chopped celery
1 cup milk	1/2 cup finely chopped red bell pepper
2 cups soft bread crumbs	1 tablespoon lemon juice
1/2 teaspoon salt	2 cups ground cooked chicken or turkey
1/8 teaspoon pepper	1/2 cup canned sliced mushrooms, drained

Preheat oven to 350 degrees F. Spray 9 x 5-inch loaf pan with nonstick cooking spray and set aside.

In large bowl, combine eggs, broth, and milk and beat until blended. Stir in bread crumbs, salt, and pepper and let stand until the bread absorbs the liquid.

Stir in remaining ingredients until combined. Pour into prepared pan. Bake for 50–60 minutes or until set.

Let cool in pan for 10 minutes, then turn out onto serving plate and slice to serve. *Serves 8*

• •

DEVILED DRUMSTICKS

"Deviled" usually means spiced with mustard and red pepper. These drumsticks will be a smash at a children's birthday party or a casual cookout. You can remove the skin or not in this recipe as you'd like; the coating keeps the meat tender.

12 chicken drumsticks	3 tablespoons honey
1 teaspoon salt	1 teaspoon salt
1 cup fine soda-cracker crumbs	1/2 teaspoon pepper
1/2 cup butter	2 tablespoons lemon juice
1 teaspoon dry mustard	12 slices bacon

Combine chicken with 1 teaspoon salt and enough water to cover in large saucepan. Bring to a boil, lower heat, and simmer chicken for 30 minutes.

Remove chicken from the water and dry thoroughly on paper towels; let stand for 15 minutes. Preheat oven to 400 degrees F.

Place cracker crumbs on a plate. In shallow saucepan, melt butter. Stir in mustard, honey, 1 teaspoon salt, pepper, and lemon juice; remove from heat.

Dip chicken into butter mixture, then roll in crumbs to coat. Wrap 1 slice of bacon around each drumstick, keeping bacon in a single layer, and place on a rack in a baking dish.

Bake for 15–25 minutes or until bacon is cooked and crisp, turning chicken occasionally. *Serves 12*

CHICKEN-BROCCOLI HOT DISH

"Hot dish" is an Upper Midwest term that means "casserole" or "one-dish recipe." These casseroles feed a crowd, and they can be made ahead of time. Most of them freeze well too, so you can double the recipes you like and freeze one for a later meal.

This recipe is a variation of Chicken Divan, but it uses rice as well as broccoli.

2 (10-ounce) packages frozen broccoli spears	2 tablespoons butter
1/2 cup grated Parmesan cheese	2 tablespoons flour
2 cups cubed cooked chicken	1 cup milk
1/2 teaspoon salt	1 tablespoon lemon juice
1/8 teaspoon pepper	1 cup sour cream
1 cup cooked rice	1/2 cup grated Parmesan cheese

Preheat oven to 400 degrees F. Cook broccoli as directed on package, then drain and place in 11 x 7-inch glass baking dish. Sprinkle $1/2$ cup Parmesan cheese over the broccoli and top that with the chicken, then sprinkle with salt and pepper. Arrange rice over the chicken.

In medium saucepan, melt butter over medium heat. Add flour; cook and stir until bubbly. Add milk; cook and stir until sauce thickens. Remove from heat and add lemon juice and sour cream.

Pour sauce over rice in casserole and sprinkle with $1/2$ cup Parmesan cheese. Bake for 15–25 minutes or until casserole is hot and cheese melts and begins to brown. *Serves 6*

• •

CHICKEN-ASPARAGUS PIE

This rich quiche is a good choice for a brunch. Serve it with a simple fruit salad and some cooked baby carrots. Make sure you use a 10-inch pie crust for this recipe; this amount of filling will overflow a smaller crust.

1 (10-ounce) package frozen asparagus spears	1 tablespoon flour
	$1/2$ teaspoon salt
1 (10-inch) pie crust, unbaked	$1/8$ teaspoon white pepper
$11/2$ cups chopped cooked chicken	2 cups light cream
4 slices bacon, cooked and crumbled	$1/4$ cup grated Parmesan cheese
1 cup shredded Swiss cheese	$1/2$ teaspoon paprika
4 eggs	

Preheat oven to 375 degrees F. Cook asparagus according to package directions and drain well. Arrange the spears in pie crust like the spokes of a wheel.

Sprinkle chicken and bacon over the asparagus and top with Swiss cheese.

In medium bowl, beat eggs until foamy. Stir in flour, salt, pepper, and cream and beat with wire whisk. Pour into pie crust and sprinkle with Parmesan cheese and paprika.

Bake for 40–50 minutes or until filling is set and beginning to turn golden brown. Let stand 10 minutes, then cut into wedges to serve. *Serves 6–8*

• •

BEEF AND LAMB

The Upper Midwest is populated by beef lovers and ranches. In Minnesota, raising cattle is all in the family. More than 80 percent of cattle farms in the state are family-owned and have been in the same family for more than twenty-five years.

These home-cook-tested recipes are all excellent vehicles for using beef and lamb. Minnesota's famous "hot dish," or casserole, takes center stage when beef is the main ingredient. From ground beef to tender lamb chops to big beef roasts, you'll find great ideas for dinner tonight—and every night!

BEEF–COTTAGE CHEESE PIE

This comforting, homey pie is easy to make and so delicious. The cottage cheese topping is like a thin, rich, and cheesy quiche. You'll love it!

1 pound ground beef	1/4 cup ketchup or chili sauce
1 onion, chopped	1 (9-inch) pie crust, unbaked
3 cloves garlic, minced	2 eggs, beaten
1/4 teaspoon pepper	1 cup cottage cheese
2 tablespoons flour	1/2 teaspoon dried thyme leaves

Preheat oven to 350 degrees F. In large saucepan, combine ground beef, onion, and garlic over medium heat. Cook and stir until onion is tender and beef is thoroughly cooked. Drain if necessary. Sprinkle with pepper and flour; cook and stir for 2 minutes. Add ketchup to skillet; cook and stir for 2 minutes. Pour mixture into pie crust.

Combine eggs, cottage cheese, and thyme in blender or food processor. Blend or process until smooth. Carefully spoon over mixture in pie crust.

Bake for 30–40 minutes or until pie crust is golden and egg topping is puffed and light golden brown. Let stand for 5 minutes, then cut into wedges to serve. *Serves 6*

SHISH KABOBS

Lamb is a good buy during the summer and fall; it is tender, lean, and juicy. The succulent meat is delicious threaded onto skewers with fresh and crisp garden vegetables. Serve with a simple rice pilaf and some hot, chewy breadsticks.

2 pounds lamb shoulder, trimmed	1 teaspoon chopped fresh oregano
2 cloves garlic, minced	1 teaspoon paprika
1 teaspoon salt	1 green bell pepper
$1/3$ cup olive oil	1 red bell pepper
$1/3$ cup tarragon vinegar	2 firm, ripe tomatoes
$1/4$ teaspoon pepper	2 Vidalia onions, peeled

Cut the lamb into $1^1/2$ inch cubes. For marinade, in shallow non-metallic container, combine garlic, salt, oil, vinegar, pepper, oregano, and paprika and mix well. Add lamb cubes, cover, and refrigerate for at least 2 hours or overnight.

When ready to cook, preheat broiler or prepare and preheat grill. Cut each bell pepper into 6 pieces and cut each tomato into 6 pieces. Cut onions into quarters. Thread lamb on skewers alternately with vegetables. Broil 4 inches from heat or 6 inches above medium coals until meat is browned, about 12–15 minutes, turning often and basting frequently with marinade. Discard any remaining marinade. *Serves 6*

• •

PIZZA CASSEROLE

What a homey casserole! It's perfect for a potluck or to feed a hungry crowd of teenagers. Serve it with some cheesy garlic bread and a salad made from baby spinach leaves and grated carrots.

1 pound ground beef	$1/8$ teaspoon pepper
1 onion, chopped	1 teaspoon dried oregano leaves
3 cloves garlic, minced	1 (12-ounce) package gemelli
1 (8-ounce) package sliced	pasta
mushrooms	$1/4$ cup heavy whipping cream
1 (26-ounce) jar pasta sauce	1 (3-ounce) package thinly
1 (14.5-ounce) can diced	sliced pepperoni
tomatoes with garlic, undrained	1 cup shredded Mozzarella cheese
$1/2$ teaspoon salt	$1/4$ cup grated Romano cheese

Preheat oven to 350 degrees F. Bring a large pot of water to a boil. In heavy saucepan, cook ground beef with onion, garlic, and mushrooms over medium heat until beef is browned; drain thoroughly. Stir in pasta sauce, diced tomatoes, salt, pepper, and oregano and bring to a boil. Reduce heat to low and simmer for 10 minutes.

Meanwhile, cook pasta according to package directions. Drain well and combine with meat mixture; stir in cream. Spoon into greased 2 1/2–quart casserole.

Bake for 20 minutes, then remove from oven; top with pepperoni and sprinkle with cheeses. Return the dish to the oven for 10–15 minutes or until the cheese melts and begins to brown. Serve immediately. *Serves 8*

• •

BUDGET STEAK AND MUSHROOMS

This recipe is from 1971, well before flank steak became a popular cut. The trick to making the best flank steak is in the carving. Look at the meat; you'll see parallel lines running through it; this is the grain. When you slice the meat before serving, cut perpendicular to the lines, or "against the grain." This cuts the fibers in the meat and makes each bite tender and succulent. And "scoring" meat means cutting about 1/8 inch into the surface of the meat in long slashes so the meat can absorb flavors in the marinade.

1 pound flank steak	1/4 cup dry sherry or apple
3 tablespoons ketchup	cider vinegar
1 tablespoon low-sodium soy sauce	1 (6-ounce) jar sliced
2 cloves garlic, minced	mushrooms, drained
1/2 teaspoon dried thyme leaves	1 tablespoon butter

Score flank steak and place in large zip-top food storage bag. Add ketchup, soy sauce, garlic, thyme, and sherry. Seal bag and knead to mix all ingredients. Place in large baking dish and refrigerate for 4–6 hours to marinate.

When ready to eat, prepare and preheat grill. Remove steak from marinade, reserving marinade. Place steak on grill rack 6 inches from medium coals and grill for 7–8 minutes on each side, turning once, for medium.

Meanwhile, combine marinade in small saucepan with mushrooms and butter. Bring to a boil and simmer for 4–5 minutes.

When steak is done, remove from heat, cover with foil, and let stand for 5–6 minutes. Slice steak across the grain, place on serving platter, and top with mushroom sauce. *Serves 4*

• •

COTTAGE CHEESE MEAT LOAF

Meat loaf is homey, comforting, and can be flavored so many ways. This recipe is a real winner. Most meat loaf is really good served cold the next day in a nice sandwich made with toasted whole-grain bread, mustard, sour cream, and crisp lettuce leaves.

1 cup cottage cheese	2 tablespoons minced onion
1 egg	$1/2$ teaspoon salt
$1/2$ cup quick-cooking oatmeal	$1/8$ teaspoon pepper
$1/4$ cup ketchup	1 pound lean ground beef
2 tablespoons prepared mustard	$1/3$ cup grated Parmesan cheese

Preheat oven to 350 degrees F. In large bowl, combine cottage cheese, egg, oatmeal, ketchup, mustard, onion, salt, and pepper and mix well.

Add ground beef and mix with hands until combined. Press mixture loosely into 8-inch square baking pan.

Bake for 20 minutes, then remove from oven and sprinkle with Parmesan cheese. Return to oven and continue baking for 10–15 minutes longer or until meat thermometer registers 160 degrees F.

Remove meat loaf from oven, cover with foil, and let stand for 5 minutes. Cut into squares to serve. *Serves 6*

"From the start, I was the only woman in this big boys' club of 'CCO broadcasters," Joyce says. "There were other women in the office, of course—secretaries and receptionists and so on—but I was the only one on the air. So, I guess I was a pioneer of sorts."

CREAMY SPAGHETTI CASSEROLE

Layered casseroles are always a good choice to serve a crowd. All you need to add is a lettuce or spinach salad and some cheesy garlic bread or crisp breadsticks. This casserole can be made ahead of time. Refrigerate it for up to 24 hours before baking; then add another 15–20 minutes to the baking time.

1¹/2 pounds ground beef	¹/2 cup tomato juice
2 onions, chopped	1 (12-ounce) package spaghetti pasta
1 (8-ounce) package sliced	1 cup sour cream
mushrooms	2 cups cottage cheese
2 (8-ounce) cans tomato sauce	¹/2 cup grated Parmesan cheese
1 (6-ounce) can tomato paste	¹/2 cup chopped green onion
2 tablespoons flour	¹/2 cup chopped black olives
¹/2 teaspoon salt	1 cup shredded Mozzarella cheese
1 teaspoon dried Italian	¹/4 cup grated Romano cheese
seasoning	

Preheat oven to 400 degrees F. Bring a large pot of water to a boil. Meanwhile, cook ground beef with onions and mushrooms in large skillet over medium heat. Drain off excess fat and add tomato sauce, paste, flour, salt, Italian seasoning, and tomato juice. Bring to a boil, then reduce heat to low and let simmer.

Cook spaghetti according to package directions in boiling water; drain and combine in large bowl with sour cream, cottage cheese, Parmesan cheese, green onion, and olives.

Place the spaghetti mixture in 2-quart baking dish. Top with ground beef mixture, then top with Mozzarella and Romano cheeses. Bake for 35–45 minutes or until casserole is bubbly and cheeses are melted and begin to brown. *Serves 10–12*

• •

GERMAN-STYLE GOULASH

Gingersnaps, used to thicken Sauerbraten, a classic German recipe, add thickness and a bit of flavor to this simple recipe. For a yield of 2 cups of chopped onions, use about 4 medium-sized onions. Serve this excellent dish over frozen spaetzle noodles, cooked according to package directions.

2 tablespoons butter	¹/8 teaspoon white pepper
2 tablespoons olive oil	1 teaspoon paprika
2 cups chopped onions	1 cup water
5 cloves garlic, minced	3 plum tomatoes, chopped

1 pound beef or lamb,	1/2 cup ketchup
cut into 1-inch cubes	1 cup beef broth
3 tablespoons flour	1 tablespoon Worcestershire sauce
1/2 teaspoon salt	4 gingersnaps, crumbled

In large saucepan or Dutch oven, combine butter and olive oil over medium heat. Add onions and garlic; cook for 4–5 minutes or until crisp-tender.

Meanwhile, toss beef with flour, salt, pepper, and paprika and add to saucepan. Brown beef on all sides, about 5–7 minutes total. If there is any flour remaining, add to the pan and cook for another minute.

Add water, tomatoes, ketchup, broth, and Worcestershire sauce to saucepan. Bring to a simmer, stirring occasionally. Then cover and simmer mixture for 1 hour or until meat is tender and sauce is blended, stirring occasionally. Stir in crumbled gingersnaps and cook for 5–7 minutes longer until sauce is blended. Serve over hot cooked noodles. *Serves 4*

· ·

PARMESAN MEATBALLS

These delicious, tender little meatballs can be served as a main dish, or layered with tomato sauce in split, toasted hoagie buns for a hearty meatball sandwich. They also freeze well; freeze the meatballs in the sauce up to three months. To thaw and use, let thaw in the refrigerator overnight, then place in a saucepan and bring to a simmer. Simmer until meatballs are hot.

1/2 cup soft fresh bread crumbs	2 tablespoons olive oil
1/2 cup grated Parmesan cheese	1/4 cup flour
1 egg	1 cup beef broth
1/2 cup milk	1/2 cup dry white wine or
2 tablespoons minced onion	beef broth
1/2 teaspoon salt	1 (4-ounce) can sliced
1/4 teaspoon pepper	mushrooms, undrained
1 pound ground beef	

In large bowl, combine bread crumbs, cheese, egg, milk, onion, salt, and pepper and mix well. Work in ground beef with your hands just until combined.

Form mixture into 18 meatballs. Heat olive oil in a large skillet. Brown the meatballs on all sides, about 5–6 minutes, then remove to plate.

Add flour to drippings in skillet and cook until bubbly. Add beef broth, wine, and mushrooms with their liquid. Bring to a boil, then reduce heat and simmer for a few minutes to blend sauce.

Return meatballs to skillet and bring to a simmer. Reduce heat to low, cover pan, and simmer for 15–20 minutes or until meatballs are thoroughly cooked and no longer pink in center. Serve over hot buttered noodles. *Serves 4–6*

BEEF MACARONI CASSEROLE

Extra-lean ground beef has only 5 percent fat and is a good choice when the beef is not browned before being combined with other ingredients. This easy casserole is fun to make and serve.

2 eggs	1/2 cup sour cream
1/2 cup ketchup	1/4 cup milk
1/3 cup milk	1 cup grated processed
1/3 cup finely chopped onion	American cheese
1/2 teaspoon salt	1/4 cup dry bread crumbs
1 pound extra-lean ground beef	2 tablespoons butter, melted
2 cups elbow macaroni	1 tomato, sliced
1 green bell pepper, chopped	

Preheat oven to 350 degrees F. In large bowl, combine eggs, ketchup, milk, onion, and salt and mix well. Work in ground beef with your hands; set aside.

Bring a large pot of water to a boil. Cook macaroni until al dente according to package directions. Drain and combine in medium bowl with green bell pepper, sour cream, and milk.

Place macaroni mixture in bottom of greased 2-quart baking dish. Crumble the beef mixture over the top. Sprinkle with American cheese. In small bowl, combine bread crumbs and melted butter. Sprinkle over cheese.

Bake casserole for 30–40 minutes or until ground beef is thoroughly cooked. Place tomato slices on top of casserole, return to oven, and bake 10 minutes longer. *Serves 6*

• •

LAMB CHOPS PARMESAN

When you're purchasing lamb, look for firm meat that is an even color, with white fat. Don't buy packages that have a lot of liquid in them. Because the meat is so tender and delicate, don't trim the fat before cooking the lamb: It helps protect the meat as it cooks.

2 tablespoons olive oil	1/3 cup grated Parmesan cheese
4 shoulder lamb chops	1/2 soup can water
1/2 teaspoon salt	1 tablespoon apple cider vinegar
1/8 teaspoon white pepper	1/2 teaspoon dried oregano leaves
1 onion, sliced	4 slices Swiss cheese
3 cloves garlic, minced	3 tablespoons shredded
1 (10 3/4-ounce) can condensed	Parmesan cheese
tomato soup	

In large skillet, heat olive oil over medium heat. Sprinkle lamb chops with salt and pepper. Brown chops, turning once, 4–5 minutes total, and remove from skillet.

Cook onion and garlic in pan drippings until crisp-tender, about 4 minutes. Remove from skillet with slotted spoon. Drain fat from skillet but do not wipe out.

Add soup, $1/3$ cup Parmesan cheese, water, vinegar, and oregano to skillet and bring to a simmer. Return onion, garlic, and lamb chops to skillet. Cover skillet and simmer chops for 25–35 minutes or until fork-tender.

Uncover skillet and top each chop with a slice of Swiss cheese and some shredded Parmesan cheese. Cover skillet and cook for 2–3 minutes to melt cheese. Serve immediately. *Serves 4*

• •

SAVORY BEEF RING

This recipe has you shape a savory meat loaf mixture into a ring mold, then glaze it to perfection. This method is a great way to ensure that the beef cooks thoroughly in the center, and it's a fun presentation too. Fill the center of the ring with fluffy mashed potatoes drizzled with a bit of melted butter.

$1/3$ cup dry bread crumbs	$1/8$ teaspoon pepper
1 cup lemon-lime carbonated beverage	1 teaspoon dried marjoram leaves
2 eggs	2 pounds ground beef
1 cup minced onion	3 tablespoons Worcestershire sauce
2 cloves garlic, minced	$1/2$ cup chili sauce
1 teaspoon salt	$1/8$ teaspoon Tabasco sauce

Preheat oven to 350 degrees F. In large bowl, combine bread crumbs with the carbonated beverage; let stand for 5 minutes. Add eggs and beat well, then stir in onion, garlic, salt, pepper, and marjoram.

Add ground beef and work in lightly but thoroughly. Pack meat mixture into a deep ovenproof $1^1/2$-quart ring mold.

Turn beef out of mold onto shallow baking dish. Brush ring with the Worcestershire sauce. Bake for 45 minutes, basting occasionally with pan drippings.

In small bowl, combine chili sauce and Tabasco sauce and mix well. Spoon over meat and bake for 15–25 minutes longer or until meat thermometer inserted into ring registers 160 degrees F.

Cover ring and let stand for 5 minutes, then cut into slices to serve. *Serves 6–8*

• •

Herb-Marinated Steak

A flavorful marinade makes even an inexpensive steak tender and juicy. You can marinate steak up to 12 hours but don't let it go much longer than that, or the marinade will make the meat too soft.

1 cup dry red wine	1 teaspoon pepper
1/2 cup vinegar	1 teaspoon dried basil leaves
1/3 cup vegetable oil	1 teaspoon dried oregano leaves
2 slices onion	1/8 teaspoon cayenne pepper
2 cloves garlic, minced	3 pounds top or bottom round steak
1 teaspoon seasoned salt	

Combine all ingredients except steak in a food processor or blender. Process or blend until smooth.

Place steak in large zip-top food storage bag and pour marinade over. Seal bag and place in large bowl or baking pan. Refrigerate for at least 4 hours, turning bag occasionally.

When ready to eat, prepare and preheat grill. Drain steak, reserving about 1/2 cup of the marinade. Grill steak for 9–15 minutes on each side to desired doneness, brushing now and then with reserved marinade. Discard any marinade not used. Let steak stand for 5 minutes, then slice to serve. *Serves 6*

Stuffed Meat Loaf

Meat loaf, when properly made, can be a feast. Just follow a few rules; combine all ingredients except the meat, then add the meat last. Don't mix it too much; too much handling will make the meat loaf tough. And let it stand, covered, for 5–10 minutes after it comes out of the oven before serving to give the juices a chance to redistribute.

1/2 cup chopped onion	1/2 teaspoon dried thyme leaves
1 tablespoon olive oil	2 eggs
1 (4-ounce) jar mushroom pieces, drained	1/3 cup chili sauce
	1 teaspoon salt
1/2 cup grated sharp Cheddar cheese	1/2 teaspoon dry mustard
	2 pounds lean ground beef
1/8 teaspoon pepper	

Preheat oven to 350 degrees F. In small microwave-safe bowl, combine onion and olive oil. Microwave on high for 2 minutes, then remove and stir; onion should be tender. Let cool for 15 minutes, then add mushrooms, cheese, pepper, and thyme and set aside.

In large bowl, combine eggs, chili sauce, salt, and mustard and mix well. Add ground beef and mix gently but thoroughly.

Press half of the meat mixture into 9 x 5-inch loaf pan. Spread onion mixture onto meat, then top with remaining meat mixture; press lightly.

Bake for 1 hour, then carefully drain excess fat from pan if necessary. Return to oven and bake another 25–35 minutes or until meat thermometer registers 160 degrees F. Let stand for 10 minutes, then unmold and serve. *Serves 8*

....

STEAK ITALIANO

You could use round steak or flank steak in this classic dish. Be sure to cut the steak across the grain (the lines running through the meat) for best results. Serve it over hot cooked spaghetti or linguine.

1 pound round steak
1 tablespoon vegetable oil
3 cloves garlic, minced
1 onion, chopped
1 tablespoon dried parsley
    flakes
$1/2$ teaspoon salt
$1/2$ teaspoon dried oregano
    leaves

$1/2$ teaspoon dried basil leaves
$1/8$ teaspoon pepper
$1/4$ cup red wine
1 cup beef broth
1 cup water
1 (4-ounce) can mushroom
    pieces, undrained
2 (6-ounce) cans tomato paste

Cut steak into $1/2$ x 2-inch strips across the grain. In large heavy skillet, brown meat in the vegetable oil for about 2–4 minutes. Add garlic and onion; cook and stir for 2 minutes longer.

Add remaining ingredients, stir, and bring to a simmer over medium heat. Reduce heat to low, cover, and simmer for 30–40 minutes or until meat is tender and sauce is slightly thickened. Serve over spaghetti, rice, or mashed potatoes. *Serves 6*

....

TOMATO ROAST IN FOIL

Cooking food in foil is a great way to concentrate flavor, keep food moist, and helps cut down on cleanup. It's a win-win-win situation! This recipe is a delicious idea for Sunday supper.

4-pound chuck roast
3 tablespoons steak sauce
1 envelope onion soup mix
1 (14.5-ounce) can diced
    tomatoes, drained
1 (8-ounce) package sliced
    mushrooms

1 green bell pepper, sliced
2 tablespoons chopped flat-leaf parsley
1 teaspoon salt
$1/4$ teaspoon pepper
$1/2$ teaspoon dried oregano leaves
2 tablespoons flour
3 tablespoons water

Preheat oven to 325 degrees F. Tear off a long sheet of heavy-duty foil and place in shallow roasting pan.

Rub steak sauce over roast and place roast in center of foil. Sprinkle onion soup mix over the meat.

Arrange tomatoes, mushrooms, green bell pepper, and parsley around meat. Sprinkle meat with salt, pepper, and oregano.

Bring edges of foil together over meat and seal with double folds, leaving some room for expansion.

Bake roast for $2^1/2$–3 hours or until desired doneness. Carefully open one end of the foil package and pour juices into a saucepan.

Combine flour and water in small bowl and whisk to combine. Add to juices in saucepan and boil hard for 5–8 minutes, stirring frequently with wire whisk, until gravy is thickened. Season to taste.

Slice roast and serve with vegetables and gravy. *Serves 8–10*

Howard Viken   Rog Erickson   Joyce Lamont   Maynard Speece   Bob DeHaven   Jim Hill

"The Morning Crew"
Of The People You Know At
WCCO RADIO
Dial 8-3-0

"This photo gives an idea of what it was like as the only woman among the on-air personalities," Joyce says. "I always felt accepted by them, and they didn't give me any special treatment, that's for sure!" (Courtesy of the Pavek Museum)

OVEN BEEF BURGUNDY

Make this for your next dinner party! All you need to serve with it are some hot, buttered noodles, a spinach salad, bread, and a fabulous dessert.

3 onions, sliced	$1/2$ teaspoon dried thyme leaves
$2 1/2$ pounds round steak, cubed	$1/4$ teaspoon pepper
2 (4-ounce) cans sliced mushrooms	3 tablespoons flour
1 (16-ounce) package baby carrots	2 beef bouillon cubes
$1/4$ teaspoon garlic salt	2 cups Burgundy wine
$1/2$ teaspoon dried marjoram leaves	

Preheat oven to 350 degrees F. Arrange onions in 3-quart casserole; top with cubed beef. Drain mushrooms, reserving liquid. Arrange mushrooms and carrots over beef.

In large saucepan, combine reserved mushroom liquid, garlic salt, marjoram, thyme, pepper, flour, bouillon cubes, and wine. Bring this mixture to a boil over high heat and stir until bouillon cubes dissolve. Pour over ingredients in casserole.

Cover tightly and bake for $2 1/2$–3 hours until beef and vegetables are tender and sauce is thickened. Serve over hot, buttered noodles. *Serves 8*

• •

CAULIFLOWER–BEEF CASSEROLE

This is an unusual recipe. If you think you don't like cauliflower, try this recipe. When it's properly cooked, it's tender, sweet, and slightly nutty tasting. I like the individual layers in this casserole, and the combination is delicious.

1 medium head cauliflower	1 tablespoon flour
$1 1/2$ pounds lean ground beef	1 cup milk
1 onion, chopped	$1 1/2$ cups shredded Cheddar
2 cloves garlic, minced	cheese
$1/2$ teaspoon salt	$1/2$ cup grated Parmesan
$1/8$ teaspoon hot pepper sauce	cheese, divided
1 (8-ounce) can tomato sauce	1 cup diced bread cubes
$1/2$ teaspoon dried marjoram	3 tablespoons butter, melted
leaves	1 tablespoon chopped
1 tablespoon butter	flat-leaf parsley

Preheat oven to 375 degrees F. Break cauliflower into small florets. Bring large pot of salted water to a boil and cook cauliflower until just barely tender, about 3–5 minutes. Drain and set aside.

In large skillet, cook beef with onion and garlic over medium heat, stirring frequently, until beef is browned. Drain thoroughly, then sprinkle with salt and hot pepper sauce and add tomato sauce and marjoram. Bring to a simmer, then reduce heat to low and let simmer while preparing cheese sauce.

In small saucepan, combine 1 tablespoon butter and flour; cook over medium heat until bubbly. Add milk; cook and stir until thickened. Add Cheddar cheese and half of the Parmesan cheese; cook until cheese melts; remove from heat.

In small bowl, combine bread cubes with 3 tablespoons melted butter, parsley, and remaining 1/4 cup Parmesan cheese and toss.

In 2-quart casserole, place meat mixture. Cover with the bread mixture, then the cooked cauliflower. Pour cheese sauce over the top. Bake for 30–35 minutes or until casserole is bubbly and top begins to brown. *Serves 6*

BEEF STROGANOFF

Beef Stroganoff is one of my favorite dishes. It's rich and delicious and easier to make than you may think. Serve it with hot, buttered noodles, cooked baby carrots, a fruit salad, and a chocolate cake for dessert.

1 pound bottom round steak	2 onions, chopped
2 tablespoons flour	4 cloves garlic, minced
1/2 teaspoon salt	1 1/2 cups sliced mushrooms
1/8 teaspoon nutmeg	1 cup beef broth
1/8 teaspoon pepper	1/4 cup red wine
2 tablespoons butter	2 cups sour cream
1 tablespoon olive oil	2 tablespoons chopped chives

Cut beef into strips 1 1/2 inches long and 1/4 inch wide. Toss with flour, salt, nutmeg, and pepper.

In large skillet, combine butter and oil over medium heat. Add beef strips; sauté until browned, about 4–5 minutes. Remove beef strips from skillet and set aside.

Add onions and garlic to skillet; cook and stir until crisp-tender, about 4 minutes. Add mushrooms; cook and stir for 2 minutes longer. Return beef to skillet.

Add broth and wine; cook and stir to remove drippings from skillet. Bring to a simmer; simmer for 5–6 minutes.

Stir in sour cream, heat through, and serve immediately over hot, buttered noodles. Garnish with chives. *Serves 4–6*

TERIYAKI STEAK

Bottom round or chuck steak becomes meltingly tender when marinated in an Asian-inspired sauce. Then the marinade is simmered until slightly thick and served with the broiled beef.

1/4 cup low-sodium soy sauce
1/4 cup sherry or apple juice
2 tablespoons honey
1 teaspoon grated orange zest

1 tablespoon minced fresh ginger root
3 cloves garlic, minced
3/4 cup pineapple juice
4-pound boneless bottom round steak, 2 inches thick

In large, heavy-duty zip-top food storage bag, combine all ingredients except steak. Add steak, seal bag, and knead to mix marinade. Place in large baking dish and refrigerate for 4–6 hours, turning steak occasionally.

Remove meat from marinade. Place meat on broiler rack, and place marinade in medium saucepan. Broil steak for 15 minutes while you simmer the marinade over medium heat.

Turn steak and broil other side for 5–10 minutes for desired doneness. To serve, cut meat against the grain into thin slices. Serve with hot cooked rice and the reduced marinade. *Serves 6–8*

• •

VEGETABLE-BEEF CASSEROLE

Now this is one hearty recipe! Use your favorite vegetables in this casserole; mushrooms, bell peppers, and tomatoes would be nice additions.

2 pounds ground beef
2 onions, chopped
4 cloves garlic, minced
1/2 teaspoon freeze-dried chives
1/2 teaspoon seasoned salt
1/4 teaspoon pepper

1/4 teaspoon nutmeg
1 1/2 pounds zucchini
4 large carrots
1 (10 3/4-ounce) can cream
  of mushroom soup
12 slices processed
  American cheese

Preheat oven to 350 degrees F. In large skillet, combine beef with onions and garlic; cook and stir until beef is browned and vegetables are tender. Drain well. Add chives, seasoned salt, pepper, and nutmeg and set aside.

Slice zucchini and carrots. Bring large pot of water to a boil; cook zucchini and cook for 3–4 minutes until crisp-tender; drain and set aside in large bowl. Cook carrots in same water for 5–6 minutes until crisp-tender, drain, and place in same bowl.

Stir soup into zucchini mixture. Place half of this mixture into buttered 3-quart casserole dish. Top with half of meat mixture and half of cheese slices. Repeat layers, ending with cheese.

Bake for 30–40 minutes until casserole is hot and cheese is melted and bubbly. Let stand for 10 minutes, then serve. *Serves 8*

ROAST BEEF HASH

When you make a beef roast on Sunday or for company, use the leftover meat in this excellent recipe. Leftover cooked and diced potatoes can be used instead of the hash brown potatoes if you have them on hand. This hearty dish is an old-fashioned one that isn't served much anymore; let's bring it back!

2 tablespoons butter
1 tablespoon vegetable oil
1 1/2 pounds diced lean
　roast beef
1 onion, diced
1 1/2 cups southern-style frozen
　hash brown potatoes, thawed

2 cups beef broth
2 tablespoons Worcestershire sauce
1/4 teaspoon pepper
Dash hot pepper sauce

Preheat oven to 350 degrees F. Heat butter and oil over medium heat in large skillet. Add beef, onion, and potatoes; cook and stir until browned. Stir in broth along with remaining ingredients.

Turn into buttered 2-quart casserole. Bake for 1 hour, stirring occasionally, until liquid is absorbed and vegetables are tender. *Serves 4–6*

CHILI-BEEF PIE

This isn't really a pie but a layered casserole. It's similar to the "Frito Pie," popular in Texas, which consists of chili poured into corn chip bags and topped with cheese and onions. But this dish is easier to eat!

2 tablespoons olive oil
1 onion, finely chopped
2 cloves garlic
1 green bell pepper, chopped
1 pound lean ground beef
1–2 tablespoons chili powder
$1/2$ teaspoon salt

$1/8$ teaspoon pepper
1 (6-ounce) can tomato paste
1 teaspoon sugar
1 cup grated sharp Cheddar cheese
$1^1/2$ cups coarsely crushed
   corn chips

Preheat oven to 350 degrees F. In large skillet, heat olive oil over medium heat. Add onion and garlic; cook and stir for 3 minutes. Add bell pepper; cook and stir for 3 minutes longer. Add ground beef; cook and stir until beef is browned.

Add chili powder, salt, pepper, tomato paste, and sugar and bring to a simmer; simmer for 5 minutes.

Pour mixture into 2-quart casserole. Sprinkle with cheese and top with corn chips. Bake for 25–35 minutes or until casserole is bubbly and hot. *Serves 6*

• •

POTATO MEAT LOAF

Shredded potatoes and carrots add moisture and flavor to this simple meat loaf. Serve it with refrigerated mashed potatoes prepared according to the package directions with some sour cream stirred in, green peas, and a fruit salad.

1 tablespoon olive oil
1 onion, finely chopped
2 cups finely shredded
   raw potatoes
1 carrot, finely shredded

2 tablespoons chopped flat-leaf parsley
2 eggs
1 teaspoon garlic salt
1 cup tomato juice
2 pounds lean ground beef

Preheat oven to 350 degrees F. In small skillet, heat olive oil over medium heat. Add onion; cook and stir until tender, about 6 minutes. Remove from heat and transfer to large bowl; let cool for 15 minutes.

Add potatoes, carrot, parsley, eggs, and garlic salt to onion mixture; stir well. Add tomato juice and mix. Add ground beef; mix gently but thoroughly with your hands until combined.

Pack mixture into 9 x 5-inch loaf pan. Bake for 55–65 minutes or until meat thermometer registers 165 degrees F. Cover with foil and let rest for 10 minutes, then unmold and slice to serve. *Serves 8*

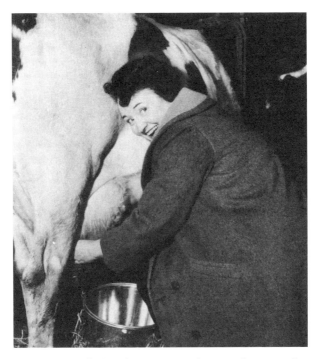

"The publicity folks brought me to a very large cow," Joyce recalls, "and told me to milk her. I patted her, said, 'Don't blame me,' and sat down. As soon as the photo was snapped, I got away from her."

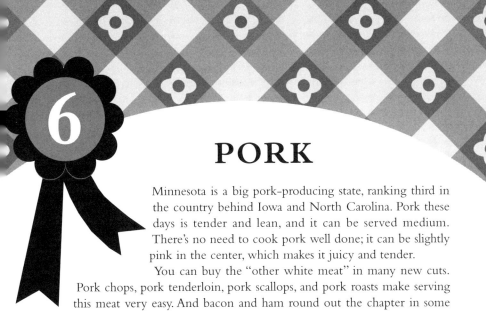

PORK

Minnesota is a big pork-producing state, ranking third in the country behind Iowa and North Carolina. Pork these days is tender and lean, and it can be served medium. There's no need to cook pork well done; it can be slightly pink in the center, which makes it juicy and tender.

You can buy the "other white meat" in many new cuts. Pork chops, pork tenderloin, pork scallops, and pork roasts make serving this meat very easy. And bacon and ham round out the chapter in some easy and hearty recipes.

SCALLOPED POTATOES WITH PORK CHOPS

On a cold winter night, there's nothing better than a hearty one-pot dinner. This recipe is pure old-fashioned comfort food. Serve it with a baby spinach salad tossed with some chopped red bell peppers and fresh mushrooms. For dessert, Coconut Bread Pudding (page 222) is the perfect finish.

6 boneless loin pork chops
5 tablespoons flour, divided
1 teaspoon seasoned salt, divided
1/4 teaspoon pepper, divided
2 tablespoons olive oil

6 russet potatoes, unpeeled
3 onions, peeled
1 (16-ounce) jar Cheddar cheese
    pasta sauce
1 cup milk

Preheat oven to 350 degrees F. On shallow plate, combine 3 tablespoons flour, 1/2 teaspoon seasoned salt, and 1/8 teaspoon pepper. Sprinkle this mixture over both sides of pork chops.

In large skillet, heat olive oil. Brown coated chops on both sides, about 5–6 minutes; remove from skillet and set aside. Remove skillet from heat; do not wash.

Thinly slice potatoes and onions. Arrange half of potato slices and half of the onions in 3-quart casserole.

Combine remaining 2 tablespoons flour, 1/2 teaspoon seasoned salt, and 1/8 teaspoon pepper in small bowl. Sprinkle half of this mixture over potatoes and onions. Add remaining potatoes and onions; sprinkle with rest of flour mixture.

Add pasta sauce and milk to skillet; heat over medium-high heat until mixture just comes to a boil. Pour over potatoes and onions. Top with browned pork chops.

Cover dish tightly with foil and bake for 1 hour. Remove foil and bake 25–35 minutes longer or until pork chops and potatoes are tender and sauce is bubbling. Let stand for 10 minutes, then serve. *Serves 6*

●●

HAM AND LIMA BEAN CASSEROLE

Lima beans are delicious, soft, and nutty. Combined with tender and salty ham, they make a wonderful, hearty casserole. This retro recipe would be delicious served with a molded fruit salad (see the Salads chapter) and some homemade cookies.

2 (15-ounce) cans lima beans	1 (10^3/4-ounce) can condensed
1 tablespoon olive oil	cream of mushroom soup
1 onion, chopped	1 teaspoon Worcestershire sauce
1 green bell pepper, chopped	^{1}/8 teaspoon pepper
2 cups cubed cooked ham	^{1}/2 cup soft bread crumbs
	2 tablespoons butter, melted

Preheat oven to 350 degrees F. Drain lima beans, reserving ^{1}/4 cup of liquid. In medium saucepan, heat olive oil over medium heat. Add onion and bell pepper; cook and stir until crisp-tender, about 4 minutes.

Remove from heat and stir in ham. Add reserved lima bean liquid, soup, Worcestershire sauce, and pepper and mix gently.

Pour into 1^1/2-quart casserole. In small bowl, combine bread crumbs with butter and mix until coated. Sprinkle over casserole. Bake for 25–35 minutes or until crumbs are golden brown. *Serves 4–6*

●●

BACON AND EGG CASSEROLE

Have you ever tried serving a breakfast item for dinner? It's a nice change of pace, and breakfast foods are usually easier and faster to make than most dinner recipes.

This casserole works well as a brunch dish, a late-night supper, or breakfast. You can cook the bacon and sauce ahead of time, then layer them with the eggs, peas, and croutons and bake.

12 slices bacon	1 1/2 cups milk
8 eggs	1 1/4 cups shredded Havarti cheese
4 tablespoons butter, divided	1/4 cup grated Parmesan cheese
1 onion, finely chopped	1 (10-ounce) package frozen peas,
2 tablespoons flour	thawed and drained
1/4 teaspoon salt	1 1/2 cups slightly crushed croutons
1/8 teaspoon white pepper	

Preheat oven to 350 degrees F. Cook bacon until crisp; crumble and set aside.

Beat eggs in medium bowl until frothy. Melt 2 tablespoons butter in medium skillet. Add eggs and cook over medium-low heat until eggs are scrambled and just set. Set aside.

In large saucepan, melt remaining 2 tablespoons butter over medium heat. Add onion; cook and stir until tender, 6–7 minutes. Add flour, salt, and pepper; cook until bubbly. Add milk; cook and stir until thickened. Add Havarti and Parmesan cheeses; stir until cheese melts and remove from heat.

In 1 1/2-quart greased casserole, alternate layers of peas, eggs, crushed croutons, and cheese sauce. Top with crumbled bacon. Bake for 20–25 minutes or until casserole is hot. Serve immediately. *Serves 6*

. . . .

CHILI-STUFFED PEPPERS

When is the last time you had stuffed peppers? This old-fashioned dish is fun to make and serve. The rich filling, made of pork sausage, kidney beans, and tomatoes, bakes inside a hollowed-out bell pepper for a beautiful presentation.

Use different colors of bell peppers for a party dish. Did you know that you can now buy bell peppers in many different colors? Green, red, orange, yellow, and purple peppers all taste about the same but look beautiful in this recipe.

6 large bell peppers	1/2 cup chili sauce
2 tablespoons butter	1 (15-ounce) can kidney beans, drained
1 onion, chopped	1/2 teaspoon salt
3 cloves garlic, minced	1 teaspoon paprika
1 pound pork sausage	1 tablespoon chili powder
1 cup chopped celery	2 cups tomato juice
1 (8-ounce) can tomato sauce	

Preheat oven to 350 degrees F. Cut tops off bell peppers and set aside. Carefully remove seeds and membranes from peppers and discard. Set peppers aside.

In large skillet, melt butter over medium heat and add onion and garlic. Cook and stir until crisp-tender, about 5 minutes. Add pork sausage and break up with fork; cook until sausage browns. Drain fat from skillet.

Add celery, tomato sauce, chili sauce, kidney beans, salt, paprika, and chili powder to pork mixture and bring to a simmer. Simmer for 5 minutes.

Stuff peppers with chili mixture. Place in baking dish that fits the peppers snugly. Top peppers with their tops. Pour tomato juice around the peppers.

Bake for 35–45 minutes or until peppers are tender when pierced with a knife. Serve immediately. *Serves 6*

Bacon Spaghetti

This recipe is similar to Spaghetti Carbonara, but it adds tomatoes and green bell pepper. The spaghetti cooks in the sauce, as well, and it will absorb the flavors of the vegetables. It's delicious!

8 slices bacon	1 1/2 cups boiling water
1 onion, chopped	1 (14.5-ounce) can diced
1 green bell pepper, chopped	tomatoes, undrained
1 (8-ounce) package spaghetti	1 tablespoon Worcestershire sauce
pasta	1/3 cup grated Parmesan cheese

In large skillet, cook bacon until crisp. Remove bacon from pan, drain on paper towels, crumble, and set aside.

Drain all but 2 tablespoons bacon drippings from pan. Add onion and bell pepper; cook and stir until crisp-tender, about 5 minutes.

Break spaghetti into 2-inch pieces and add to skillet along with water and tomatoes. Bring to a boil, then cover pan and simmer for 15–20 minutes or until spaghetti is tender, stirring occasionally.

Stir in Worcestershire sauce and bacon; cook and stir for 2–3 minutes. Sprinkle with Parmesan cheese and serve immediately. *Serves 4*

SAUSAGE AND FRIES CASSEROLE

Kids will love this casserole if you make it with sliced hot dogs. Sausages are a bit more sophisticated, but this recipe is still old-fashioned comfort food. Just five ingredients make this casserole super quick.

1 (20-ounce) package frozen French fries
1 pound fully cooked Polish sausage
1 onion, chopped
1 green bell pepper, chopped
1 (16-ounce) jar four-cheese pasta sauce

Preheat oven to 400 degrees F. Place frozen French fries in single layer on a large cookie sheet. Bake for 15 minutes.

Meanwhile, cut sausage into 1-inch pieces and place in large saucepan. Cook until some of fat renders, then add onion and bell pepper. Cook and stir over medium heat until vegetables are crisp-tender, about 5 minutes. Add pasta sauce and remove from heat.

In 1^1/$_2$-quart casserole, place half of the hot French fries. Top with half of the sausage mixture, then repeat layers. Bake for 20–30 minutes or until casserole is hot and bubbling. *Serves 4–6*

....

DENVER SCRAMBLED EGGS

This is like a Denver omelet but much simpler to make. It's a wonderful use for the leftover ham you have on hand after Easter or Christmas.

3 tablespoons butter
1/2 cup chopped onion
1/3 cup chopped green pepper
1 cup chopped cooked ham
8 eggs

2 tablespoons milk
1/4 teaspoon salt
1/8 teaspoon pepper
3 English muffins, split
2 tablespoons butter

In large skillet, melt 3 tablespoons butter over medium heat. Add onion and green pepper; cook and stir until crisp-tender, about 4 minutes. Add ham and heat through.

In medium bowl, combine eggs, milk, salt, and pepper and beat until foamy. Add to skillet; cook and stir over low heat until eggs are glossy and moist but set.

Meanwhile, spread English muffin halves with butter and toast until golden brown. Serve eggs on top of hot English muffins. *Serves 6*

....

RIB AND BEAN BARBECUE

Spareribs are true comfort food, especially when slowly baked in the oven with a simple marinade. This one-dish meal is delicious on a fall night when the kids get home from a high school football game; serve it with a mixed green salad and some garlic bread.

4 pounds pork spareribs
1/3 cup soy sauce
1/4 cup honey
1/8 teaspoon pepper
1 teaspoon Chinese five-spice
    powder
3 tablespoons olive oil
4 onions, sliced

4 cloves garlic, minced
1/2 teaspoon dried thyme leaves
1/2 teaspoon minced fresh
    rosemary leaves
2 (16-ounce) cans baked beans
1/2 cup barbecue sauce
1 green bell pepper, chopped
1 cup chopped celery

Preheat oven to 350 degrees F. Cut ribs into 2-rib portions. Place in large roasting pan. In small bowl, combine soy sauce, honey, pepper, and five-spice powder and mix well. Brush half of the honey mixture over ribs; cover and refrigerate the rest.

Cover pan and bake for 2 hours. Half an hour before the 2 hours are up, heat olive oil in large saucepan and cook onions and garlic, stirring frequently, until tender, about 6–7 minutes. Add thyme, rosemary, baked beans, barbecue sauce, bell pepper, and celery and bring to a simmer. Simmer for 5 minutes.

Remove ribs from oven and uncover. Remove ribs from roasting pan and set aside. Skim surface fat from drippings in the pan.

Pour bean mixture into roasting pan and mix with drippings. Top with ribs and brush with remaining honey mixture. Bake for 30–40 minutes longer or until ribs are tender and glazed and bean mixture is bubbling around the edges. Serve immediately. *Serves 8*

· ·

HAWAIIAN UPSIDE-DOWN HAM LOAF

Ground ham makes a well-flavored meat loaf with pineapple, mustard, and brown sugar. I love this flavor combination!

9 slices canned pineapple rings
  in syrup
1/2 cup brown sugar
1 tablespoon flour
2 tablespoons prepared mustard
1/8 teaspoon nutmeg
2 tablespoons reserved pineapple
  syrup

2 pounds ground ham
1 cup soft bread crumbs
1/3 cup chopped flat-leaf parsley
1/2 cup reserved pineapple syrup
2 eggs
1 teaspoon dry mustard
1/8 teaspoon ground cloves

Preheat oven to 350 degrees F. Drain pineapple rings, reserving syrup. In small bowl, combine brown sugar, flour, prepared mustard, nutmeg, and 2 tablespoons of reserved pineapple syrup. Spread evenly in 9-inch square pan and arrange pineapple rings evenly over this mixture; set aside.

In large bowl, combine remaining ingredients and mix well until combined. Pack this mixture over pineapple rings. Bake for 40–50 minutes or until set.

Remove pan from oven and let stand for 5 minutes. Unmold onto heated platter and cut into squares to serve. *Serves 6–8*

FRANKFURTER-STUFFED POTATOES

This is an old-fashioned recipe that kids will love. You can bake the potatoes in the oven (350 degrees F for about 60 minutes) or in the microwave oven (4 minutes on high, turn, 2 minutes on high, and let stand 2 minutes).

2 large russet potatoes
2 tablespoons butter
1/4 cup whole milk
1 cup sour cream
3 tablespoons prepared
  horseradish

1 tablespoon brown sugar
6 frankfurters, sliced
1 (3-ounce) can French fried onions
1/2 cup grated Parmesan cheese,
  divided

Bake potatoes. While still hot, cut potatoes in half lengthwise and scoop the centers into a medium bowl. Add butter and mash. Stir in milk and set aside.

Preheat oven to 400 degrees F. In small bowl, combine sour cream, horseradish, and brown sugar and mix well. Stir in sliced frankfurters. Crush the onions and add to sour cream mixture along with 1/4 cup cheese.

Pile mixture back into potato shells and sprinkle with remaining cheese. Bake for 15–25 minutes or until potatoes are hot and tops begin to brown. Serve immediately. *Serves 4*

PORK FRIED RICE

Cold rice works best when making fried rice. If you don't want to cook and chill rice, you can buy some from your local Chinese take-out place and keep it in the fridge until you're ready to make this delicious recipe.

1 tablespoon vegetable oil	1/4 cup chicken broth
1/2 cup chopped onion	2 cups cold cooked rice
1/4 cup bean sprouts	1 tablespoon low-sodium soy sauce
1 egg	Dash of pepper
1/2 teaspoon salt	1 tablespoon sugar
1 cup diced cooked pork	1 green onion, chopped
2 teaspoons sherry	

In large skillet or wok, heat vegetable oil over medium-high heat. Add onion and bean sprouts; cook and stir for 3 minutes.

In small bowl, beat egg with salt. Add to skillet; cook egg until just set but still moist. Add pork to skillet and stir. Then add sherry and chicken broth; simmer 1 minute.

Add rice and stir thoroughly. Sprinkle with soy sauce, pepper, sugar, and green onion. Stir-fry until mixture is hot; serve immediately. *Serves 2*

•••

GREEN TOMATO AND HAM CASSEROLE

Fall and the first frost come early to the Upper Midwest. We can have a killing frost in early September. Gardeners can cover their plants during the night to extend the growing season, but many prefer to pick delicate fruits, especially tomatoes, and cook with the unripe ones.

Fried green tomatoes are a famous Southern dish, but this casserole uses the fruit in a new way. The green tomatoes are more piquant than the juicy ripe ones, and that flavor with sweet-salty ham and a cheese sauce is really delicious.

2 cups cubed ham	1/4 cup milk
5 large green tomatoes, sliced	1 teaspoon paprika
1/8 teaspoon pepper	1/4 cup grated Parmesan cheese
1 (16-ounce) jar Cheddar cheese	2 tablespoons minced
pasta sauce	flat-leaf parsley

Preheat oven to 350 degrees F. Layer ham and tomatoes in 2-quart casserole dish, sprinkling each layer with pepper.

In medium bowl, combine pasta sauce, milk, and paprika and mix well. Pour over tomatoes and ham. Sprinkle with Parmesan cheese.

Bake for 50–60 minutes or until casserole is bubbling and tomatoes are tender. Sprinkle with parsley and serve. *Serves 6*

Quick Bacon-Rice Casserole

This simple casserole is great for a late-night supper or for a company brunch. It's also an excellent way to use leftover cooked rice. Serve it with a fruit salad and some Chocolate-Applesauce Bars (page 174).

6 slices bacon	3 cups cooked rice
1 cup diced celery	1 cup shredded Cheddar
1 (4-ounce) can sliced mushrooms	cheese, divided
1 (14.5-ounce) can diced tomatoes	2 tablespoons grated
1 envelope dry onion soup mix	Parmesan cheese

Preheat oven to 375 degrees F. Cook bacon in large skillet until crisp; remove bacon to paper towels to drain. Crumble and set aside.

Drain all but 1 tablespoon bacon fat from skillet. Cook celery in remaining bacon fat until crisp-tender, 2–3 minutes; set aside.

Drain mushrooms and reserve liquid. Drain tomatoes and reserve liquid. Combine reserved liquids in 2-cup glass measuring cup and add enough water to make $1^1/2$ cups, if necessary.

In large mixing bowl, combine this liquid with the mushroom slices, drained diced tomatoes, soup mix, cooked rice, and $1/2$ cup Cheddar cheese. Mix well, then stir in the celery and crumbled bacon.

Spoon into buttered 2-quart casserole. Sprinkle with remaining $1/2$ cup Cheddar cheese and the Parmesan cheese. Bake for 25–35 minutes or until casserole is hot and cheese is melted and begins to brown. Serve immediately.
Serves 4–6

• •

Cheese Macaroni Loaf

Well-seasoned macaroni is mixed with a cheese sauce and baked in a loaf pan until it's firm, then sliced and served with tomato sauce. This unusual recipe is delicious. If you omit the bacon, this would make an excellent vegetarian entrée recipe.

6 slices bacon	2 eggs, beaten
$1/4$ cup finely minced onion	$1/2$ teaspoon salt
2 cups elbow macaroni	1 tablespoon dried parsley flakes
1 (8-ounce) package processed	1 ($10^3/4$-ounce) can condensed
American cheese, diced	cream of tomato soup
1 (12-ounce) can evaporated milk	$1/4$ cup milk

Preheat oven to 325 degrees F. Grease 9 x 5-inch loaf pan with solid shortening and set aside.

Bring a large pot of salted water to a boil. Cook bacon in large skillet until crisp; remove from pan, crumble, and set aside. Remove all but 1 tablespoon

115

bacon fat from pan; cook onion in the fat until tender, then remove from pan with slotted spoon.

Cook macaroni until al dente according to package directions. Drain, place in large bowl, and stir in bacon and onions.

In heavy saucepan, combine cheese and evaporated milk over low heat. Cook and stir until cheese melts. Slowly stir in eggs, then add salt, parsley, and the macaroni mixture.

Spoon mixture into prepared loaf pan. Set pan in a larger baking pan and place in oven. Carefully pour hot water into the larger baking pan so it comes about 1 inch up the sides of the loaf pan.

Bake for 45–55 minutes or until macaroni mixture is set. While loaf is baking, in small saucepan combine soup with $1/4$ cup milk and heat to boiling. When loaf is done, unmold onto serving plate, slice it, and serve with the sauce. *Serves 8*

. . . .

PORK CHOP DINNER CASSEROLE

One-dish meals are Minnesota favorites. But remember, you can't partially cook meat, refrigerate it, then finish cooking, so this casserole can't be assembled ahead of time.

1 (20-ounce) package frozen green beans
4 cups peeled, sliced potatoes
1 ($10^3/4$-ounce) can cream of mushroom soup
1 ($10^3/4$-ounce) can cream of celery soup

$1/3$ cup grated Parmesan cheese
$1/4$ teaspoon pepper
2 tablespoons olive oil
6 center-cut loin pork chops
1 (3-ounce) can French fried onions

Preheat oven to 350 degrees F. Spread the beans in 2-quart baking pan and let thaw. Meanwhile, cook potatoes in boiling water for 5 minutes or until almost tender. Drain potatoes well.

In small bowl, combine cans of soup with cheese and pepper. Spread half of this mixture over green beans. Top with potato slices, then top with remaining soup mixture.

Heat olive oil in large skillet over medium heat. Brown pork chops on both sides, about 5 minutes total. Place on top of soup mixture, then cover pan with foil.

Bake for 45 minutes. Remove foil, sprinkle onions over all, and return to oven 5–10 minutes longer until casserole is bubbly. *Serves 6*

Ham and Cheese Casserole

This layered casserole is unique and delicious. The combination of ham, cheese, and tangy tomato soup will become a family favorite at your house.

1 tablespoon olive oil
1 onion, chopped
1 green bell pepper, chopped
1 cup sliced mushrooms
2 cups cubed ham
2 cups grated processed
   American cheese

1 (8-ounce) package narrow
   egg noodles
1 (10³/4-ounce) can condensed
   tomato soup
1 cup milk

Preheat oven to 350 degrees F. Bring large pot of salted water to a boil. Grease 3-quart casserole and set aside.

In medium saucepan, heat olive oil over medium heat. Add onion; cook and stir for 3 minutes. Add bell pepper and mushrooms; cook and stir for 3–4 minutes longer until vegetables are crisp-tender.

Remove pan from heat and let cool for 10 minutes, then stir in ham and cheese.

Cook noodles in boiling water until al dente according to package directions. Drain well. Layer noodles and ham mixture in prepared casserole.

In small bowl, combine soup with milk and stir until blended. Pour over food in casserole. Bake for 55–65 minutes or until casserole is bubbly. *Serves 6*

• •

Ham Loaf with Mustard Topping

You can get ground ham from the butcher, or you can grind it yourself, either in an old-fashioned hand grinder or in the food processor. Don't over-process the ham: you still want some texture in the loaf. This old-fashioned recipe is delicious.

³/4 cup soft bread crumbs
³/4 cup milk
2 eggs
2 tablespoons prepared mustard
1/8 teaspoon pepper

1¹/2 pounds ground ham
1 pound ground lean pork
1/3 cup brown sugar
2 tablespoons Dijon mustard

Preheat oven to 350 degrees F. In large bowl, combine bread crumbs, milk, eggs, 2 tablespoons prepared mustard, and pepper; mix well. Add ground ham and pork and mix well with hands.

Press into 9 x 5-inch loaf pan. In small bowl, combine brown sugar with Dijon mustard and mix well. Spread over the loaf.

Bake for 85–95 minutes or until meat thermometer registers 165 degrees F. Let stand for 5 minutes, then turn out onto serving plate and slice to serve. *Serves 6–8*

BARBECUED COUNTRY RIBS

This recipe is richly flavored and satisfying. It's perfect for a summer cook-out, but you don't have to fire up the grill! Serve these tender ribs with baked beans, potato salad, lots of fresh fruit, and ice cream for dessert.

3 pounds country-style spareribs
1/3 cup vinegar
3 tablespoons brown sugar
1 cup ketchup
1 envelope dry onion soup mix

3 cloves garlic, minced
2 teaspoons chili powder
1 teaspoon pepper
1/8 teaspoon Tabasco sauce
1 1/2 cups hot water

Preheat oven to 450 degrees F. Place the ribs in a shallow baking pan. Roast for 30 minutes, then drain off fat.

Meanwhile, in quart jar combine remaining ingredients. Cover jar tightly and shake well to blend.

Remove meat from the oven, turn down oven temperature to 350 degrees F, and pour ketchup mixture over ribs.

Bake for 60–75 minutes or until ribs are tender and glazed, basting occasionally with the ketchup mixture. Serve immediately. *Serves 4–6*

HAM SQUARES

This unusual recipe is a real treat. It's similar to scrapple, but richer and more elegant. Serve it after Easter when you have a lot of ham in the refrigerator. It makes an excellent dish to pair with scrambled eggs. The kids will love it!

6 tablespoons butter
1/4 cup minced onion
1/4 cup minced celery
1/2 cup flour
1/8 teaspoon white pepper

1 1/2 cups milk
3 cups finely diced ham
2 eggs
1 cup fine dry bread crumbs
4 tablespoons peanut oil

In large saucepan, melt butter over medium heat. Add onion and celery; cook and stir until crisp-tender, about 4 minutes.

Add flour and pepper; cook and stir until bubbly. Then gradually stir in the milk. Cook over medium heat until sauce bubbles and thickens. Remove from heat and add ham; mix well.

Spread mixture into 9-inch square baking pan. Cover and refrigerate until mixture is firm, at least 4 hours.

When ready to eat, beat eggs in shallow bowl; place bread crumbs on a plate. Place peanut oil in large skillet and heat over medium heat.

Cut ham mixture into 9 squares. Dip into eggs, then into bread crumbs to coat. Fry the coated squares, turning once, until golden brown, 4–6 minutes per side. Serve immediately. *Serves 9*

BACON ONION TART

This method for making a pie crust is super easy. You can use it for many other pie recipes, as well. This pie is a variation on the classic Quiche Lorraine, but it's easier to make.

1 cup biscuit mix	2 eggs
1/3 cup whole milk	1/2 cup whole milk
4 slices bacon	1/4 teaspoon salt
1 tablespoon butter	1/8 teaspoon white pepper
1 cup sliced green onion	1/4 cup grated Parmesan cheese
1 (8-ounce) package cream cheese, softened	

Preheat oven to 350 degrees F. In medium bowl, combine biscuit mix with milk until a dough forms. Form dough into a ball and pat it onto the bottom and up sides of a buttered 9-inch pie plate; set aside.

In medium skillet, cook the bacon until crisp; remove from pan, drain on paper towels, crumble and set aside. Remove all but 1 tablespoon bacon drippings from pan.

Add butter to pan and cook green onion over medium heat until softened, about 4 minutes. Place in pie crust along with bacon.

In medium bowl, beat cream cheese until soft and fluffy. Add eggs, one at a time, beating well after each addition. Add milk, salt, and pepper and mix until smooth.

Pour this mixture over bacon and onions in the pie crust. Sprinkle with Parmesan cheese. Bake for 25–35 minutes or until filling is set and golden brown. Serve immediately. *Serves 6*

....

ASPARAGUS AND HAM CASSEROLE

Asparagus has a sweet and slightly bitter flavor that pairs well with sweet and salty ham. This casserole can be made ahead of time, so it's perfect for company, and you can use up leftover Easter eggs and ham in one recipe!

2 pounds asparagus	3 tablespoons flour
2 cups refrigerated sliced home-fry potatoes	1 1/2 cups milk
	1/2 teaspoon salt
4 hard-cooked eggs, sliced	1/2 teaspoon dry mustard
2 cups diced ham	1/4 teaspoon pepper
1/4 cup butter	1/2 cup soft bread crumbs
1/2 cup minced onion	2 tablespoons butter, melted

Preheat oven to 375 degrees F. Prepare asparagus by snapping off the ends where they break easily, then rinse well. Place in large saucepan and cover with cold water. Bring to a boil, then reduce heat and simmer, uncovered, for 5–7 minutes until asparagus is crisp-tender; drain and set aside.

Prepare potatoes according to package directions; drain if necessary.

In 2-quart casserole, place half of the asparagus. Top with the potatoes, eggs, and ham, then the rest of the asparagus.

In large saucepan, melt butter over medium heat. Add onion; cook and stir for 5 minutes. Add flour, cook and stir until bubbly. Gradually add milk; cook and stir until sauce thickens and bubbles.

Remove from heat and add salt, mustard, and pepper. Pour into casserole. In small bowl, combine bread crumbs and melted butter; sprinkle over casserole.

Bake for 25–35 minutes or until casserole is bubbling and the bread crumbs begin to toast. Serve immediately. *Serves 6*

• •

SEAFOOD

Even though there's no saltwater within hundreds of miles, Minnesotans enjoy their seafood. Back in the 1960s and 1970s, fresh seafood was hard to come by, so we relied on canned. Unless, of course, we were lucky enough to know a fisherman who could supply us with fresh walleye and trout pulled from one of Minnesota's thousands of lakes.

Now fresh and fresh-frozen seafood of all kinds is readily available, including wild salmon, and is much more affordable. Still, the old-fashioned recipes are delicious and fun to make and eat.

. . . .

TANGY TOPPED SALMON LOAF

Seasoned croutons are a great shortcut ingredient that flavors this tender salmon "meat loaf" perfectly. The tangy topping seals in the moisture and adds a wonderfully tart flavor.

$1/3$ cup sour cream
$1/2$ cup milk
3 egg yolks
2 cups herb-seasoned croutons
2 tablespoons butter
$1/2$ cup finely chopped onion
$1/4$ cup finely chopped celery
1 (15-ounce) can red sockeye salmon, drained, skinned, boned
1 tablespoon chopped flat-leaf parsley

2 tablespoons lemon juice
2 tablespoons Dijon mustard, divided
$1/2$ teaspoon salt
$1/8$ teaspoon pepper
3 egg whites
$1/2$ cup mayonnaise
$1/4$ cup sour cream
2 tablespoons chopped flat-leaf parsley

Preheat oven to 375 degrees F. In large mixing bowl, combine sour cream, milk, and egg yolks and beat well. Mix in croutons and let stand for 10 minutes until croutons are softened. Beat until smooth.

In small saucepan, melt butter. Add onion and celery and cook until tender, about 6–7 minutes. Add to crouton mixture along with salmon, 1 tablespoon parsley, lemon juice, 1 tablespoon mustard, salt, and pepper. In small bowl, beat egg whites until stiff. Fold two thirds of the egg whites into the salmon mixture; reserve remaining egg whites. Spread salmon mixture into a greased

121

$1^1/_2$-quart rectangular baking dish. Bake at 375 degrees F for 30 minutes until knife inserted in center comes out clean.

While salmon mixture is baking, in small mixing bowl, combine mayonnaise, sour cream, and 1 tablespoon mustard. Gently fold in reserved beaten egg whites until blended.

Remove salmon loaf from oven and spread mayonnaise mixture evenly over top. Return to oven and continue baking for 10–15 minutes until topping is firmly set and lightly browned. Remove from oven and sprinkle 2 tablespoons chopped parsley over the top. Let stand for 10 minutes, then slice to serve. *Serves 6*

• •

DILLY SALMON PIE

Remember back in the 1980s when the book *Real Men Don't Eat Quiche* was so popular? Well, real men eat whatever they want!

This excellent recipe is a rich quiche, filled with salmon, cheese, and seasonings. Dill seed is not dill weed; be sure to read labels. The seed has a richer, smokier flavor than the weed, which is made from the feathery stalks of the dill plant.

1 (10-inch) pie crust	$1/_4$ cup flour
$1^1/_2$ cups shredded dilled Havarti cheese	$1/_2$ teaspoon salt
	$1/_8$ teaspoon white pepper
1 (15-ounce) can salmon, drained	1 teaspoon dill seed
3 tablespoons butter	$1/_2$ cup milk
1 onion, chopped	1 cup sour cream
3 cloves garlic, minced	2 eggs
1 cup sliced fresh mushrooms	$1/_4$ cup grated Parmesan cheese

Preheat oven to 325 degrees F. Place Havarti cheese in bottom of pie crust. Remove skin and bones from salmon and break into chunks; arrange over cheese. Set aside.

In large saucepan, combine butter, onion, garlic, and mushrooms over medium heat. Cook and stir until vegetables are tender, 5–7 minutes. Add flour, salt, pepper, and dill seed; cook and stir until bubbly.

Add milk and sour cream; cook and stir until thick. Remove from heat and beat in eggs, one at a time. Pour this mixture slowly into pie crust over the salmon and cheese.

Sprinkle top of pie with Parmesan cheese. Bake for 30–40 minutes or until pie is puffed and top is golden brown. Let stand 10 minutes before serving. *Serves 6*

• •

Baked Almond Shrimp

Shrimp is quite a treat. This recipe stretches it so it serves eight people easily. Serve this rich casserole with a spinach salad, a fruit salad, and some bakery rolls. For dessert, I'd choose Apple Upside-Down Cake (page 191).

1/4 cup butter	1 cup chopped green olives,
1 onion, chopped	if desired
3 cloves garlic, minced	1 cup chopped fresh tomatoes
2 pounds medium cooked shrimp	1 cup frozen baby green peas
3 cups cooked rice	1 cup heavy whipping cream
1/2 teaspoon salt	1/4 cup dry sherry
1/8 teaspoon Tabasco sauce	1/2 cup sliced almonds
1/8 teaspoon nutmeg	1/3 cup ground almonds

Preheat oven to 350 degrees F. In medium saucepan, melt butter over medium heat. Add onion and garlic; cook and stir until tender, 5–6 minutes.

In large bowl, combine onion mixture and remaining ingredients except for ground almonds; mix gently but thoroughly to combine. Turn into buttered 2-quart baking dish. Sprinkle with ground almonds. Bake for 30–40 minutes or until lightly browned. *Serves 8*

• •

Salmon Steaks with Dill Sauce

Salmon is delicious, with a smooth and velvety texture and mild flavor. This fun recipe adds potato chips for a crisp crust and a creamy dill sauce for even more flavor. Think about using unsalted potato chips; there's now a new type made from sweet potatoes that would be delicious in this recipe.

1 cup finely crushed potato chips	1 cup sour cream
1/2 teaspoon dried dill weed	2 tablespoons mayonnaise
1 tablespoon minced flat-leaf parsley	1 teaspoon dried dill weed
1/4 teaspoon pepper	2 tablespoons olive oil
4 salmon steaks	

On shallow plate, combine potato chips, 1/2 teaspoon dill weed, parsley, and pepper and mix well. Press salmon into mixture, coating both sides.

In small bowl, combine sour cream, mayonnaise, and 1 teaspoon dill weed and mix well; set aside.

In large skillet, heat olive oil over medium heat. Cook salmon steaks, turning once, until crust is golden brown and salmon is opaque, about 5–6 minutes on each side. Serve with the dill sauce. *Serves 4*

TUNA-RICE LAYERED CASSEROLE

Did you know that you should eat some fatty fish like tuna, mackerel, or salmon twice a week for good health? This comforting casserole is quick and easy to make and has a nice blend of textures and flavors.

3 tablespoons butter	1 cup chopped flat-leaf parsley
1 onion, chopped	1 (12-ounce) can white chunk tuna,
1 yellow summer squash, chopped	drained
3 cloves garlic, minced	1 (10³/₄-ounce) can cream of
4 stalks celery, chopped	mushroom soup
2 cups cooked rice	³/₄ cup whole milk

Preheat oven to 400 degrees F. Butter 2-quart casserole and set aside. In large saucepan, melt butter over medium heat. Add onion and summer squash; cook and stir until crisp-tender, about 4 minutes. Add garlic and celery; cook and stir for 1 minute longer.

Remove pan from heat and stir in rice and parsley. Place mixture in prepared casserole. Scatter the chunks of tuna on top.

In same large saucepan, combine soup and milk; heat to a simmer, stirring to blend. Pour over casserole.

Bake for 20–25 minutes or until casserole is bubbly and top starts to brown. *Serves 6*

• •

SALMON TETRAZZINI

When you're grilling or broiling salmon fillets or steaks, make a couple of extras and save them for this delicious recipe. You can use drained canned salmon if you'd like, but fresh salmon really makes this dish special.

3 tablespoons butter	1 (4-ounce) jar sliced mushrooms,
¹/₂ cup finely chopped onion	drained
3 tablespoons flour	1 cup frozen baby peas, thawed
¹/₄ teaspoon salt	2 (6-ounce) salmon fillets, cooked
¹/₂ teaspoon dried thyme leaves	and flaked
¹/₈ teaspoon nutmeg	3 tablespoons dried bread crumbs
2 cups whole milk	2 tablespoons butter, melted
2 tablespoons dry sherry	2 tablespoons grated Parmesan
1 (8-ounce) package spaghetti	cheese

Preheat oven to 350 degrees F. Bring a large pot of water to a boil. In large saucepan, melt butter over medium heat. Sauté onion until tender, about 5 minutes. Add flour, salt, thyme, and nutmeg and cook and stir until bubbly.

Stir in milk; cook and stir until sauce bubbles and thickens. Add sherry and remove from heat.

Cook pasta according to package directions until al dente. Drain and add to sauce with mushrooms, peas, and flaked salmon. Pour into $1^1/2$-quart casserole.

In small bowl, combine bread crumbs, butter, and cheese. Sprinkle evenly over salmon mixture in casserole. Bake for 35–40 minutes or until casserole is bubbling and top is browned. *Serves 6*

··

SCRAMBLED EGGS WITH SHRIMP

This elegant recipe is perfect for a brunch or for a late-night supper after the theater. It is simple and easy to make but is gorgeous too. Serve it with a fresh fruit salad and some homemade or bakery muffins.

8 eggs	1 tablespoon chopped pimento
$1/2$ cup milk	$1/2$ teaspoon salt
1 cup frozen cooked shrimp, thawed	$1/8$ teaspoon white pepper
$1^1/2$ cups cooked rice	$1/4$ cup grated sharp Cheddar
3 tablespoons butter	cheese

In large bowl, beat eggs with milk until foamy. Add shrimp and rice. In large saucepan, melt butter over medium heat. Add egg mixture; cook and stir until eggs are set and shrimp are hot.

Add pimento, salt, and pepper and stir gently. Top with cheese, cover pan, and remove from heat. Let stand for 2–3 minutes to melt cheese, then serve immediately. *Serves 4*

"We always cultivated a personal relationship with our sponsors," Joyce says. Here she helps celebrate ten years of sponsorship of *First Bank Notes* in 1964, with Larry Haeg, general manager of WCCO Radio; Si Rogers, St. Paul First National advertising manager; Bob DeHaven; Lyman Wakefield, Minneapolis First National vice president, and Jim Paul, WCCO Radio sales representative.

CREAMY SALMON CASSEROLE

Cream cheese makes a wonderful base for a silky sauce that surrounds salmon, vegetables, and egg noodles in this classic casserole. You can make it ahead of time; just add 10–15 minutes to the baking time.

1 tablespoon olive oil	1 (8-ounce) package cream
1 red bell pepper, chopped	cheese, softened
1 onion, finely chopped	1 1/2 cups sour cream
2 cloves garlic, minced	1 teaspoon Worcestershire sauce
1 (8-ounce) package egg noodles	1 (15-ounce) can salmon
	1/4 cup grated Parmesan cheese

Preheat oven to 350 degrees F. Bring large pot of salted water to a boil.

Meanwhile, place olive oil in medium pan over medium heat. Sauté bell pepper, onion, and garlic until crisp-tender, 5–6 minutes. Remove from heat.

Cook egg noodles until al dente according to package directions; drain and set aside.

In medium bowl, beat cream cheese until soft and fluffy. Gradually beat in sour cream and Worcestershire sauce. Add vegetables, salmon, and cooked noodles.

Spoon into 1 1/2-quart casserole. Sprinkle Parmesan cheese over all. Bake for 30–40 minutes or until casserole is bubbling and cheese melts and begins to brown. Serve immediately. *Serves 6*

• •

FILLETS OF SOLE WITH MUSHROOMS

Any mild white fish—like mahi mahi, red snapper, or walleye—will work in this simple recipe. Serve with a fruit salad and some cooked baby carrots.

1 pound fillets of sole	2 tablespoons flour
2 tablespoons butter	1/4 teaspoon salt
1/2 cup finely chopped onion	1/8 teaspoon pepper
3 tablespoons lemon juice	1/2 teaspoon dried thyme leaves
2 tablespoons butter	1/4 teaspoon dried mint leaves
1 (8-ounce) package sliced	1 cup milk
mushrooms	1/4 cup grated Parmesan cheese

Preheat oven to 350 degrees F. Place fish in ungreased baking dish. In medium saucepan, melt 2 tablespoons butter and add onion; cook and stir for 3 minutes. Remove from heat, add lemon juice, and pour over fish. Bake fish for 15–20 minutes or until fish flakes when tested with fork.

Meanwhile, in same saucepan, melt remaining 2 tablespoons butter and add mushrooms. Cook and stir for 5–6 minutes until tender. Stir in flour, salt, pepper, thyme, and mint and cook until bubbly, about 2 minutes.

Stir in milk and cook until thick, about 4 minutes. Stir in cheese.

Remove fish from oven, pour mushroom sauce over, and serve. *Serves 4*

TUNA SKILLET

Tuna is a great boon for cooks on a budget. It's very inexpensive, and everyone likes it. It is also good for you; any fatty fish has lots of omega-3 fatty acids, necessary for good health.

3 tablespoons butter	1 tablespoon chopped fresh
1 onion, chopped	tarragon
1 green bell pepper, sliced	2 (6-ounce) cans tuna, drained
1 cup sliced celery	1 tablespoon cornstarch
1 (13-ounce) can pineapple	2 tablespoons water
tidbits	1 (4-ounce) can diced pimento
1 cup chicken broth	3 cups toasted chow mein noodles
1/2 teaspoon salt	

In large skillet, melt butter over medium heat. Add onion and bell pepper; cook and stir for 3 minutes. Add celery; cook and stir for 2 minutes longer. Add pineapple, including juice, chicken broth, salt, and tarragon. Bring to a boil, then reduce heat, cover pan, and simmer for 2 minutes.

Add tuna and bring back to a simmer. In small bowl, combine cornstarch and water; add to tuna mixture and simmer until thickened. Stir in pimento.

Serve over the chow mein noodles. *Serves 6*

SALMON-STUFFED AVOCADOS

This is another one of those recipes perfect for an elegant lunch or brunch. You could substitute any cooked seafood for the salmon if you'd like. Serve it with a simple tomato soup and some bakery breadsticks.

1 pound salmon fillets	1/8 teaspoon pepper
1 (8-ounce) package cream cheese,	2 teaspoons fresh dill weed
softened	1 cup grape tomatoes
1/2 cup mayonnaise	3 ripe avocados
2 teaspoons Worcestershire sauce	2 tablespoons lemon juice

Cook salmon fillets by broiling or grilling. When done, let cool for 30 minutes, or refrigerate until you're ready to make the salad.

In medium bowl, combine cream cheese, mayonnaise, Worcestershire sauce, pepper, and dill weed and beat until light and fluffy. Flake the cooked and cooled salmon and add to cream cheese mixture along with tomatoes.

Cut avocados in half and remove pits. Brush cut surface of avocados with lemon juice to prevent browning. Fill each avocado half with some of the salmon mixture. Cover and refrigerate for 1 hour before serving. *Serves 6*

Fish with Sour Cream

If you have a fisherman (or woman) in the family, use the harvest from Minnesota's many lakes in this excellent recipe. It's rich and delicious. Serve it with roasted asparagus and a fruit salad.

$1/2$ cup flour	$1^1/2$ cups whole milk
1 teaspoon salt	1 cup soft bread crumbs
$1/4$ teaspoon white pepper	$1/4$ cup butter, melted
6 fish fillets	1 cup sour cream
1 tablespoon butter, melted	2 tablespoons chopped flat-leaf parsley

Preheat oven to 350 degrees F. On plate, combine flour, salt, and pepper. Dip fillets in the flour mixture to coat both sides.

Coat a shallow baking dish with 1 tablespoon melted butter. Arrange coated fish in the dish. Pour milk over the fish. Bake for 45 minutes or until fish is tender.

Remove fish from oven and increase the oven temperature to 450 degrees F. In small bowl, combine bread crumbs with $1/4$ cup melted butter and mix to coat.

Carefully remove most of the milk from the dish, using a turkey baster or a large spoon. Then spread sour cream over each fillet and top with buttered bread crumbs and parsley. Bake 10–12 minutes longer or until bread crumbs are browned. Serve immediately. *Serves 6*

• •

Tuna-Potato Puffs

Combining meat with potatoes and baking until puffy is an old-fashioned idea that uses up leftovers beautifully. If you don't have leftover mashed potatoes, you can use the refrigerated mashed potatoes found in the dairy aisle of the supermarket or make some from dried potato flakes.

1 (6-ounce) can tuna, drained	Dash pepper
$1^1/2$ cups mashed potatoes	2 egg whites
2 egg yolks	$1/3$ cup grated Parmesan cheese
2 tablespoons minced onion	

Preheat oven to 350 degrees F. Grease 6 custard cups with solid shortening and set aside.

In medium bowl, combine tuna, potatoes, egg yolks, onion, and pepper and mix well. In small bowl, beat egg whites until stiff peaks form.

Fold egg whites and half of cheese into tuna mixture. Spoon into prepared custard cups. Place custard cups onto a heavy duty cookie sheet and sprinkle with remaining cheese.

Bake for 25–35 minutes or until puffed and light golden brown. Serve immediately. *Serves 6*

SALMON-RICE LOAF

Seafood recipes in the 1960s and 1970s almost always used canned fish. Fresh fish was hard to come by and usually quite expensive. Recipes like this one stretched the food budget, and everyone loved them too!

1 1/2 tablespoons unsalted butter
1/2 cup fine dry bread crumbs
1 (15-ounce) can salmon, drained
2 cups cooked rice
3 eggs, beaten
1/2 cup chopped green onion
1/2 cup chopped green pepper

1/4 cup chopped flat-leaf parsley
1 tablespoon minced capers
1/8 teaspoon Tabasco sauce
1 tablespoon lemon juice
1/4 teaspoon salt
1/8 teaspoon white pepper

Preheat oven to 350 degrees F. Line 9 x 5-inch loaf pan with aluminum foil and grease it, using the unsalted butter. Press the bread crumbs into the bottom and up the sides of the pan; set aside.

Flake the salmon and place in large bowl. Add remaining ingredients and stir until well mixed. Turn into prepared pan.

Bake for 55–65 minutes or until loaf is set and light golden brown. Remove from oven and let stand for 5 minutes, then invert onto serving plate, remove foil, and serve. *Serves 6*

• •

SHRIMP-CREAM CHEESE CASSEROLE

This elegant recipe can be made ahead of time, so it's perfect for company. Serve it to shrimp lovers: they'll thank you! You could use another cheese if you'd like: Havarti with dill would be delicious.

1 (8-ounce) package cream
    cheese, softened
1/2 cup sour cream
1/2 cup cottage cheese
1/4 cup chopped green onions
1/4 teaspoon garlic powder
1 (8-ounce) package small pasta shells

1/2 pound medium cooked
    shrimp, shelled
2 tomatoes, sliced
1/8 teaspoon salt
1 1/2 cups shredded sharp
    processed American cheese

Preheat oven to 350 degrees F. Bring large pot of salted water to a boil. In medium bowl, beat cream cheese until fluffy. Gradually add sour cream and cottage cheese, beating until smooth. Stir in green onions and garlic powder.

Cook pasta shells until al dente according to package directions. Drain and stir into the cream cheese mixture.

Place half of the cream cheese mixture into 2-quart casserole dish. Top with the shrimp, then remaining cream cheese mixture. Arrange sliced tomatoes on top; sprinkle with salt.

Bake for 30 minutes, then sprinkle the cheese over the top. Bake for another 5–10 minutes or until cheese is melted and bubbly. *Serves 6–8*

SALMON SOUFFLÉ

Soufflés are easier to make than you think! Just fold the egg whites gently into the base and make sure your guests are waiting for the soufflé, rather than the other way around. Even if it falls, it will still be delicious.

1 (15-ounce) can sockeye salmon, drained	2 tablespoons minced flat-leaf parsley
2 tablespoons butter	1 teaspoon Worcestershire sauce
2 tablespoons flour	1 tablespoon sherry
1/4 teaspoon salt	1 teaspoon onion juice
1/8 teaspoon white pepper	2 eggs, separated
1 cup milk	1/3 cup grated Parmesan cheese
	1/8 teaspoon cream of tartar

Preheat oven to 350 degrees F. Butter the bottom of $1^1/_2$-quart baking or soufflé dish and set aside.

Remove skin and bones from salmon, flake, and place on a plate. In medium saucepan, melt butter over medium heat. Add flour, salt, and white pepper; cook and stir until bubbly.

Add milk; cook and stir until sauce bubbles and thickens. Remove from heat and add salmon, parsley, Worcestershire sauce, sherry, onion juice, egg yolks, and cheese; mix and set aside.

In small bowl, combine egg whites with cream of tartar and beat until stiff peaks form. Carefully fold egg whites into the salmon mixture.

Spoon into prepared dish. Bake for 40–50 minutes or until soufflé is puffed and golden brown. Serve immediately. *Serves 4*

• •

SCALLOPED OYSTERS

Traditionally, oysters were served at Christmas; I think it's time to bring that tradition back to life. This super-rich and classic recipe is easy to make and delicious too. Serve it with a vegetable casserole, a molded fruit salad, and Chocolate Oatmeal Pie (page 218) for dessert.

You can get fresh shucked oysters from the butcher in most grocery stores. You may have to order them, so check ahead of time.

1 1/2 cups soda-cracker crumbs	1/8 teaspoon pepper
3 cups fresh shucked oysters, drained	1/4 cup butter, melted
1/2 cup butter, melted	

Preheat oven to 400 degrees F. Butter $1^1/2$-quart baking dish. Spread half of the cracker crumbs in dish.

Combine oysters with $1/2$ cup melted butter and toss gently to coat. Arrange oysters in a single layer over the crumbs; sprinkle with pepper. Pour any leftover butter over the oysters.

Sprinkle with the remaining crumbs and drizzle $1/4$ cup melted butter over all. Bake for 12–18 minutes or until crumbs are lightly browned. Serve immediately. *Serves 4–6*

Joyce smiles bravely from the steering wheel of a tractor.
Farmers and farm families made up the backbone of 'CCO-land.

SALMON SALAD

Cold pasta salads can be a mainstay in the hot summer months. This one is delicate and flavorful, with a mild mustard dressing complementing the salmon and pasta.

2 cups small shell pasta	3 tablespoons minced flat-leaf parsley
1/4 cup French salad dressing	1 (7-ounce) pouch salmon, drained
2/3 cup mayonnaise	1/2 cup diced celery
1/4 teaspoon garlic salt	2 tablespoons sweet pickle relish
1 tablespoon prepared mustard	2 hard-cooked eggs, diced
1/8 teaspoon pepper	1/3 cup chopped green onion

Cook pasta in boiling salted water according to package directions. Drain and combine in large bowl with French salad dressing.

In small bowl, combine mayonnaise, garlic salt, mustard, pepper, and parsley and mix well. Stir into pasta mixture along with salmon, celery, pickle relish, eggs, and green onion. Cover and chill for 2–4 hours before serving. *Serves 6*

· ·

TUNA-BROCCOLI CASSEROLE

This simple casserole is easy to make, with ingredients you probably already have around the house. I like serving it over hot cooked brown rice.

2 (10-ounce) packages frozen broccoli	1 (4-ounce) can sliced mushrooms, drained
1 tablespoon butter	1/2 cup grated Parmesan cheese
1 onion, chopped	1/2 teaspoon dried dill weed
1 (10 3/4-ounce) can cream of celery soup	1/8 teaspoon pepper
	2 tablespoons lemon juice
	1 (6-ounce) can tuna

Preheat oven to 325 degrees F. Cook broccoli according to package directions, drain, and arrange in $1^{1}/2$-quart baking dish.

Melt butter in large skillet over medium heat. Add onion; cook and stir until crisp-tender, about 5 minutes. Add soup, mushrooms, cheese, dill weed, pepper, and lemon juice and bring to a simmer.

Drain tuna, reserving liquid. Add liquid to the skillet and bring to a simmer. Stir in tuna and remove from heat.

Pour this mixture over the broccoli in the baking dish. Bake for 25–35 minutes or until casserole is bubbling. Serve over hot cooked rice. *Serves 6*

Shrimp and Spinach Quiche

Frozen shrimp and spinach make this pie easy. To thaw shrimp, place it under cold running water for 3–5 minutes. If the shrimp still have their tails attached, gently pull them off once the shrimp has thawed.

1 (10-ounce) package frozen chopped spinach, thawed
1 (3-ounce) package cream cheese, softened
1 1/2 cups shredded Monterey Jack cheese
1/4 teaspoon salt
1/4 teaspoon white pepper
1 pound medium cooked shrimp, thawed if frozen
1 (10-inch) pie crust, unbaked
4 eggs
1 cup milk
1/4 cup grated Parmesan cheese

Preheat oven to 350 degrees F. Drain thawed spinach in a colander, then press in kitchen towel to remove as much moisture as possible.

In medium bowl, beat cream cheese until soft and fluffy. Add Monterey Jack cheese, spinach, salt, and pepper and mix well.

Arrange shrimp in pie crust and top with the spinach mixture. In medium bowl, beat four eggs until foamy; stir in milk. Pour into pie crust and sprinkle with the Parmesan cheese.

Bake for 40–50 minutes or until quiche is set and puffed. Let stand for 10 minutes, then cut into wedges and serve. *Serves 6*

SIDE DISHES AND VEGETABLES

Side dishes don't have to be boring. In fact, they can be a whole meal. When planning a menu, think about four things: taste, texture, color, and temperature. Make sure that your menu encompasses all these characteristics. One of the easiest ways to do that is to serve an inventive and flavorful side dish.

. . . .

FRESH TOMATO CASSEROLE

If you grow tomatoes in your backyard, you are one lucky person! If not, visit a farmers' market or produce stand in the summer for the next best thing. Fresh tomatoes in the summertime are one of life's joys. This casserole is a wonderful way to use tomatoes; serve it alongside a juicy grilled steak.

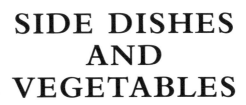

1/3 cup butter	1 green bell pepper, chopped
1 cup tomato juice	1/4 cup chopped green onions
1 (8-ounce) package herb-seasoned stuffing cubes	1/4 cup minced flat-leaf parsley
3 tomatoes	1 teaspoon lemon zest

Preheat oven to 350 degrees F. In large saucepan, combine butter and tomato juice over medium heat. Heat together until steam rises. Add stuffing cubes and mix. Remove from heat.

Cut tomatoes into wedges and add to stuffing mixture along with remaining ingredients. Spoon into greased 1 1/2-quart casserole. Cover and bake for 20 minutes, then uncover and bake 5–10 minutes longer. Garnish with lemon zest and serve. *Serves 6–8*

. . . .

GOLDEN PARMESAN POTATOES

Roasted potatoes are such a nice side dish, especially when you're serving roast chicken or meat loaf. This recipe is special because the potatoes are coated in a mixture that adds a crisp, cheesy coating. Yum.

6 russet potatoes	$1/8$ teaspoon pepper
$1/4$ cup flour	2 tablespoons water
$1/4$ cup grated Parmesan cheese	$1/3$ cup butter, melted
$1/2$ teaspoon salt	2 tablespoons chopped flat-leaf parsley

Preheat oven to 375 degrees F. Peel potatoes and cut them into chunks. On a plate, combine flour, cheese, salt, and pepper and mix well.

Sprinkle potatoes with water, then toss in the flour mixture to thoroughly coat.

Place melted butter into 13 x 9-inch pan. Add the potatoes. Bake for 55–65 minutes, turning potatoes with a spatula twice during baking time until tender. Sprinkle with parsley and serve immediately. *Serves 6–8*

• •

PERFECT CORN ON THE COB

This unusual method of cooking fresh ears of corn yields tender corn that is bursting with juice and flavor. It works every single time. Serve the corn, of course, with lots of softened butter. If you'd like, you could try flavored butters: blend in everything from honey to jalapeno peppers and chili powder.

Fresh ears of corn	1 tablespoon sugar
1 tablespoon lemon juice	

Make sure to refrigerate the corn as soon as you get it home. One hour before you want to serve it, husk the corn and remove the silk. Place the corn in a deep container of ice water.

When you're ready to cook, bring a large pot of water to a boil. Add lemon juice and sugar to water. Do not add salt; it toughens the kernels.

Add corn when the water comes back to a boil. Let the water come to a boil a second time, and let it boil for 2 minutes, no more, no less. Remove pan from heat.

Let corn stand in the hot water, uncovered, for 10 minutes. Then serve with lots of butter.

• •

Cheese-Potato Soufflés

Individual soufflés are a special treat, and they're actually easier to make than larger soufflés. Because the overall volume is smaller, there's a better chance they will rise perfectly, and they'll hold their shape longer before collapsing. Serve these little soufflés with grilled chicken and a molded fruit salad for a nice dinner.

1 (24-ounce) package refrigerated
    mashed potatoes
4 egg yolks
1 cup grated sharp Cheddar cheese
1 teaspoon Worcestershire sauce
1/8 teaspoon cayenne pepper

4 egg whites
1/4 teaspoon cream of tartar
1/3 cup grated Parmesan cheese
1 (10 3/4-ounce) can condensed
    cream of mushroom soup
1 cup sour cream

Preheat oven to 400 degrees F. Grease bottoms only of 6 1-cup-capacity soufflé dishes and set aside.

Prepare mashed potatoes as directed on package. Stir egg yolks, Cheddar cheese, Worcestershire sauce, and cayenne pepper into hot potatoes.

In medium bowl, combine egg whites and cream of tartar; beat until stiff peaks form. Fold into potato mixture. Divide among prepared soufflé dishes. Sprinkle top with Parmesan cheese.

Place soufflés on a cookie sheet. Bake for 20–30 minutes or until soufflés are golden brown and puffed.

If desired, combine soup and sour cream in small saucepan and heat until it comes to a boil. Stir this sauce and serve with the soufflés. *Serves 6*

•••

Broccoli with Lemon Sauce

Fresh broccoli, when cooked properly in a large amount of water, is delicious and mild flavored. Lemon is the perfect complement to broccoli. This easy dressing can also be used as a salad dressing.

1/2 cup vegetable oil
1/2 cup lemon juice
1/2 teaspoon paprika
2 tablespoons grated onion

1 teaspoon sugar
1/2 teaspoon salt
2 pounds broccoli
2 hard-cooked eggs, chopped

In small glass jar with a tight lid, combine oil, lemon juice, paprika, onion, sugar, and salt and mix well. Set aside.

Trim broccoli and cut into individual florets. Bring large pot of salted water to a boil. Add broccoli; bring to a boil again and cook for 4–6 minutes or until broccoli is crisp-tender and still very bright green.

Drain broccoli and place on serving plate. Drizzle half of the lemon dressing over all, garnish with the eggs, and serve remaining dressing on the side. *Serves 6–8*

SCALLOPED POTATOES WITH MUSHROOMS

Using liquid from canned mushrooms to make sauce for potatoes adds a depth of flavor you just can't get from water or milk. This classic dish is perfect for Thanksgiving or Christmas. It bakes for a long time, so you can put it in the oven and forget about it until it's time to eat.

8 white potatoes	3 tablespoons flour
2 (6-ounce) cans sliced mushrooms	1$1/2$–2 cups milk
1 onion, very thinly sliced	$1/2$ teaspoon salt
$1/4$ cup butter	$1/8$ teaspoon white pepper

Peel potatoes and slice $1/8$-inch thick. Drain mushrooms, reserving liquid. Alternate layers of potatoes, onion, and mushrooms in buttered 2-quart casserole; set aside.

In large saucepan, melt butter over medium heat. Stir in flour and cook and stir until bubbly. Combine reserved mushroom liquid with enough milk to make 3 cups. Add to butter-flour mixture; cook and stir until mixture thickens and just comes to a boil, about 10–12 minutes. Season with salt and pepper.

Pour sauce slowly over vegetables in casserole. Cover with foil and bake for 45 minutes. Then uncover casserole and bake until potatoes are tender and top is light golden brown, 30–40 minutes longer. Serve immediately. *Serves 8*

• •

ESCALLOPED ASPARAGUS

Fresh asparagus is plentiful in the spring in Minnesota grocery stores, and the price is quite reasonable. It's delicious combined with a bit of onion and green pepper, baked in a cream sauce.

2 pounds fresh asparagus	6 tablespoons flour
2 cups water	1 cup milk
$1/2$ teaspoon salt	4 hard-cooked eggs, chopped
6 tablespoons butter	$1/2$ cup soft bread crumbs
$1/2$ cup chopped onion	2 tablespoons butter, melted
$1/2$ cup chopped green bell pepper	

Preheat oven to 375 degrees F. Snap off ends of asparagus and rinse well in cool water. Combine asparagus and water in large shallow saucepan. Bring to a boil, then reduce heat and simmer for 4 minutes. Drain asparagus, reserving 1 cup liquid.

In large saucepan over medium heat, melt 6 tablespoons butter. Cook onion and green bell pepper until crisp-tender, about 4 minutes. Add flour; cook and stir until bubbly.

Stir in milk and 1 cup reserved asparagus cooking liquid; cook and stir until thickened.

Place half of asparagus in 1^1/2-quart casserole. Top with chopped eggs, then remaining asparagus. Pour sauce over top. Combine bread crumbs and 2 tablespoons melted butter in small bowl and sprinkle over all.

Bake casserole for 20–25 minutes or until sauce is bubbling around the edges and bread crumbs are browned. *Serves 6*

Company Vegetable Casserole

You can make this casserole ahead of time; refrigerate it until you're ready to bake it, then bake for 10–15 minutes longer. You can vary the types of vegetables, as well, using your favorites.

1 tablespoon olive oil
1 red bell pepper, chopped
1 onion, minced
2 (10-ounce) packages frozen cut green beans, thawed
1 (4-ounce) can water chestnuts, drained
1 (4-ounce) can or jar mushroom pieces, drained
1 (10-ounce) container refrigerated four-cheese Alfredo sauce
1 (3-ounce) can fried onion rings

Preheat oven to 350 degrees F. In saucepan, heat olive oil over medium heat. Add bell pepper and onion; cook and stir until crisp-tender, 4–5 minutes.

Combine all ingredients except onion rings in shallow 2-quart casserole. Bake for 25 minutes, then top with the onion rings and bake for 10–15 minutes more or until casserole is hot and bubbly. *Serves 6*

CRANBERRY APPLESAUCE

This applesauce has the most gorgeous pink color. Serve it as an accompaniment to roast pork or as a Thanksgiving side dish. Your kids will also love it as a snack.

2 cups sugar	1 teaspoon grated orange zest
2 cups water	1/2 teaspoon grated lemon zest
2 apples, peeled and chopped	1 cinnamon stick
4 cups fresh cranberries	

In large saucepan, combine sugar and water and bring to a boil. Boil for 5 minutes until sugar dissolves completely.

Add apples and cook for 5–6 minutes until tender. Add cranberries, orange zest, lemon zest, and cinnamon and bring back to a boil.

Boil the sauce, without stirring, for 5 minutes. Then remove sauce from heat and pour into heatproof bowl. Chill until very cold and then remove cinnamon stick and serve. *Yields 5 cups applesauce*

· ·

DELMONICO POTATOES

When you're serving a juicy steak, this is an excellent side dish. It's an old-fashioned recipe that is also a great way to use leftover cooked potatoes. Or use canned potatoes, drained and sliced. You can omit the hard-cooked eggs if you'd like, but they do add richness to the recipe.

3 tablespoons butter	3 cups cold, sliced cooked potatoes
1/2 cup finely chopped onion	2 hard-cooked eggs
2 tablespoons flour	1/2 cup grated Parmesan cheese
1/2 teaspoon salt	3/4 cup corn-flake crumbs
1/8 teaspoon white pepper	3 tablespoons butter, melted
1 cup whole milk	

Preheat oven to 350 degrees F. Butter a $1^{1}/_{2}$-quart baking dish and set aside.

In medium saucepan, melt butter over medium heat. Add onion; cook and stir until crisp-tender, about 4 minutes. Add flour, salt, and pepper; cook and stir until bubbly.

Gradually add milk, stirring constantly with a wire whisk. Remove from heat.

Alternate layers of potatoes, eggs, cheese, and sauce in prepared baking dish. In small bowl, combine corn-flake crumbs with melted butter and sprinkle over top.

Bake for 25–35 minutes or until casserole is bubbling and top is beginning to brown. *Serves 6*

· ·

SAVORY BAKED BEANS

Baked beans can, of course, be served straight from the can, but with these simple additions, they are transformed into an elegant side dish. You could top these with some browned pork chops and make a one-dish meal.

1 tablespoon butter	1 tablespoon prepared mustard
1 onion, chopped	1 tablespoon brown sugar
2 (16-ounce) cans pork and beans	Dash pepper
1 (3-ounce) can deviled ham	

Preheat oven to 350 degrees F. In small saucepan, melt butter over medium heat. Cook onion, stirring frequently, until tender, about 5 minutes.

Combine with remaining ingredients in $1^1/2$-quart casserole dish. Cover tightly with foil and bake for $1^1/2$ hours. *Serves 4–6*

• •

NEW POTATOES AND PEAS

In the spring, new potatoes start appearing in the market, and they are a good buy. They are tender and fun to eat. Combined with a savory cheese sauce and some baby peas, they can be a meal in themselves.

4 slices bacon	$1^2/3$ cups whole milk
1 (16-ounce) package frozen baby peas, thawed	20 new potatoes (about 2 pounds)
2 tablespoons butter	1 cup shredded processed American cheese
2 tablespoons flour	$1/2$ cup shredded Colby cheese
$1/2$ teaspoon salt	
$1/8$ teaspoon pepper	

Cook bacon until crisp; drain bacon on paper towels, crumble, and set aside. Thoroughly drain the thawed peas but do not cook them.

To bacon fat in pan, add butter and heat over medium heat. Add flour, salt, and pepper and cook until bubbly. Add whole milk; cook and stir until bubbly; remove from heat.

Scrub the potatoes and peel off a narrow strip of peel around the center of each potato. Cook potatoes in boiling salted water until tender, about 10–15 minutes. Drain potatoes and return to hot pot along with peas.

Return sauce to heat; add cheeses and cook and stir until melted. Pour cheese sauce over potatoes and peas; heat for 1–2 minutes over low heat. Pour into serving dish and top with reserved bacon. *Serves 10*

CHEESE-ALMOND RICE

Rice pilaf made in the oven is very easy, and you can forget about it while you prepare the rest of the meal. This is an excellent accompaniment to meat loaf; try Stuffed Meat Loaf (page 97).

1 (8-ounce) jar sliced mushrooms	$1/8$ teaspoon pepper
$1/4$ cup minced onion	2 cups beef broth
$1/3$ cup sliced almonds	1 tablespoon soy sauce
1 cup shredded Colby cheese	2 tablespoons chopped
$1^1/4$ cups uncooked	flat-leaf parsley
long-grain rice	2 tablespoons chopped pimento

Preheat oven to 375 degrees F. Butter 2-quart casserole and set aside.

Drain mushrooms, reserving liquid. Place liquid in a 4-cup measuring glass. Combine mushrooms, onion, almonds, cheese, rice, and pepper in prepared casserole.

Add beef broth, soy sauce, and enough water to the mushroom liquid to equal $3^1/2$ cups. Microwave on high for 2–4 minutes or until mixture just starts to simmer. Carefully pour over rice mixture in casserole.

Cover tightly with foil and bake for 45–55 minutes or until liquid is absorbed and rice is tender. Stir in parsley and pimento and serve. *Serves 6–8*

••

NOODLES ROMANOFF

This can be served as a vegetarian entrée or as a side dish for meat loaf or a roast chicken. It's similar to noodle kugel but is more highly flavored.

$1/2$ cup minced onion	2 tablespoons Worcestershire
2 cloves garlic, minced	sauce
1 tablespoon olive oil	$1/2$ teaspoon salt
1 (8-ounce) package egg noodles	$1/8$ teaspoon hot pepper sauce
2 cups cottage cheese	1 cup shredded sharp Cheddar
1 cup sour cream	cheese

Preheat oven to 350 degrees F. Grease 2-quart baking dish. Bring a large pot of salted water to a boil.

In small saucepan, combine onion, garlic, and olive oil over medium heat. Cook and stir until vegetables are tender, about 6 minutes. Set aside.

Cook noodles until they are just tender, then drain. While noodles are cooking, in large bowl combine cottage cheese with remaining ingredients including sautéed onions and garlic. Add drained noodles and mix well.

Spoon mixture into prepared dish and bake for 30–40 minutes or until casserole is hot and bubbly. *Serves 6*

Broccoli Amandine

"Amandine" means "with almonds." The crunch of this tender nut adds great interest to this simple side-dish recipe.

1/2 cup sliced almonds	1 teaspoon grated lemon zest
1 tablespoon butter	1 tablespoon lemon juice
2 (3-ounce) packages cream cheese	1/4 teaspoon salt
1/3 cup milk	1 1/2 pounds fresh broccoli

Bring large pot of salted water to a boil. In small skillet, combine almonds with butter over medium heat; cook and stir until almonds are toasted and fragrant. Remove from heat.

In small saucepan, combine cream cheese, milk, lemon zest, lemon juice, and salt. Cook and stir over medium-low heat until cheese melts and mixture is smooth.

Meanwhile, cut broccoli into spears. Cook in boiling water until crisp-tender, 5–7 minutes.

When broccoli is done, drain and place on serving platter. Pour cream cheese mixture over and sprinkle with almonds. Serve immediately. *Serves 6*

• •

Quick Potato Patties

This is a fun recipe! It's a great way to turn leftover potato chips into a side dish for dinner. You could use flavored potato chips if you'd like; sour cream and onion would be delicious.

3 eggs	1 tablespoon minced flat-leaf parsley
1/2 cup milk	2 tablespoons minced onion
1/8 teaspoon pepper	3 cups finely crushed potato chips
1/4 cup canned chopped mushrooms, drained	2 tablespoons butter

In medium bowl, combine eggs, milk, and pepper and beat well. Add mushrooms, parsley, onion, and potato chips and stir to combine.

Melt butter in large skillet over medium heat. Add large spoonfuls of the potato mixture; fry until golden brown, then turn and brown the other side. Serve immediately. *Serves 6*

• •

Fresh Tomato-Zucchini Casserole

In late summer, Minnesota gardens are bursting with zucchini and tomatoes. And if a garden isn't in your backyard, farmers' markets and roadside stands will more than fulfill your needs. This classic casserole is delicious made with a combination of zucchini and summer squash.

1/4 cup olive oil
3 cloves garlic, split
2 zucchini
3 yellow summer squash
1 cup shredded Cheddar cheese
1/4 cup grated Parmesan cheese

1 tablespoon minced fresh basil
1 tablespoon minced fresh oregano
5 tomatoes, sliced 1/4-inch thick
1/2 teaspoon salt
2 tablespoon butter, melted
1/2 cup dried bread crumbs

Preheat oven to 350 degrees F. In large skillet, heat olive oil over low heat. Add garlic; simmer for 4–5 minutes.

Meanwhile, slice zucchini and summer squash into 1/4-inch slices. Remove garlic from oil and discard. Add zucchini and squash to the oil; simmer for 3–4 minutes; remove from oil with slotted spoon and set aside. Discard oil.

In small bowl, combine cheeses, basil, and oregano and mix well; set aside.

Butter 1 1/2-quart casserole. Alternately layer sautéed zucchini, cheese mixture, and tomato slices, sprinkling each layer with a bit of salt.

In small bowl, combine butter and bread crumbs; sprinkle over top of casserole. Bake for 25–35 minutes or until bread crumbs are browned and casserole is bubbling. *Serves 6*

•••

Baked Broccoli with Rice

When you need a side dish in a hurry, this is a good recipe. It's also an easy way to use up leftover cooked rice.

1 tablespoon butter
1 onion, chopped
1 (10-ounce) package frozen
   chopped broccoli, thawed

2 cups cooked rice
1 (10 3/4-ounce) can condensed
   cream of broccoli soup
1/2 cup grated Cheddar cheese

Preheat oven to 350 degrees F. Butter 1 1/2-quart casserole and set aside. In large saucepan, melt butter over medium heat. Add onion; cook and stir until tender, 5–6 minutes. Add broccoli; cook and stir for 2–3 minutes longer.

Remove from heat and stir in rice and soup. Turn mixture into prepared pan and sprinkle top with cheese. Bake for 30–40 minutes or until casserole is bubbly and cheese melts and begins to brown. *Serves 6*

Fried Eggplant

Eggplant is very mild but can be slightly bitter. Sprinkling the slices with salt and letting them sit draws out the bitter liquid. When fried until crisp, this unusual vegetable is delicious.

1 large eggplant	1 cup crushed soda crackers
1 tablespoon salt	1 teaspoon seasoned salt
3/4 cup pancake mix	2 cups peanut oil
1 cup milk	

Peel eggplant and slice into 1/2-inch slices. Place slices in a large bowl, sprinkle with salt, and toss to coat. Then add enough water to cover completely. Soak for 15 minutes, then drain the slices, rinse well, and dry in a kitchen towel. Then pat with paper towels to dry thoroughly.

In shallow bowl, combine pancake mix and milk. On a plate, combine cracker crumbs and seasoned salt. Pour oil into heavy, deep skillet and place over medium-high heat, until a thermometer registers 350 degrees F.

Dip eggplant slices into batter, shaking off excess, then into crumbs. Fry on both sides until golden brown, 4–6 minutes per side. Drain on paper towels, then serve immediately. *Serves 6*

....

Sour Cream–Scalloped Potatoes

Scalloped potatoes are a classic side dish; when sour cream is added to the mixture, this recipe becomes a favorite for company. Using hash brown potatoes makes preparation easy.

2 eggs	1/8 teaspoon pepper
1 cup sour cream	1 cup shredded sharp
1/2 cup milk	Cheddar cheese
1/2 cup chopped green onions	4 cups frozen hash brown
1/2 teaspoon salt	potatoes, thawed and drained
	1/4 cup grated Parmesan cheese

Preheat oven to 325 degrees F. Butter a $1^1/2$-quart shallow baking dish and set aside.

In large bowl, beat eggs with sour cream. Add milk, green onions, salt, pepper, and Cheddar cheese; mix well. Stir in potatoes and pour into prepared baking dish.

Sprinkle with Parmesan cheese; bake for 25–35 minutes or until casserole is bubbly and top is lightly browned. *Serves 4–6*

Green Rice Casserole

This easy and elegant casserole is perfect served with grilled steak or chicken. The color is gorgeous, and it's a wonderful way to make rice more interesting.

1 cup uncooked long-grain white rice	3 eggs
$1/2$ cup butter	1 cup milk
1 green bell pepper, chopped	$1/2$ teaspoon salt
1 onion, chopped	$1/2$ pound diced sharp Cheddar cheese
$1/2$ cup chopped flat-leaf parsley	

Cook rice according to package directions until tender. Drain if necessary.

Meanwhile, in large saucepan, melt butter over medium heat. Add green bell pepper and onion; cook and stir until crisp-tender, about 5 minutes.

Preheat oven to 325 degrees F. When rice is done, stir into saucepan along with parsley. In small bowl, combine eggs with milk and salt and beat well. Stir into rice mixture, then stir in cheese.

Pour rice mixture into $1^1/2$-quart casserole. Cover casserole and bake for 55–65 minutes or until casserole is set. *Serves 6–8*

· ·

Oven–Baked Cranberry Relish

For Thanksgiving, nothing beats a homemade cranberry relish. Leftovers are fabulous served as a sandwich spread with turkey and whole-grain bread, or combined with sour cream and served as an appetizer dip.

1 pound fresh cranberries	1 cup orange marmalade
$2^1/2$ cups sugar	$1/2$ cup dried, sweetened cranberries
1 cup coarsely broken walnuts	$1/8$ teaspoon salt
3 tablespoons lemon juice	

Preheat oven to 350 degrees F. Combine cranberries and sugar in shallow baking dish. Cover tightly and bake for 1 hour.

Meanwhile, place the walnuts on a cookie sheet and toast in same oven for 10 minutes until fragrant. Remove from oven and let cool.

When the cranberry mixture is done, stir in the walnuts, lemon juice, marmalade, dried cranberries, and salt and mix well. Let cool for 30 minutes, then cover and refrigerate until serving time. The relish can be stored in the refrigerator for up to one week. *Yields 3 cups*

· ·

BABY LIMA BEANS IN SOUR CREAM

Lima beans are delicious—soft and pillowy with a wonderful mild and nutty taste. I don't know why people don't like them! Even lima bean–haters will like this casserole. Smother vegetables in enough sour cream and cheese, and even kids will eat them!

2 (10-ounce) package frozen
   baby lima beans
1/4 cup butter
1 cup crushed herb-seasoned
   stuffing mix

2 cups sour cream
1/2 teaspoon onion salt
1 cup grated processed
   American cheese

Cook lima beans in large saucepan according to package directions. Remove from heat, drain, and set aside.

In another saucepan, melt butter and add stuffing mix crumbs. Cook and stir over medium heat until the crumbs are coated with butter and toasted.

Stir the sour cream, onion salt, and American cheese into the lima beans; return to low heat. Cook and stir until heated through. Sprinkle with toasted buttered crumbs and serve immediately. *Serves 6–8*

- -

BROWNED POTATO LOAF

This is a beautiful and unusual way to serve potatoes as a side dish. In fact, it could be an excellent vegetarian main dish. Serve it with salsa or a hot tomato sauce spiced with Italian seasoning.

8 medium red potatoes
1/4 cup butter
1/4 cup flour
1/2 teaspoon salt
1/8 teaspoon white pepper

1 1/3 cups milk
2 tablespoons minced flat-leaf parsley
1/4 cup grated Parmesan cheese
1 cup grated sharp Cheddar cheese

Grease a 9 x 5-inch loaf pan with solid shortening and set aside. Boil potatoes in their jackets, then peel and cut into small cubes. Meanwhile, melt butter in large saucepan and stir in flour, salt, and pepper. Cook and stir until bubbly.

Add milk; cook and stir until sauce becomes thick. Add potatoes, parsley, and Parmesan cheese. Pack into prepared loaf pan, cover, and chill overnight.

When ready to serve, preheat oven to 375 degrees F. Unmold potatoes from pan, place on a baking dish, and sprinkle with Cheddar cheese. Bake until heated through and browned, 45–55 minutes. Slice to serve. *Serves 6*

- -

CHEDDAR ZUCCHINI

When zucchini is overflowing in the garden, this simple and flavorful side dish is a good way to prepare it. Serve it with a grilled steak and some fresh fruit.

3 tablespoons butter	1/2 teaspoon salt
1 onion, chopped	1/8 teaspoon pepper
3 cloves garlic, minced	1 (8-ounce) can tomato sauce
6 cups thinly sliced zucchini	1 cup shredded Cheddar cheese, divided

Preheat oven to 375 degrees F. Butter a 1^1/2-quart casserole and set aside.

In large skillet, melt butter. Add onion and garlic; cook and stir for 2 minutes. Add zucchini; cook and stir 3 minutes longer. Add salt, pepper, and tomato sauce and bring to a simmer. Simmer for 5 minutes, stirring frequently.

Stir in half of the cheese and pour mixture into prepared casserole. Sprinkle with remaining cheese. Bake for 20–30 minutes or until casserole is bubbling and cheese melts. *Serves 6*

9

QUICK BREADS AND COFFEE CAKES

In the 1950s, bread baking was a part of almost every American kitchen. As more women entered the work force, yeast-bread baking at home declined.

Quick breads remain popular because they are, well, quick to make! All you have to do is stir together a few ingredients, pour the batter into a pan, and bake.

Most quick breads improve upon standing; let the breads cool completely, then wrap in plastic wrap and let stand overnight before serving. Corn bread and popovers are the exceptions; they must be served hot, with butter melting onto each piece.

• •

LETTUCE BREAD

Lettuce in a quick bread! This unusual ingredient adds nice moisture and a pretty green color to this easy bread. Serve it for a brunch and have your guests guess what's in it.

$1/2$ head iceberg lettuce
1 cup all-purpose flour
$1/2$ cup whole-wheat flour
2 teaspoons baking powder
$1/2$ teaspoon baking soda
$1/4$ teaspoon salt
$1/8$ teaspoon ground ginger
$1/4$ teaspoon ground nutmeg
$1/8$ teaspoon ground cardamom
$1/2$ cup sugar

$1/2$ cup brown sugar
$1/2$ cup butter
1 teaspoon grated lemon zest
1 teaspoon vanilla
2 eggs, beaten
1 cup chopped walnuts
1 cup powdered sugar
2 tablespoons lemon juice
1 tablespoon butter, melted

Rinse lettuce and refrigerate for 1 hour to crisp. Finely chop enough lettuce to measure 1 cup; set aside. Reserve remaining lettuce for another use.

Preheat oven to 350 degrees F. Spray $8^1/2$ x $4^1/2$-inch loaf pan with non-stick cooking spray containing flour and set aside.

In large bowl, combine all-purpose flour, whole-wheat flour, baking powder, baking soda, salt, ginger, nutmeg, cardamom, sugar, and brown sugar and mix well.

Cut in butter until particles are fine. Add lemon zest, vanilla, eggs, and lettuce and mix just until combined. Fold in walnuts and spoon batter into prepared loaf pan.

Bake for 50–60 minutes or until bread is firm, deep golden brown, and begins to pull away from sides of pan. Remove from pan and cool on wire rack.

While bread is cooling, combine powdered sugar, lemon juice, and butter in small bowl until smooth. Drizzle over warm bread. Cool completely, then slice to serve. *Serves 12*

• •

WHEAT GERM CORN BREAD

Wheat germ adds a wonderful crunch and nutty flavor to tender, moist cornbread. Serve it hot out of the oven with sweet, soft butter melting onto each piece.

1 cup all-purpose flour	$1/2$ cup wheat germ
$1/4$ cup whole-wheat flour	2 eggs
$1/3$ cup brown sugar	$1/4$ cup honey
3 teaspoons baking powder	$3/4$ cup milk
1 teaspoon baking soda	$1/2$ cup plain yogurt
$1/2$ teaspoon salt	$1/3$ cup butter, melted
1 cup cornmeal	

Preheat oven to 425 degrees F. Grease a 9 x 9-inch square pan with solid shortening and set aside. In a large mixing bowl, combine all-purpose flour, whole-wheat flour, brown sugar, baking powder, baking soda, and salt. Stir in cornmeal and wheat germ and mix well.

In small bowl, combine eggs, honey, milk, yogurt, and melted butter and beat until blended. Pour egg mixture into flour mixture all at once; stir just to moisten. Turn into prepared pan and bake for 25–30 minutes until bread is golden brown. Serve hot. *Serves 9*

• •

ORANGE WHEAT GERM MUFFINS

Wheat germ is so good for you, but it's quite perishable. Store it, tightly covered, in the refrigerator. It adds nutrition and crunch to these tender little muffins. I especially like the crumbly, fragrant topping.

1 cup wheat germ	1/3 cup vegetable oil
1 1/3 cups flour	1 egg
1/3 cup sugar	2/3 cup orange juice
2 teaspoons baking powder	2 tablespoons wheat germ
1 teaspoon baking soda	3 tablespoons brown sugar
1/4 teaspoon salt	1/2 teaspoon cinnamon
1 teaspoon grated orange zest	2 tablespoons butter, melted

Preheat oven to 400 degrees F. Spray 12 muffin cups with nonstick baking spray containing flour and set aside.

In medium bowl, combine 1 cup wheat germ, flour, sugar, baking powder, baking soda, and salt and mix well.

In large bowl, combine orange zest, oil, egg, and orange juice and beat until smooth. Add dry ingredients all at once and mix just until combined.

Fill muffin cups 2/3 full of batter. In small bowl, combine 2 tablespoons wheat germ, brown sugar, cinnamon, and melted butter and mix until crumbly. Sprinkle this mixture over muffin batter.

Bake for 18–22 minutes or until muffins are rounded and firm to the touch. Remove from cups and cool on wire rack. *Yields 12 muffins*

• •

CUSTARD CORN BREAD

This unusual method makes a very moist and tender corn bread. Be sure to follow the directions to the letter. This bread is excellent served hot out of the oven with Bean and Bacon Soup (page 58) or Fresh Vegetable Beef Soup (page 57).

3/4 cup cornmeal	1 cup buttermilk
1/4 cup flour	1 egg
3 tablespoons brown sugar	1/2 cup frozen corn kernels, thawed
1/2 teaspoon salt	2 tablespoons butter
1/2 teaspoon baking powder	1/2 cup whole milk
1/2 teaspoon baking soda	

Preheat oven to 400 degrees F. In medium bowl, combine cornmeal, flour, brown sugar, salt, baking powder, and baking soda and mix well.

In small bowl, combine buttermilk, egg, and corn and beat until combined. Add to flour mixture and stir just until dry ingredients are moistened.

Place butter in a heavy duty 8-inch square baking pan and melt butter in hot oven for about 5 minutes. Remove pan from oven and immediately pour batter over butter. Pour whole milk over batter; do not stir.

Bake for 25–35 minutes or until bread is light golden brown and begins to pull away from sides of pan. Serve hot. *Serves 9*

Easy Cranberry Nut Bread

Cranberry bread is really a good choice for the holidays. The color is perfect, and there's something about the combination of sweet bread with tart cranberries that is very satisfying.

Like most quick breads, this one is better the day after it is made. So make it, let it cool, and wrap in plastic wrap. Let it sit at room temperature overnight and then enjoy the bread the next day.

2 cups flour	1 cup whole-berry cranberry sauce
3/4 cup brown sugar	1 teaspoon grated lemon zest
2 teaspoons baking powder	1 cup chopped walnuts
1 teaspoon baking soda	1/2 cup quick-cooking oatmeal
1/2 teaspoon salt	1 (3-ounce) package cream
1 teaspoon cinnamon	cheese, softened
1 egg	1/2 cup whole-berry cranberry sauce
2 tablespoons vegetable oil	

Preheat oven to 350 degrees F. Spray a 9 x 5-inch loaf pan with nonstick baking spray containing flour and set aside.

In large bowl, combine flour, brown sugar, baking powder, baking soda, salt, and cinnamon and mix well.

In small bowl, combine egg and vegetable oil and beat well. Stir in 1 cup cranberry sauce and lemon zest. Add to dry ingredients and mix just until combined, then stir in walnuts and oatmeal. Spoon batter into prepared pan.

Bake for 50–60 minutes or until bread is set and deep golden brown. Remove from pan and cool on wire rack.

In small bowl, combine cream cheese with 1/2 cup cranberry sauce and mix gently. Serve as a spread with bread. *Serves 8*

• •

Pear-Blueberry Coffee Cake

This cake is excellent for breakfast on the run or for a coffee klatch. Muffin mix makes it easy, and the fruits make it delicious.

Did you know that dried blueberries made from wild blueberries are one of the best sources of antioxidants? Antioxidants are some of the most important compounds you can eat for good health.

3 pears	1 teaspoon cinnamon
2 teaspoons lemon juice	1/2 cup chopped pecans
1/4 cup butter, softened	2 (7-ounce) packages blueberry muffin mix
1/2 cup brown sugar	2 eggs
1/3 cup flour	1 cup sour cream
1/4 teaspoon nutmeg	1/2 cup pear nectar

Preheat oven to 400 degrees F. Peel, core, and thinly slice pears; sprinkle with lemon juice and set aside.

For streusel, in small bowl, combine butter, brown sugar, flour, nutmeg, and cinnamon and mix until crumbly. Stir in pecans and set aside.

In large bowl, combine muffin mixes, eggs, sour cream, and pear nectar and mix just until combined.

Butter a 9-inch square baking pan. Spoon and spread batter into pan. Arrange pears over batter and sprinkle with streusel topping.

Bake for 25–35 minutes or until coffee cake is golden brown and starts to pull away from sides of pan. Let cool for 20 minutes, then serve warm. *Serves 9*

Joyce visits a farm family's root cellar in the 1960s during Farm-City Days. Many of the recipes Joyce read on the air were sent in by wives and mothers throughout the listening area.

Applesauce Bran Muffins

Muffins make the perfect breakfast, especially on busy weekday mornings. You can make these muffins ahead of time. To reheat them, microwave each muffin on a microwave-safe piece of paper towel for about 15–20 seconds on high. Serve these with softened butter and whipped honey.

1¼ cups flour	⅓ cup brown sugar
½ teaspoon cinnamon	⅓ cup buttermilk
¼ teaspoon cloves	⅔ cup applesauce
¼ teaspoon nutmeg	1 egg
2 teaspoons baking powder	¼ cup vegetable oil
1 teaspoon baking soda	1 cup whole bran cereal flakes
½ teaspoon salt	

Preheat oven to 400 degrees F. Spray 12 muffin cups with nonstick baking spray containing flour and set aside.

In large bowl, combine flour, cinnamon, cloves, nutmeg, baking powder, baking soda, salt, and brown sugar and mix well. In small bowl, combine buttermilk, applesauce, egg, and vegetable oil and beat well.

Add buttermilk mixture all at once to dry ingredients and stir just until batter is mixed; stir in cereal. Spoon batter into prepared muffin cups. Bake for 20 minutes or until muffins are set. Cool on wire racks. *Yields 12 muffins*

•••

Cream Cheese Coffee Cake

Now this is a coffee cake for a celebration! It's perfect for Christmas morning to slice thinly and offer to family as everyone is busy opening presents. Make it a day ahead of time and let it stand, well covered, overnight at room temperature. The flavor will get even better, and the texture will be perfect for slicing.

Remember, it's important to use unsalted butter to grease the pan; otherwise, the coffee cake may stick.

2 tablespoons unsalted butter	1 cup sugar
¾ cup chopped pecans	½ cup brown sugar
½ cup sugar	2 teaspoons vanilla
¼ cup brown sugar	4 eggs
3 tablespoons cocoa powder	3 cups flour
2 teaspoons cinnamon	1½ teaspoons baking powder
1 cup butter, softened	½ teaspoon baking soda
1 (8-ounce) package cream cheese, softened	1 cup dried currants

Preheat oven to 325 degrees F. Generously grease a 10-inch tube pan with the unsalted butter. Sprinkle pan with chopped pecans, pressing so they stick to the bottom and sides of the pan; set aside.

In small bowl, combine $1/2$ cup sugar and $1/4$ cup brown sugar with cocoa powder and cinnamon; set aside.

In large bowl, combine 1 cup butter, cream cheese, 1 cup sugar, and $1/2$ cup brown sugar and beat until light and fluffy. Add vanilla, then beat in eggs, one at a time, beating well after each addition.

Stir in flour, baking powder, baking soda, and dried currants. Batter will be very thick.

Spoon half of batter into the prepared pan. Sprinkle with half of the cocoa mixture. Spoon on two-thirds of the remaining batter, then sprinkle with half of the remaining cocoa mixture.

Stir remaining cocoa mixture into remaining batter and swirl on top of the batter in pan.

Bake for 65–75 minutes or until cake is golden brown and toothpick inserted in center comes out clean. Cool in pan about 15 minutes, then remove to wire rack to cool completely. Store, covered, at room temperature. *Serves 16*

....

BLUE RIBBON APPLE BREAD

Applesauce adds moistness and great flavor to this simple quick bread. I don't know if it actually won a blue ribbon at a state fair, but it tastes like it did! Since it's made with applesauce instead of peeled and grated apples, the preparation time is very quick.

$2/3$ cup butter, softened	2 teaspoons baking powder
$3/4$ cup sugar	1 teaspoon baking soda
$1/2$ cup brown sugar	$1/2$ teaspoon salt
4 eggs	1 tablespoon grated lemon zest
$1^1/2$ cups applesauce	$1^1/2$ cups chopped pecans
$1/2$ cup whole milk	1 cup finely chopped dates or raisins
4 cups flour	

Preheat oven to 350 degrees F. Spray two 9 x 5-inch loaf pans with non-stick baking spray containing flour and set aside.

In large bowl, combine butter, sugar, and brown sugar and beat until light and fluffy. Add eggs, one at a time, beating well after each addition.

Combine applesauce and milk in small bowl. Combine flour, baking powder, baking soda, and salt in medium bowl. Alternately add flour mixture and milk mixture to butter mixture, beginning and ending with dry ingredients.

Add lemon zest, pecans, and dates. Divide mixture among prepared loaf pans. Bake for 45–55 minutes or until toothpick inserted in center comes out clean. Let cool on wire rack for 10 minutes, then remove bread from pans and cool completely. *Serves 12*

CRANBERRY BANANA BREAD

Wisconsin, Minnesota's neighbor to the east, produces most of the cranberries the nation consumes. But some intrepid Minnesotans are trying to start cranberry bogs in the northern part of the state. The fruit is native to Minnesota, but for some reason cranberry farming never caught on.

The bright red, tender berries are sharply acidic, a perfect complement to banana bread. This recipe is wonderful for the holidays.

1/4 cup butter, softened	1 tablespoon grated orange zest
1/2 cup sugar	1 cup mashed bananas
1/2 cup brown sugar	(about 2 medium)
1 egg	1/2 cup buttermilk
2 cups flour	1 cup chopped cranberries
2 teaspoons baking powder	1 cup chopped pecans
1 teaspoon baking soda	2 tablespoons sugar
1/4 teaspoon salt	1/2 teaspoon cinnamon
1/2 teaspoon cinnamon	

Preheat oven to 350 degrees F. Spray a 9 x 5-inch loaf pan with nonstick baking spray containing flour and set aside.

In large bowl, combine butter, sugar, and brown sugar and beat until light and fluffy. Add egg and beat well.

In medium bowl, combine flour, baking powder, baking soda, salt, and 1/2 teaspoon cinnamon. In small bowl, combine orange zest, bananas, and buttermilk.

Add dry ingredients alternately with banana mixture to egg mixture, beginning and ending with dry ingredients. Stir in cranberries and pecans.

In small bowl, combine 2 tablespoons sugar and 1/2 teaspoon cinnamon.

Turn batter into prepared pan. Sprinkle with cinnamon sugar. Bake for 65–75 minutes or until bread is dark golden brown and pulls away from sides of pan. Let cool for 10 minutes, then turn out onto wire rack to cool completely. *Serves 8*

• •

WHOLE-WHEAT HONEY NUT BREAD

In the 1970s, recipes with whole wheat, oat bran, and other whole grains started becoming more popular. This excellent recipe uses wholesome ingredients in a quick bread. Store the bread overnight, well wrapped, before serving for easier slicing and the best flavor.

1 1/2 cups all-purpose flour	1 1/4 cups buttermilk
1 1/2 teaspoons baking powder	1 egg
1/2 teaspoon baking soda	1/2 cup honey
1/4 teaspoon salt	2 tablespoons vegetable oil
1 cup whole-wheat flour	1 cup raisins or dried currants
1/4 cup brown sugar	1 cup chopped walnuts

Preheat oven to 375 degrees F. Spray a 9 x 5-inch loaf pan with nonstick baking spray containing flour and set aside.

In large bowl, combine all-purpose flour, baking powder, baking soda, salt, whole-wheat flour, and brown sugar and mix well until combined.

In medium bowl, combine buttermilk, egg, honey, and oil and beat with wire whisk until smooth. Add all at once to the flour mixture and stir just until blended. Stir in raisins and walnuts.

Spoon batter into prepared pan. Bake for 45–55 minutes or until a toothpick inserted in the center comes out clean. Cool in pan for 10 minutes, then turn out onto wire rack and cool completely. Store overnight before serving. *Serves 8*

• •

ORANGE–DATE BREAD

Date breads are old-fashioned; they were featured in many home economics classes for junior high students in the 1960s and 1970s. And they are delicious. The dates help keep the bread moist. And dates are so good for you; they are naturally sweet and full of fiber and lots of B vitamins.

1 cup chopped dates	2 eggs
1 teaspoon grated orange zest	2 cups flour
1 cup orange juice	1 teaspoon baking powder
1/2 cup boiling water	1 teaspoon baking soda
1/2 cup sugar	1/2 teaspoon salt
1/2 cup brown sugar	2 tablespoons instant mashed
2 tablespoons vegetable oil	potato flakes
1 teaspoon vanilla	1 cup chopped pecans

Preheat oven to 350 degrees F. Spray a 9 x 5-inch loaf pan with nonstick baking spray containing flour and set aside.

In large bowl, combine dates, orange zest, orange juice, and boiling water; stir for 3 minutes. Add sugar, brown sugar, oil, vanilla, and eggs and beat until combined.

Add flour, baking powder, baking soda, salt, and potato flakes and stir just until combined. Stir in pecans and spoon mixture into prepared pan.

Bake for 60–70 minutes until loaf is golden brown and toothpick inserted into center comes out clean. Cool in pan for 5 minutes, then turn out onto wire rack to cool completely. *Serves 8*

• •

Santa Fe French Toast

French toast that is first fried, then baked until puffy is quite a treat. Serve with powdered sugar and some warmed honey or maple syrup, with lots of crisply cooked bacon on the side.

6 (3/4-inch thick) slices firm white bread
4 eggs
1 cup light cream
2 teaspoons vanilla
1/4 teaspoon salt
1/4 cup sugar
1/4 cup butter
1/4 cup vegetable oil

Preheat oven to 400 degrees F. Cut bread pieces diagonally in half.

In shallow bowl, combine eggs, cream, vanilla, salt, and sugar and beat until combined. Add bread to this mixture, turning the slices occasionally, allowing bread to absorb as much liquid as possible without falling apart.

Heat butter and oil in large saucepan for about 5 minutes, until a chopstick bubbles furiously when lowered into the hot fat. Fry bread on both sides until golden brown.

Drain French toast briefly on paper towels and place on baking sheet. Bake for 4–8 minutes until puffed. Serve immediately. *Serves 6*

Apricot Loaf

Dried apricots are sweet and tart and have a wonderful texture, whether plain or rehydrated. Betty Crocker still makes a pound-cake mix. If you can't find it in the grocery store, ask the grocer to order some for you or order it online.

3/4 cup chopped dried apricots
1/2 cup chopped walnuts
1/4 cup brown sugar
1/4 cup flour
1 (16-ounce) package
    pound-cake mix
1/4 cup milk
1/4 cup orange juice
3 eggs
1 teaspoon grated orange zest
1/2 teaspoon cinnamon
1/4 cup powdered sugar
2 tablespoons apricot nectar

Preheat oven to 325 degrees F. Spray a 9 x 5-inch loaf pan with nonstick baking spray containing flour and set aside.

In small bowl, combine apricots, walnuts, brown sugar, and flour and mix well; set aside.

In large bowl, combine pound-cake mix, milk, and orange juice; beat for 1 minute. Add eggs, orange zest, and cinnamon and beat for 2 minutes longer.

Fold in apricot mixture until just combined. Spoon batter into prepared loaf pan. Bake for 65–75 minutes or until bread is golden brown and begins to pull away from sides of pan. Cool in pan for 10 minutes, then turn out onto wire rack to cool.

In small bowl, combine powdered sugar and apricot nectar; mix until smooth. Drizzle over warm bread, cool completely, then store at room temperature. *Serves 8*

Joyce Lamont and Howard Viken are photographed during the 1963 Farm-City Days, in the farm home of Mr. and Mrs. Ralph Most, Jr. near Prescott, Wisconsin. Farm-City Days, a project of WCCO, was designed to increase understanding between farm and city people.

FROZEN BRAN MUFFINS

Now this is a great way to save time in the morning! Make muffin batter, spoon it into cups, and freeze solid. Then when you want some fresh, hot muffins, bake the frozen batter until golden brown and tender. These are spectacular served hot out of the oven with soft butter.

1 (15-ounce) package raisin bran cereal	1 teaspoon salt
4 cups all-purpose flour	4 eggs
1 cup whole-wheat flour	4 cups buttermilk
2 cups sugar	1 cup vegetable oil
1 cup brown sugar	1 cup raisins
5 teaspoons baking soda	

In very large bowl, combine cereal, all-purpose flour, whole-wheat flour, sugar, brown sugar, baking soda, and salt and mix gently.

In large bowl, combine eggs, buttermilk, and oil and beat until combined. Add to flour mixture and stir just until dry ingredients are moistened; stir in raisins.

Spoon batter into paper-lined muffin cups, filling each cup $3/4$ full. Freeze until frozen solid. Remove frozen batter from muffin cups, pack into hard-sided freezer containers, label, seal, and freeze up to four months.

To bake frozen muffins, bake in preheated 400-degree-F oven for 25–35 minutes or until muffins are golden brown. Remove from muffin cups and cool on wire rack. *Yields 5 dozen muffins*

· ·

CARROT NUT BREAD

You're probably familiar with carrot cake, but carrot bread isn't as well known. It's moist and tender with a wonderful flavor, and it's so good for you too.

I like to use baby carrots and grate them on a box grater or in a food processor until quite fine. That way they melt into the batter as it bakes.

$1^1/2$ cups all-purpose flour	2 eggs
$1^1/2$ teaspoons baking powder	1 cup milk
1 teaspoon baking soda	$1/4$ cup butter, melted
$1/2$ teaspoon salt	$1^1/2$ cups finely grated carrots
$1/2$ teaspoon cinnamon	$1/2$ cup chopped walnuts
1 cup whole-wheat flour	2 tablespoons sugar
$2/3$ cup brown sugar	$1/2$ teaspoon cinnamon

Preheat oven to 350 degrees F. Spray 9 x 5-inch loaf pan with nonstick baking spray containing flour and set aside.

In large bowl, combine all-purpose flour, baking powder, baking soda, salt, and $1/2$ teaspoon cinnamon and mix well. Stir in whole-wheat flour and brown sugar and mix with wire whisk until blended.

In small bowl, combine eggs, milk, and melted butter and mix until smooth. Add to the dry ingredients and stir just until moistened. Fold in carrots and walnuts.

Spoon batter into prepared pan. In small bowl, combine sugar and $1/2$ teaspoon cinnamon and sprinkle over batter. Bake for 45–55 minutes or until bread is dark golden brown and pulls away from sides of pan. Remove and cool on wire rack. *Serves 8*

....

QUICK CHEESE BREAD

When you're serving a soup for supper, it's nice to have a warm loaf of bread to accompany it. This recipe is delicious, with lots of cheese and a bit of wheat germ for crunch.

3 cups flour	2 eggs
3 tablespoons sugar	$1^{1}/3$ cups milk
$1/2$ cup wheat germ	$1/4$ cup vegetable oil
4 teaspoons baking powder	$1^{1}/2$ cups diced Swiss cheese
$1/2$ teaspoon salt	2 tablespoons grated Parmesan cheese

Preheat oven to 350 degrees F. Spray 9 x 5-inch loaf pan with nonstick baking spray containing flour and set aside.

In large bowl, combine flour, sugar, wheat germ, baking powder, and salt and mix well.

In small bowl, combine eggs, milk, and vegetable oil and beat until combined. Add all at once to the flour mixture and mix until combined, then add the Swiss cheese.

Spoon batter into prepared pan and sprinkle with Parmesan cheese. Bake for 55–65 minutes until bread is golden brown and firm. Turn loaf out onto wire rack and let cool for at least 20 minutes before serving. *Serves 10–12*

....

ZUCCHINI BREAD

In the fall, Minnesota gardens are overflowing with zucchini. Use it to make this delicious bread that has a fun green color and wonderful flavor.

3 eggs
1 1/2 cups sugar
1/2 cup brown sugar
3/4 cup vegetable oil
2 cups raw, unpeeled,
  grated zucchini
1 teaspoon cinnamon

2 teaspoons vanilla
3 cups flour
1/2 teaspoon salt
1 teaspoon baking soda
1/2 teaspoon baking powder
1 cup chopped pecans

Preheat oven to 350 degrees F. Spray two 9 x 5-inch loaf pans with non-stick baking spray containing flour and set aside.

In large mixing bowl, beat eggs until light and fluffy. Gradually add the sugar, beating until thick. Add brown sugar and beat until blended.

Add remaining ingredients and mix well. Spoon batter into prepared pans. Bake for 40–50 minutes until bread is golden brown and toothpick inserted in center comes out clean. Remove from pans and cool on wire rack. *Serves 16*

....

NEVER-FAIL POPOVERS

Popovers look so impressive, and many people think they're difficult to make. They're not—you just need to follow a few rules. Beat the batter just until combined, don't open the oven door while they're baking, and grease the popover cups thoroughly. Oh, and make sure your oven temperature is accurate by using an oven thermometer. Then enjoy!

2 eggs
1 cup milk

1 cup flour
1/2 teaspoon salt

Generously grease 6 custard cups with solid shortening or unsalted butter. Place the cups on a cookie sheet and set aside.

In medium bowl, place eggs. Add milk, flour, and salt and mix with an eggbeater until combined; the mixture may be lumpy.

Fill each prepared custard cup 3/4 full of batter. Place in a cold oven, then turn the oven to 450 degrees F. Let popovers bake for exactly 30 minutes; do not open the oven door.

Remove popovers from the oven and puncture each one in a few places with a sharp knife. Turn the oven off, and return popovers to the oven for 10 minutes longer, then serve immediately.

You can make the popovers ahead of time. Let them cool completely on a wire rack, then bake in preheated 350-degree-F oven for exactly 5 minutes, just before serving. *Serves 6*

BISHOP'S BREAD

This delicious quick bread is full of candied fruits, chocolate, and nuts. It's similar to a fruitcake but isn't as dense. Drizzled with a simple lemon frosting, this bread is nice for the holidays.

2 cups flour
3 teaspoons baking powder
$1/2$ teaspoon salt
1 cup chopped walnuts
1 cup chopped, drained maraschino
cherries or mixed candied fruit
1 cup miniature semisweet
chocolate chips

4 eggs, separated
1 cup sugar
$1/8$ teaspoon cream of tartar
1 cup powdered sugar
2 tablespoons lemon juice

Preheat oven to 325 degrees F. Grease 9 x 5-inch loaf pan with solid shortening and line bottom with parchment paper; set aside.

In medium bowl, sift together flour, baking powder, and salt. In another medium bowl, combine walnuts, cherries, and chocolate chips. Sprinkle $1/3$ cup of the flour mixture over the nut mixture and toss to coat.

In large bowl, beat egg yolks until light colored, gradually adding the sugar. Add the nut mixture and blend well.

In medium bowl, combine egg whites with cream of tartar and beat until stiff peaks form. Fold into the egg yolk mixture, then fold in the rest of the flour mixture.

Turn batter into prepared pan. Bake for 70–80 minutes or until deep golden brown. Remove loaf from pan and peel off the paper. Let cool on wire rack.

In small bowl, combine powdered sugar and lemon juice; drizzle over cooled bread. *Serves 12*

· ·

LEMON-GLAZED BLUEBERRY MUFFINS

Muffins are a wonderful food for eating breakfast on the run. Kids always love them too, so they are a good choice for busy school mornings. And they're also great to serve with a salad for lunch on the porch.

$1 3/4$ cups flour
$1/3$ cup sugar
2 teaspoons baking powder
1 teaspoon baking soda
$1/2$ teaspoon salt
$1/3$ cup wheat germ
1 egg

$3/4$ cup milk
$1/4$ cup lemon juice
$1/4$ cup vegetable oil
1 cup fresh blueberries
2 tablespoons sugar
2 teaspoons grated lemon zest

163

Preheat oven to 375 degrees F. Spray 12 muffin cups with nonstick baking spray containing flour; set aside.

In large bowl, combine flour, sugar, baking powder, baking soda, salt, and wheat germ and mix well.

In small bowl, combine egg with milk and beat well; add lemon juice and oil and mix to combine. Add all at once to the dry ingredients, stirring just until batter forms. Fold in blueberries.

Spoon batter into prepared muffin cups, filling each 2/3 full. In small bowl, combine 2 tablespoons sugar and lemon zest; mix well and sprinkle over muffin batter.

Bake for 20–30 minutes or until muffins are light golden brown. Turn out onto wire rack and let cool for 20 minutes before serving. *Yields 12 muffins*

BUTTERSCOTCH NUT BREAD

Nut breads, like most quick breads, should be made ahead of time so the texture can set and the flavors blend. The only trick is guarding the loaf from your family while you wait for it to ripen!

2 cups flour	1 cup buttermilk
1 teaspoon baking powder	1 cup chopped walnuts
1/2 teaspoon baking soda	2 tablespoons sesame seeds
1/2 teaspoon salt	2 tablespoons sugar
2 eggs	1 tablespoon brown sugar
1 teaspoon vanilla	1/2 teaspoon cinnamon
1 cup brown sugar	1/4 teaspoon nutmeg
3 tablespoons butter, melted	

Preheat oven to 350 degrees F. Spray a 9 x 5-inch loaf pan with nonstick baking spray containing flour and set aside.

Sift flour, baking powder, baking soda, and salt into a medium bowl. In large bowl, beat eggs and vanilla until light and fluffy. Beat in 1 cup brown sugar until combined, then beat in melted butter.

Alternately add flour mixture with buttermilk to the egg mixture, beginning and ending with dry ingredients. Stir in walnuts.

Spoon and spread batter into prepared pan. In small bowl, combine sesame seeds, sugar, 1 tablespoon brown sugar, cinnamon, and nutmeg and mix well. Sprinkle over the batter.

Bake for 55–65 minutes or until bread is golden brown and firm. Remove from pan and cool on wire rack, then wrap tightly in plastic wrap and store overnight at room temperature. *Serves 12*

Enjoying each other's company as much as their listeners enjoyed listening to them, Joyce shares a laugh with her colleague Howard Viken.

ALMOND-CRUSTED PINEAPPLE BREAD

This bread is gorgeous: sliced almonds form a crust for a tender and sweet quick bread. The pineapple caramelizes while the bread bakes, creating a very rich and complex flavor.

1 tablespoon unsalted butter	1 teaspoon grated orange zest
1/2 cup sliced almonds	2 1/2 cups flour
1/2 cup butter, softened	2 teaspoons baking powder
1/2 cup sugar	1/2 teaspoon baking soda
1/4 cup brown sugar	1/2 teaspoon salt
1 egg	1 (8-ounce) can crushed pineapple
1 teaspoon vanilla	1/3 cup sour cream

Preheat oven to 350 degrees F. Grease 9 x 5-inch loaf pan with 1 tablespoon butter. Sprinkle almonds into the pan and press to coat bottom and sides.

In large bowl, beat 1/2 cup butter with sugar and brown sugar until light and fluffy. Add egg, vanilla, and orange zest; beat until fluffy.

In sifter, combine flour, baking powder, baking soda, and salt. Add alternately with undrained pineapple and sour cream to butter mixture, beginning and ending with dry ingredients.

Carefully spoon batter into the prepared pan. Bake for 55–65 minutes or until bread is deep golden brown and toothpick inserted in center comes out clean. Cool in pan for 5 minutes, then remove from pan and cool completely on wire rack. *Serves 12*

• •

BREAKFAST BREAD

This unusual recipe has a wonderful flavor and texture. Crushed corn flakes add a subtle corn flavor and a little bit of crunch. Try toasting this bread after a day or two and serve it with whipped honey or raspberry jam.

1 1/2 cups corn flakes	1/2 cup brown sugar
2 cups flour	2 eggs
2 teaspoons baking powder	1 tablespoon grated orange zest
1 teaspoon baking soda	1 cup orange juice
1/2 teaspoon salt	1/2 cup chopped walnuts
1/2 cup butter, softened	1/2 cup raisins

Preheat oven to 350 degrees F. Spray 9 x 5-inch loaf pan with nonstick baking spray containing flour and set aside.

Crush corn flakes into fine crumbs. In a sifter, combine flour, baking powder, baking soda, and salt; set aside. In large bowl, combine butter and brown sugar; beat until fluffy. Add eggs and orange zest; beat until combined.

Add orange juice to batter alternately with the flour mixture, stirring just until batter forms. Stir in the corn-flake crumbs, walnuts, and raisins. Spoon into prepared loaf pan.

Bake for 55–65 minutes or until bread is golden brown and firm. Remove bread from oven, cool in pan for 10 minutes, then remove from pan and cool completely on wire rack. *Serves 12*

· ·

MAPLE GINGERBREAD

Gingerbread is an old-fashioned recipe that is perfect as an after-school treat or as a breakfast bread. Be sure to use real maple syrup in this simple recipe, not pancake syrup or imitation. Maple syrup comes in several grades, depending on its color. A lower grade of syrup, like "B" or "A Dark Amber" is less expensive and works well in this recipe.

1 cup maple syrup	1 teaspoon baking soda
1 cup sour cream	1$1/2$ teaspoons ground ginger
1 egg	$1/2$ teaspoon salt
2$1/3$ cups flour	$1/4$ cup butter, melted

Preheat oven to 350 degrees F. Spray 13 x 9-inch baking pan with non-stick baking spray containing flour and set aside.

In large bowl, combine syrup, sour cream, and egg and beat until smooth. Add flour, baking soda, ginger, and salt and stir to combine. Stir in melted butter.

Spoon batter into prepared pan. Bake for 20–30 minutes or until gingerbread is dark golden brown and top springs back when lightly touched in center. Cut into squares and serve warm. *Serves 8–10*

· ·

GRANOLA-PEACH BREAD

Fresh peaches are delectable in this delicious quick bread. Drizzle the finished bread with a glaze made from powdered sugar and lemon juice or serve it plain.

3 ripe peaches, peeled and sliced
1 tablespoon orange juice
1 3/4 cups flour
1 teaspoon baking powder
1/2 teaspoon baking soda
1/4 teaspoon salt
6 tablespoons butter, softened

1/3 cup sugar
1/3 cup brown sugar
2 eggs
1 teaspoon vanilla
1 teaspoon grated orange zest
2/3 cup granola
1/2 cup chopped walnuts

Preheat oven to 350 degrees F. Spray 9 x 5-inch loaf pan with nonstick baking spray containing flour and set aside.

Place peaches in blender or food processor; blend or process until smooth; stir in orange juice and set aside. Sift together flour, baking powder, baking soda, and salt; set aside.

In large bowl, combine butter, sugar, and brown sugar and beat until light and fluffy. Add eggs, vanilla, and orange zest and beat until combined.

Add the peach puree and flour mixture, stirring just until combined. Add granola and walnuts. Spoon into prepared pan.

Bake for 50–60 minutes or until toothpick inserted in bread comes out clean. Let cool in pan for 5 minutes, then turn out onto wire rack to cool.
Serves 12

COOKIES
AND
CANDIES

Cookies just say "Mom" and "home." In decades past, lucky children coming home from school often found freshly baked cookies and bars waiting for them for an after-school treat.

We don't have to wish those days were here again—we can recreate them! These easy cookies are delicious and fun to make. In fact, change the tradition a bit and let your kids make their own cookies. They'll learn a lot about math and science and have a great snack too.

TREASURE CHEST BARS

The recipe is packed full of nuts, chocolate, and fruit: it's a literal treasure chest! This bar cookie is a must at Christmas and is great lunch-box fodder any time of the year.

2 cups flour
$1^1/_2$ teaspoons baking powder
$1/_2$ teaspoon salt
$1/_2$ cup butter, softened
1 cup brown sugar
2 eggs
1 teaspoon vanilla
$1/_4$ cup pineapple juice
$1/_2$ cup milk

1 cup maraschino cherries or
   cranberries, cut in half
1 cup chopped salted mixed nuts
1 cup milk chocolate chips
$1/_4$ cup butter
1 (3-ounce) package cream cheese
2 cups powdered sugar
1 teaspoon vanilla

Preheat oven to 325 degrees F. Grease and flour 15 x 10-inch jelly roll pan and set aside.

Sift together flour, baking powder, and salt and set aside. In large bowl, combine $1/_2$ cup softened butter and brown sugar and beat well. Add eggs, one at a time, beating well after each addition. Stir in 1 teaspoon vanilla and beat until fluffy.

Add sifted dry ingredients to butter mixture alternately with pineapple juice and milk, beating well after each addition. Stir in cherries, nuts, and chocolate chips.

169

Turn batter into prepared pan. Bake at 325 degrees F for 25–30 minutes until bars are light golden brown and begin to pull away from sides of pan. Let cool completely on wire rack.

For frosting, in large saucepan, melt $1/4$ cup butter and cook over medium heat until butter is brown, 7–9 minutes. Remove from heat and stir in cream cheese, mixing until smooth. Then stir in 2 cups powdered sugar and 1 teaspoon vanilla and beat until smooth. Frost bars, cool, and cut into squares. *Yields 36 bars*

to sweet!

NO-BAKE APPLE CINNAMON COOKIES

No-bake cookies are great for hot summer days. It's fun to make cookies that don't have to go into the oven, and it keeps your kitchen cooler too. These cookies are flavorful and chewy, with a nice crunch from the walnuts.

$1/2$ cup butter	$1/8$ teaspoon salt
2 tablespoons flour	3 cups quick-cooking oatmeal
$1 1/2$ cups sugar	1 cup chopped walnuts
$1/2$ cup brown sugar	1 teaspoon vanilla
$1/2$ teaspoon cinnamon	1 (16-ounce) container
1 cup peeled, grated apple	vanilla frosting

In large saucepan, combine butter and flour. Cook over medium heat until mixture bubbles; cook for 2 minutes, stirring constantly. Add sugar, brown sugar, cinnamon, apple, and salt and bring to a boil. Boil hard for 1 minute, stirring constantly.

Remove from heat and immediately add oatmeal, walnuts, and vanilla; mix well. Drop by teaspoonfuls onto waxed paper and let stand until set. Frost with frosting, if desired.

You can also pour the oatmeal mixture into greased 9-inch square pan and refrigerate until set. Frost with frosting and refrigerate again. Cut into small bars to serve. *Yields 36 cookies*

Peanut Butter Bars

Peanut butter and chocolate is, of course, a classic combination. These chewy bars are perfect to tuck into lunchboxes and also make a terrific after-school snack.

3/4 cup sugar	1 cup flour
1/2 cup brown sugar	1 teaspoon baking powder
1/3 cup peanut butter	1/4 teaspoon salt
1/3 cup butter, softened	1 cup chopped peanuts
2 eggs	2 cups semisweet chocolate chips
1 1/2 teaspoons vanilla	1/3 cup peanut butter

Preheat oven to 350 degrees F. In large bowl, combine sugar, brown sugar, 1/3 cup peanut butter, and butter and beat until smooth. Add eggs and vanilla and beat until fluffy.

Add flour, baking powder, and salt and mix until a dough forms. Stir in chopped peanuts.

Spread dough into ungreased 13 x 9-inch pan and press evenly. Bake for 20–25 minutes or until golden brown and set. Place on wire rack.

In small microwave-safe bowl, combine chocolate chips and 1/3 cup peanut butter. Heat on 50-percent power for 2 minutes, then remove and stir. Continue microwaving on 50-percent power for 1-minute intervals, stirring between each interval, until chocolate is melted and mixture is smooth.

Pour chocolate mixture over warm bars and spread to cover. Let cool completely, then cut into bars. *Yields about 36 bars*

"This is a good 'action' shot of the radio personalities at work," Joyce says. "Bob DeHaven and I are doing *Good Neighbor Time*, while Jergen Nash stands by, ready to take over."

Coconut Candy Cookies

Back in 1971, using chopped candy in recipes wasn't very common. If you want these cookies to be extra special, dip them into some melted chocolate to coat after they have cooled and let the chocolate coating harden by placing the cookies on waxed paper–lined cookie sheets. Yum!

1 cup butter, softened	2 cups flour
1 cup brown sugar	1 teaspoon baking soda
1/2 cup sugar	1/2 teaspoon salt
2 eggs	5 ounces chocolate-coated
2 tablespoons milk	coconut candy bars, chopped
1 1/2 teaspoons vanilla	

Preheat oven to 375 degrees F. In large bowl, combine butter, brown sugar, and sugar and beat until light and fluffy. Add eggs, one at a time, beating well after each addition. Add milk and vanilla.

Stir in flour, baking soda, and salt and mix well. Then add chopped candy bars.

Drop dough by heaping teaspoonfuls onto ungreased cookie sheets. Bake for 9–12 minutes or until cookies are set. Cool on pans for 2 minutes, then carefully remove to wire racks to cool. *Yields 4 dozen cookies*

Fudge Marshmallows

Food giants Pillsbury and General Mills used to make dry frosting mixes, which were used in lots of recipes in the 1960s and 1970s. When they started producing canned "ready-to-use" frosting, they discontinued the dry mixture. Some recipes, like the famous Tunnel of Fudge cake, were reworked, while others were simply discarded.

But the Jiffy folks still make the dry frosting mix that you can use in this recipe. Have fun dipping the coated marshmallows in all kinds of toppings, from toasted chopped nuts to miniature chocolate-covered candies.

1 (7-ounce) package dry fudge-frosting mix	TOPPINGS, IF DESIRED:
	Chopped toasted nuts
1 (14-ounce) can sweetened condensed milk	Toasted coconut
	Tiny chocolate-covered candies
1 teaspoon vanilla	Chocolate jimmies
16–24 large marshmallows	Multicolored jimmies

In medium microwave-safe bowl, combine frosting mix and condensed milk; stir well with a wire whisk. Microwave on high for 1 minute, then remove and stir. Continue microwaving for 1-minute intervals on high, stirring after each interval, until mixture is smooth and blended. Stir in vanilla.

Skewer marshmallows and, holding each marshmallow over the chocolate mixture, spoon chocolate mixture over marshmallows to coat. Shake off excess, then roll coated marshmallows in toppings, if desired. Place on waxed paper.

You may need to rewarm the chocolate mixture if it hardens; microwave on 30-percent power for 30–40 seconds, then stir well and continue with the recipe. *Yields 16–24 candies*

· ·

ENGLISH TOFFEE BARS

This is a variation on one of the best and easiest bar cookies around. In the 1980s, toffee baking bits started appearing in the grocery store. These little candies are a great substitute for nuts in almost any recipe, and they eliminate the work of crushing toffee used in lots of desserts.

1 cup butter, softened	1 cup miniature semisweet
1 cup brown sugar	chocolate chips
1 egg yolk	1 cup toffee baking bits
1$3/4$ cups flour	1 (12-ounce) package semisweet
1 teaspoon cinnamon	chocolate chips
1/4 teaspoon ground cardamom	1/3 cup peanut butter
	1/2 cup toffee baking bits

Preheat oven to 300 degrees F. In large bowl, combine butter and brown sugar and mix well until fluffy. Add egg yolk and beat until combined. Stir in flour, cinnamon, and cardamom and mix until a dough forms. Stir in miniature chocolate chips and 1 cup toffee baking bits.

Press into 15 x 10-inch jelly roll pan. Bake for 35–45 minutes or until bars are set and golden brown. Let cool on wire rack for 15 minutes.

In small microwave-safe bowl, combine semisweet chocolate chips and peanut butter. Microwave at 50-percent power for 2 minutes, then remove and stir. Return to microwave and cook on 50-percent power for 1–2 minutes longer until chips are melted. Stir until mixture is smooth.

Pour over warm bars and spread to coat. Sprinkle with $1/2$ cup toffee baking bits and let cool. Cut into bars to serve. *Yields 6 dozen bars*

· ·

173

CHOCOLATE COCONUT CANDY

Using mashed potatoes to make this candy has been done for years. But adding coconut oil to the potatoes is something new! This adds a subtle coconut flavor to the base and makes a smoother candy.

And did you know that coconut oil isn't bad for you? In fact, it can lower cholesterol levels. You can find it in health food stores and food co-ops.

2/3 cup refrigerated mashed
    potatoes
2 tablespoons coconut oil
4 cups powdered sugar
1 teaspoon vanilla

1/2 teaspoon almond extract
4 cups shredded coconut
1 cup semisweet chocolate chips
1 cup milk chocolate chips

Heat mashed potatoes as directed on package. While potatoes are hot, stir in coconut oil and mix until combined. Let cool, then chill until cold.

Work in powdered sugar, vanilla, and almond extract and mix with hands until blended. Knead in coconut. Form into 1-inch balls. Place on waxed paper–lined cookie sheets and chill until firm.

In microwave-safe glass measuring cup, combine semisweet chocolate chips with 3/4 cup milk chocolate chips. Microwave on 50-percent power for 2 minutes, then remove and stir. Microwave for 1 minute longer, then remove and stir until chips are melted. Add remaining 1/4 cup milk chocolate chips, stirring constantly until mixture is melted and smooth. (This tempers the chocolate so it stays solid at room temperature.)

Dip the coconut balls into the chocolate mixture, shaking off excess. Place on waxed paper–lined cookie sheets and let stand until chocolate hardens. Store tightly covered at room temperature. *Yields about 4 dozen candies*

• •

CHOCOLATE-APPLESAUCE BARS

This recipe was ahead of its time! In the 1980s, home economists started substituting pureed prunes and applesauce for the fat in many baked products to reduce the fat and cholesterol content. These ingredients also add flavor and moisture to cookies, bars, and breads. This excellent recipe is delicious served as-is, or top it with a chocolate frosting.

2 (1-ounce) squares unsweetened
    chocolate, chopped
1/2 cup butter
1 cup sugar
2 eggs
1 cup applesauce
11/4 cups flour

1/4 teaspoon nutmeg
1/2 teaspoon baking powder
1/2 teaspoon baking soda
1/4 teaspoon salt
1/2 teaspoon cinnamon
1 cup chopped walnuts

Preheat oven to 350 degrees F. Spray two 8-inch square baking pans with nonstick baking spray containing flour and set aside.

In large microwave-safe bowl, combine chopped chocolate and butter. Microwave on 50-percent power for 2 minutes, then remove and stir. If necessary, continue microwaving on 50-percent power for 1-minute intervals, stirring in between each interval, until chocolate is melted and mixture is smooth.

Stir in sugar, then beat in eggs and applesauce. Add dry ingredients and mix until combined. Then stir in chopped nuts.

Spread batter into prepared pans (do not substitute 13 x 9-inch pan in this recipe). Bake for 25–35 minutes or until bars are just set. Cool completely, then cut into bars. Can frost bars when cool. *Yields 24 bars*

• •

PINEAPPLE BARS

This delicious recipe is a variation on Dream Bars, where a shortbread cookie crust is covered with a sweet custard filling. The pineapple is a nice addition. Sprinkle with powdered sugar and cut into small squares.

1 (20-ounce) can crushed pineapple	1 tablespoon milk
1 cup flour	1 egg
1/4 cup brown sugar	1/4 cup butter, melted
1 teaspoon baking powder	1 cup sugar
1/2 cup butter, softened	1 cup coconut
1 egg	1 teaspoon vanilla

Preheat oven to 350 degrees F. Spray an 8-inch square baking pan with nonstick baking spray containing flour and set aside.

Place pineapple in a sieve and drain thoroughly, pressing down with the back of a spoon to remove as much liquid as possible. Let stand while preparing rest of recipe.

In medium bowl, combine flour, brown sugar, and baking powder. Cut in softened butter with a pastry blender until crumbs form. In small bowl, beat 1 egg with milk until blended, then stir into flour mixture.

Spread mixture into prepared pan. Top with drained pineapple.

In small bowl, combine 1 egg, melted butter, sugar, coconut, and vanilla and mix well. Spoon over pineapple in pan. Bake for 35–40 minutes or until bars are light golden brown and set. Cool completely, then cut into squares. *Yields 16 bars*

• •

GOLDEN CORNMEAL SUGAR COOKIES

Cornmeal adds crunch and a subtle sweet flavor to these crisp little sugar cookies. To prevent waste, I like to cut the cookies into squares or rectangles using one of those pastry cutters that makes a wavy edge. But you can use cookie cutters if you'd like!

1 cup butter, softened	1 cup yellow cornmeal
1 1/2 cups sugar	1 1/2 teaspoons baking powder
3 eggs	1/2 teaspoon nutmeg
1/2 teaspoon lemon extract	1/4 teaspoon salt
1 teaspoon vanilla	Granulated sugar
3 cups flour	

In large bowl, combine butter and sugar; beat until light and fluffy. Add eggs, one at a time, beating well after each addition. Stir in lemon extract and vanilla.

Add flour, cornmeal, baking powder, nutmeg, and salt and mix until a dough forms. Cover dough and chill for at least 2 hours.

Preheat oven to 400 degrees F. On lightly floured surface, roll dough 1/8-inch thick. Cut with 2-inch cookie cutters or cut into squares or triangles. Place on ungreased cookie sheet and sprinkle each with some sugar.

Bake for 8–11 minutes or until cookies are light golden brown. Remove from cookie sheet and cool on wire rack. Can be frosted with a buttercream frosting if you'd like. *Yields 6 dozen cookies*

· ·

CHERRY-COCONUT BARS

This beautiful bar is really nice for a holiday cookie tray. Slice it into small squares and arrange with cut-out cookies and other bars.

1 cup butter, softened	1 teaspoon baking powder
6 tablespoons powdered sugar	2 teaspoons vanilla
2 1/4 cups flour	1 1/2 cups coconut
1 cup sugar	1 cup slivered almonds
1 cup brown sugar	1/2 cup chopped maraschino
4 eggs	cherries or chopped dried cherries
1/2 cup flour	2 tablespoons powdered sugar
1/2 teaspoon salt	

Preheat oven to 350 degrees F. In large bowl, combine butter, 6 tablespoons powdered sugar, and 2 1/4 cups flour and mix until crumbly. Press into bottom of 13 x 9-inch pan and bake for 15–20 minutes or until light golden brown.

Meanwhile, in same bowl combine sugar, brown sugar, and eggs and beat until light and fluffy. Add flour, salt, baking powder, and vanilla and beat just until combined. Stir in coconut, almonds, and cherries.

When crust is done, remove from oven and reduce oven temperature to 325 degrees F. Pour filling over base. Bake for 30–40 minutes or until filling is set and light golden brown. Place on wire rack and cool for 20 minutes, then sift 2 tablespoons powdered sugar over bars. Cool completely and cut into squares. *Yields 4 dozen bars*

Joyce and Howard Viken, bundled against the frigid temperatures, broadcast from the St. Paul Winter Carnival. "I knew it was important not to let my teeth chatter," she says.

CHOCOLATE FUDGE BARS

These brownie-like bars are topped with a crunchy mixture of chocolate chips, coconut, and walnuts. Be careful not to overbake these bars; they're so good when fudgy and soft.

1 cup flour	2 eggs
1/2 cup sugar	2 (1-ounce) squares unsweetened
1/2 cup brown sugar	chocolate, melted
1/2 teaspoon salt	1 teaspoon vanilla
1/2 teaspoon baking soda	1/2 cup chopped walnuts
1/2 cup sour cream	1 cup semisweet chocolate chips
1/4 cup butter, softened	1/2 cup coconut
1/3 cup chocolate milk	1/2 teaspoon cinnamon

Preheat oven to 350 degrees F. Spray 13 x 9-inch pan with nonstick baking spray containing flour and set aside.

In large bowl, combine flour, sugar, brown sugar, salt, and baking soda and mix until blended. Add sour cream, butter, chocolate milk, and eggs and mix until combined. Stir in melted chocolate and vanilla and beat for 1 minute.

Spoon and spread batter into prepared pan. In small bowl, combine walnuts, chocolate chips, coconut, and cinnamon and toss. Sprinkle over batter.

Bake for 20–25 minutes until bars are just set. Cool completely, then cut into bars. *Yields 48 bars*

∙∙

HONEY APPLE COOKIES

Honey is another big Minnesota crop. In 2006, beekeepers in the state produced 10 million pounds of the sweet stuff. Combine that goodness with apples, and you have a fabulous cookie.

Did you know that if you consume honey produced from your county or neighborhood, it can help reduce allergic reactions? Exposure to the pollen in honey can act as an immune-booster. Try to find honey produced as close as possible to your home for best effect.

1/2 cup butter	1 teaspoon baking soda
1/2 cup sugar	1/2 teaspoon salt
1/4 cup brown sugar	1 teaspoon cinnamon
1/2 cup honey	1/8 teaspoon cloves
2 eggs	1/4 teaspoon nutmeg
1/4 cup sour cream	1 1/2 cups peeled, finely chopped apples
1 teaspoon vanilla	Powdered sugar
2 cups flour	

Preheat oven to 350 degrees F. In large bowl, combine butter, sugar, and brown sugar; beat until fluffy. Add honey and beat until smooth.

Add eggs, one at a time, beating well after each addition. Stir in the sour cream and vanilla. Add flour, baking soda, salt, cinnamon, cloves, and nutmeg and stir until a dough forms. Stir in apples.

Drop dough by teaspoons onto parchment paper–lined cookie sheets about 3 inches apart. Bake for 12–16 minutes or until cookie edges start to brown. Cool on cookie sheets for 2 minutes, then carefully remove to wire racks to cool.

Sift powdered sugar over cooled cookies. Store in airtight container at room temperature. *Yields about 5 dozen cookies*

....

CHOCOLATE MARBLE BARS

This easy bar cookie is a take-off on the popular marshmallow cereal bars, but it doesn't use marshmallows. A combination of corn syrup, sugar, and peanut butter coats cereal, which is marbled with chocolate. All I can say is yum!

1 cup corn syrup	5 cups rice cereal flakes
1 cup brown sugar	1 cup semisweet chocolate chips
1 cup peanut butter	

In large microwave-safe bowl, combine corn syrup and brown sugar. Microwave on high for 2 minutes. Remove from microwave and stir. Return mixture to microwave and cook on high for 2 minutes longer. Rinse off spoon in hot water.

Stir in peanut butter until mixture is smooth. Add cereal flakes and stir until coated. Then add the chocolate chips and stir just until mixture is marbled.

Press mixture into buttered 13 x 9-inch pan. Let stand until firm, then cut into bars to serve. *Yields about 48 bars*

....

GRAHAM CRACKER BROWNIES

Now these are some tasty, chewy bar cookies! This is a quick recipe, one that can be dressed up by sprinkling nuts or chocolate chips over the top before baking. You can omit the white chocolate topping if you'd like to make this even easier.

1/2 cup sugar	14 graham crackers, finely crushed
1/2 cup brown sugar	2 eggs
1/8 teaspoon salt	1 teaspoon vanilla
1/2 teaspoon cinnamon	1 cup white chocolate chips
1/4 cup chopped walnuts	

Preheat oven to 350 degrees F. Spray an 8-inch square pan with nonstick baking spray containing flour and set aside.

In medium bowl, combine sugar, brown sugar, salt, cinnamon, walnuts, and graham-cracker crumbs and mix well.

In small bowl, beat eggs until light and lemon colored. Stir into graham cracker mixture along with vanilla and mix well.

Spread mixture evenly in prepared pan. Bake for 22–28 minutes or until bars are set; do not overbake. Immediately sprinkle with white chocolate; cover bars with foil. Let stand for 5 minutes.

Spread melted white chocolate over the brownies. Cut into squares while still warm. *Yields 24 bars*

• •

PINEAPPLE OATMEAL COOKIES

These soft cookies are delicious spread with the cream cheese frosting. The pineapple caramelizes slightly when it bakes, adding wonderful flavor.

2/3 cup butter, softened	1 teaspoon vanilla
1 cup brown sugar	1 cup rolled oats
1 egg	1 cup chopped walnuts
2 cups flour	1 (8-ounce) package cream
2 teaspoons baking powder	cheese, softened
1/2 teaspoon baking soda	3 tablespoons butter, softened
1/2 teaspoon salt	2 cups powdered sugar
1 (8-ounce) can crushed pineapple	1/2 teaspoon vanilla

Preheat oven to 350 degrees F. In large bowl, combine butter and brown sugar; beat until light and fluffy. Add egg and beat until combined.

Combine flour, baking powder, baking soda, and salt in small bowl. Add alternately to butter mixture with the crushed pineapple (juice and all). Stir in vanilla, oats, and walnuts.

Drop batter by teaspoons onto greased baking sheets. Bake for 13–17 minutes or until cookies are set and light golden brown. Remove from cookie sheets and cool completely on wire racks.

For frosting, combine cream cheese, 3 tablespoons butter, powdered sugar, and vanilla and beat well. Frost cooled cookies. Store in tightly covered container at room temperature. *Yields 4–5 dozen cookies*

•••

CHOCOLATE POTATO BROWNIES

Potatoes are the surprise ingredient in these moist brownies. Minnesota's Red River Valley produces a lot of potatoes. And to make sure those potatoes are best quality, the horticulture department at the University of Minnesota's St. Paul campus conducts a lot of research, including taste-test panels, on potato varieties.

You could use leftover mashed potatoes, refrigerated prepared potatoes, or rehydrate some dried potato flakes for this unusual recipe. The potatoes make the brownies very moist and chewy, without affecting the flavor.

2/3 cup cold mashed potatoes	1/2 cup brown sugar
2/3 cup hot water	2 eggs
1/3 cup butter	1/3 cup flour
2 squares unsweetened chocolate, chopped	1/2 teaspoon salt
	1/2 teaspoon baking powder
1/2 cup sugar	1/2 cup chopped walnuts

Preheat oven to 350 degrees F. Butter an 8-inch square pan with unsalted butter and set aside.

In medium bowl, combine potatoes with hot water and stir with wire whisk. In small microwave-safe bowl, combine butter with chopped chocolate. Microwave on 50-percent power for 2 minutes, then remove and stir. Continue microwaving on 50-percent power for 30-second intervals until chocolate is melted and mixture is smooth.

Stir chocolate mixture into potato mixture. Add sugar, brown sugar, and eggs and stir until combined. Add flour, salt, baking powder, and walnuts and stir just until mixed.

Spoon batter into prepared pan. Bake for 20–30 minutes or until brownies are set; do not overbake. Let cool in pan. *Yields 16 brownies*

•••

ALOHA SQUARES

This recipe makes a lot of bars, perfect for a bake sale or school celebration. It's an unusual recipe that is very delicious, rich, and fresh-tasting all at the same time.

1/2 cup sugar
2 tablespoons cornstarch
2 (8-ounce) cans crushed pineapple, undrained
2 tablespoons lemon juice

2 cups flour
2 cups brown sugar
1/2 teaspoon salt
5 cups quick-cooking oats
2 cups butter

Preheat oven to 375 degrees F. Spray bottoms of 3 8-inch square baking pans with nonstick baking spray containing flour and set aside.

In medium saucepan, combine sugar, cornstarch, and crushed pineapple including juice. Cook and stir over medium heat until mixture turns clear and has thickened, 7–9 minutes. Stir in lemon juice.

In large mixing bowl, combine flour, brown sugar, salt, and oats and mix well. Cut in butter until coarse crumbs form.

Press half of crumbs in the bottom of prepared baking pans. Top each with one-third of the pineapple mixture. Top with remaining crumbs.

Bake for 15–25 minutes or until bars are light golden brown and set. Cool completely, then cut into squares. *Yields 75 squares*

• •

POTATO CHIP KISSES

These unusual and very simple cookies are chewy, as well as sweet and salty. Try them soon; kids especially like them.

1 egg white
1 cup brown sugar

1/2 teaspoon orange extract
1 1/4 cups plain potato-chip crumbs

Preheat oven to 325 degrees F. In large bowl, beat egg white until stiff. Gradually beat in the brown sugar until the mixture is glossy like a meringue. It will become softer as the moisture in the brown sugar interacts with the egg white.

Add the orange extract and beat well. Then fold in potato-chip crumbs by hand.

Drop mixture by teaspoons onto parchment paper–lined cookie sheets. Bake for 8–12 minutes until light golden brown. Cool for 10 minutes on cookie sheets, then remove to wire rack to cool completely. *Yields 2 dozen cookies*

• •

HONEY-COCONUT BARS

These simple bars are really good for packing into lunchboxes. The recipe makes a lot of bars, but the honey helps keep them moist and tender for several days—if they last that long!

$1/2$ cup butter, softened	$1/2$ teaspoon baking soda
$1/2$ cup brown sugar	$1/2$ teaspoon baking powder
$1/2$ cup honey	$1/4$ teaspoon salt
1 egg	1 cup quick-cooking oats
1 teaspoon vanilla	1 cup coconut
$3/4$ cup flour	$1/2$ cup chopped walnuts

Preheat oven to 350 degrees F. Spray 15 x 10-inch jelly roll pan with non-stick baking spray containing flour and set aside.

In large bowl, combine butter with brown sugar and honey; beat well until fluffy. Add egg and vanilla and mix well.

Add flour, baking soda, baking powder, and salt to the mixture and stir. Then add the oats, coconut, and nuts.

Spread batter evenly in prepared pan. Bake for 20–25 minutes or until bars are light golden brown and starting to pull away from edges of pan. Cool completely, then cut into bars. *Yields 36 bars*

••

SPICED APPLE BARS

Use Minnesota's most famous homegrown apple, the Haralson, in these spicy-sweet bars. They're ideal for an after-school snack, especially on the first day of school.

$2/3$ cup butter, softened	1 teaspoon cinnamon
$1/2$ cup sugar	$1/2$ teaspoon nutmeg
$1/2$ cup brown sugar	$1/8$ teaspoon cloves
2 eggs	1 cup peeled, diced apples
1 cup flour	1 cup rolled oats
1 teaspoon baking powder	$1/2$ cup chopped walnuts
$1/2$ teaspoon baking soda	2 tablespoons powdered sugar

Preheat oven to 350 degrees F. Spray a 13 x 9-inch pan with nonstick baking spray containing flour and set aside.

In large bowl, combine butter with sugar and brown sugar; beat until light and fluffy. Add eggs and beat well. Stir in flour, baking powder, baking soda, cinnamon, nutmeg, and cloves.

Stir in apples, oats, and walnuts. Spread batter into prepared pan. Bake for 25–35 minutes or until bars are light golden brown. Cool in pan, then sprinkle with powdered sugar and cut into bars. *Yields 24–30 bars*

CRISP ORANGE–COCONUT COOKIES

It seems that most cookbooks offer rich and decadent, chewy and soft cookies. It's nice to have a simple, crisp cookie to offer guests or your kids on a rainy weekend. These cookies are delicious.

2 eggs	$1/2$ teaspoon grated orange zest
$2/3$ cup vegetable oil	$2^1/2$ cups flour
1 cup sugar	2 teaspoons baking powder
$1/4$ cup frozen orange juice	$1/2$ teaspoon salt
concentrate, thawed	1 cup shredded coconut

In large bowl, beat eggs until light and fluffy. Stir in oil and sugar and mix well, then add the orange juice concentrate and orange zest.

Stir in flour, baking powder, and salt until a dough forms. Stir in coconut. Cover dough and chill for 2–3 hours or until firm.

Preheat oven to 400 degrees F. Shape dough into $3/4$-inch balls and place on ungreased cookie sheet. Press balls flat using the bottom of a drinking glass dipped into granulated sugar.

Bake for 9–12 minutes or until cookies are very light golden brown. Remove from cookie sheets and cool on wire rack. *Yields about 36 cookies*

• •

CHEESECAKE COOKIES

Thumbprint cookies are fairly common, but a cheesecake filling for them isn't! Store these delicate little cookies in the refrigerator but bring them out about 20 minutes before serving to take a bit of the chill off.

1 cup butter, softened	$2^1/3$ cups flour
1 (3-ounce) package cream	1 teaspoon baking powder
cheese, softened	1 (3-ounce) package cream
$3/4$ cup sugar	cheese, softened
$1/4$ cup brown sugar	2 tablespoons sugar
1 egg	1 egg yolk
1 teaspoon grated lemon zest	$1/4$ teaspoon grated lemon zest
1 tablespoon lemon juice	1 cup fine graham-cracker crumbs

In large bowl, combine butter with 1 package cream cheese, $3/4$ cup sugar, and brown sugar and beat until fluffy. Add egg, 1 teaspoon lemon zest, and lemon juice and beat to combine.

Stir in flour and baking powder until a dough forms. Chill dough for 1 hour. Meanwhile, for filling, in small bowl, combine 1 package cream cheese with 2 tablespoons sugar, egg yolk, and $1/4$ teaspoon lemon zest and beat until fluffy.

Preheat oven to 325 degrees F. Divide chilled dough into fourths. Divide each fourth into thirds, then divide that mixture into fourths, making 48 balls of dough.

Roll balls in cracker crumbs and place on ungreased cookie sheet. Flatten each cookie slightly and make a small indentation in the middle of each cookie. Spoon 1/2 teaspoon of cream cheese filling into the indentation in each cookie.

Bake for 20–25 minutes or until cookies are set and very light golden brown. Remove from cookie sheet and cool on wire racks. Sprinkle with powdered sugar when cool. *Yields 48 cookies*

● ●

APPLE-WALNUT CANDY

The pectin in apples will help this candy become firm. It's a great way to use up fall's apples and treat your kids and yourself too. There's nothing as good as homemade candy.

8 large apples	1/4 cup water
1/4 cup water	1 cup chopped walnuts
2 cups brown sugar	1 tablespoon lemon juice
2 (0.25-ounce) envelopes unflavored gelatin	1/2 cup powdered sugar

Peel apples, core them, and cut into small pieces. Combine in a large, heavy saucepan with 1/4 cup water. Cook apples, stirring frequently, over medium heat until very tender, about 15–20 minutes.

Push the apple mixture through a sieve or food mill. Return the puree to saucepan with the brown sugar; cook over low heat for 30 minutes, stirring frequently, until thick.

Soften gelatin in 1/4 cup water, then add to the hot apple mixture, stirring until gelatin dissolves. Chill this mixture until it begins to thicken, then stir in walnuts and lemon juice.

Pour mixture into a 9-inch square pan and refrigerate until firm and set. Cut candy into squares and roll in powdered sugar to coat. Store tightly covered at room temperature. *Yields about 3 dozen candies*

● ●

SOUTHERN PECAN BARS

If you like nuts and pecan pie, this is the cookie recipe for you! It tastes like pecan pie, but it's easier to cut and serve, and you can eat it while still warm. Be sure to use dark corn syrup: it adds more flavor than the light.

$1/2$ cup butter, softened
$1/3$ cup brown sugar
1 cup flour
$1/4$ teaspoon baking powder
$1/4$ cup chopped pecans
2 eggs

$3/4$ cup dark corn syrup
$1/4$ cup brown sugar
2 tablespoons flour
$1/4$ teaspoon salt
1 teaspoon vanilla
1 cup chopped pecans

Preheat oven to 350 degrees F. In medium bowl, combine butter with $1/3$ cup brown sugar and beat until fluffy. Add 1 cup flour, baking powder, and $1/4$ cup pecans.

Press this mixture into bottom of a 9-inch square pan. Bake for 10 minutes.

Meanwhile, in same bowl, beat eggs until light, then add dark corn syrup, $1/4$ cup brown sugar, 2 tablespoons flour, salt, and vanilla; beat well to blend.

Pour this mixture over the hot baked crust and sprinkle with 1 cup chopped pecans. Bake for another 15–25 minutes or until filling is just set; do not overbake.

Cool on wire rack; cut into bars while still warm. *Yields 24 bars*

As the food expert at WCCO, Joyce received a huge number of requests for copies of her recipes. She mailed out as many as ten thousand newsletters every month.

CAKES

Whether you bake cakes from scratch or prefer to start with a cake (or muffin!) mix, these recipes will satisfy the need for any occasion. Cakes are easy to make, as long as you follow the instructions.

Be sure that your oven is properly calibrated. Use an oven thermometer to check the temperature. If it's off, have it adjusted by a repairman.

And be sure to measure flour correctly. Improperly measured flour is one of the main reasons baked goods fail. Spoon the flour lightly into a measuring cup and level off with the back of a knife. Don't scoop the cup into the flour, or you'll add too much, which makes cakes tough and dry.

· ·

ALMOND PRALINE BANANA CAKE

The topping on this easy cake is sometimes called "Lazy Daisy," because it's just mixed, spread on the cake, then broiled to finish. This is a good lunch-box cake, hearty and delicious.

1 (18-ounce) package yellow cake mix	1 cup chopped almonds
1¹⁄₄ cups mashed bananas	1 cup brown sugar
¹⁄₂ cup oil	¹⁄₄ cup light cream
3 eggs	¹⁄₄ cup butter, melted
1 teaspoon grated lemon zest	1 teaspoon vanilla

Preheat oven to 350 degrees F. Spray 13 x 9-inch pan with nonstick cooking spray containing flour and set aside.

In large bowl, combine cake mix, bananas, oil, eggs, and lemon zest and mix until combined. Beat on medium speed for 2 minutes. Pour into prepared pan. Bake for 25–35 minutes or until cake is done. Remove to wire rack.

In medium bowl, combine almonds, brown sugar, cream, melted butter, and vanilla and mix well. Drop by small spoonfuls over warm cake and carefully spread to coat.

Turn oven to broil. Broil cake 4 inches from heat source for 2–5 minutes, turning once during broiling, until entire topping is bubbly. Watch carefully, as this can burn easily. Cool completely. *Serves 16*

UPSIDE-DOWN PEAR SPICE CAKE

Upside-down cakes are old-fashioned and deserve to make a comeback. Glazed fruit is arranged in the bottom of a cake pan, and a batter is poured over. After baking, the cake is flipped upside down so the fruit and a sweet glaze are on top.

1/4 cup butter
1/2 cup brown sugar
1/4 cup honey
4 pears
2 tablespoons lemon juice
1/2 cup pecan halves

1 (18-ounce) package spice cake mix
1 teaspoon cinnamon
1/2 teaspoon ground ginger
1 cup dried currants
1/2 cup chopped pecans

Preheat oven to 350 degrees F. Spray 13 x 9-inch baking pan with non-stick baking spray containing flour and set aside.

In small saucepan, melt butter over low heat and stir in brown sugar and honey until smooth. Pour into prepared pan. Peel, core, and slice pears 1/4-inch thick, dipping each slice into lemon juice as you work. Arrange pears over the butter mixture in the pan and sprinkle with any remaining lemon juice; top with pecan halves.

Prepare cake mix according to package directions, adding cinnamon, ginger, currants, and chopped pecans to the batter. Pour carefully over pears in pan.

Bake for 30–40 minutes or until cake tests done. Cool in pan. To serve, cut into squares and carefully flip upside down. Serve with whipped cream. *Serves 12*

• •

ONE-BOWL CHOCOLATE CAKE

Using canned fruit cocktail in the cake batter adds moisture, texture, and lots of flavor to this simple chocolate cake. And the topping, which bakes into the cake, saves time because you don't have to frost the cake!

2 1/4 cups flour
1/3 cup cocoa powder
2 teaspoons baking soda
1/2 teaspoon salt
1 cup brown sugar
2 eggs

1/4 cup butter, softened
1 (16-ounce) can fruit cocktail
1 teaspoon cinnamon
1 teaspoon vanilla
1 cup semisweet chocolate chips
1 cup chopped pecans

Preheat oven to 350 degrees F. Spray 13 x 9-inch baking pan with non-stick baking spray containing flour and set aside.

In large mixer bowl, combine flour, cocoa powder, baking soda, salt, brown sugar, eggs, butter, fruit cocktail (syrup and all), cinnamon, and vanilla. Beat until blended, then beat for 2 minutes at medium speed. Pour batter into prepared pan.

Sprinkle top with chocolate chips and pecans. Bake for 35–45 minutes or until cake springs back when lightly touched in center and begins to pull away from sides of pan. Cool completely on wire rack. *Serves 16*

APPLE UPSIDE-DOWN CAKE

Simmering apples in apple juice is a wonderful way to intensify the flavor. Use Granny Smith apples in this recipe as they turn brown more slowly than other varieties. Serve this cake warm with softly whipped cream flavored with some brown sugar and vanilla.

3 tart apples	$1/2$ cup coarsely chopped walnuts
1 cup apple juice	$1/2$ cup chopped dried cherries
$1/3$ cup butter	1 (18-ounce) package spice cake mix
1 cup brown sugar	$1/2$ cup butter, softened
$1/2$ teaspoon cinnamon	4 eggs

Preheat oven to 350 degrees F. Peel and core apples; slice $1/8$-inch thick. In large saucepan, combine apples and apple juice; simmer until apples are tender, 4–5 minutes. Drain apples, reserving juice.

Do not wipe out pan. In same pan, combine $1/4$ cup reserved apple juice, $1/3$ cup butter, brown sugar, and cinnamon; cook and stir over medium heat until butter melts and mixture is smooth. Pour into 13 x 9-inch baking pan and spread evenly. Arrange apples over sauce in pan and sprinkle with walnuts and dried cherries.

In large bowl, combine cake mix, remaining reserved apple juice, $1/2$ cup butter, and eggs. Beat at low speed until combined, then beat at medium speed for 2 minutes. Carefully pour batter over mixture in pan.

Bake for 40–50 minutes or until cake tests done. Cool in pan for 5–6 minutes, then carefully invert onto serving plate. Serve warm. *Serves 12*

• •

AUTUMN HARVEST CAKE

There's a lot going on in this cake! It's delicious frosted with the cream cheese frosting, but you can also top it with whipped cream and serve it in single-layer wedges.

$1/2$ cup butter, softened	2 teaspoons baking soda
1 cup sugar	1 teaspoon baking powder
1 cup brown sugar	$1^1/2$ teaspoons pumpkin pie spice
$1/4$ cup apple juice	$1/2$ cup finely chopped walnuts
1 cup applesauce	1 cup chopped dates
1 (15-ounce) can pumpkin pie filling	$1/2$ cup butter, softened
2 eggs	1 (8-ounce) package cream
1 teaspoon vanilla	cheese, softened
$2^1/2$ cups flour	4–5 cups powdered sugar
$1/2$ teaspoon salt	1 teaspoon vanilla

Preheat oven to 350 degrees F. Spray 2 9-inch round cake pans with non-stick baking spray containing flour and set aside.

In large bowl, combine $1/2$ cup butter, sugar, brown sugar, and apple juice and beat until light and fluffy. Add applesauce and pumpkin pie filling; beat for 2 minutes. Add eggs, one at a time, beating after each addition. Stir in vanilla.

Sift together flour, salt, baking soda, baking powder, and pumpkin pie spice. Gradually add this mixture to the pumpkin mixture, then beat for 2 minutes. Stir in walnuts and dates.

Spoon batter into prepared pans. Bake for 35–40 minutes or until toothpick inserted in center comes out clean. Cool in pans for 5 minutes, then remove cake from pans and cool completely on wire racks.

For frosting, combine $1/2$ cup butter and cream cheese in medium bowl; beat until smooth. Add 2 cups powdered sugar and vanilla and beat well. Gradually add enough remaining powdered sugar until desired frosting consistency is reached. Fill and frost cake and store, covered, at room temperature. *Serves 16*

APPLESAUCE-MARSHMALLOW CAKE

Now this is a clever cake! The marshmallows will rise during baking to form a topping as the cake bakes. It's a good hearty cake that kids will love.

$2^3/4$ cups flour	$1/2$ teaspoon allspice
1 cup sugar	$1/2$ cup butter, softened
1 cup brown sugar	2 eggs
$1^1/2$ teaspoons baking soda	2 cups unsweetened applesauce
$1/4$ teaspoon baking powder	1 cup coarsely chopped walnuts
$1/2$ teaspoon salt	20 large marshmallows
1 teaspoon cinnamon	

Preheat oven to 350 degrees F. Spray 13 x 9-inch pan with nonstick baking spray containing flour and set aside.

In large bowl, combine flour, sugar, brown sugar, baking soda, baking powder, salt, cinnamon, and allspice and mix with beater to combine. Stir in butter, eggs, and applesauce and beat until moistened. Then beat for 1 minute until well blended.

Stir in walnuts, then pour batter into prepared pan. Press the whole marshmallows into the batter to the bottom of the pan in 4 rows, 5 in each row.

Bake for 45–55 minutes or until cake pulls away from sides of pan. Cool on wire rack, then cut into squares to serve. *Serves 16*

MAYONNAISE SPICE CAKE

There is a recipe for mayonnaise cake made with chocolate, but this spice cake recipe is different. Frost it with a caramel frosting or serve it warm from the oven with caramel sauce.

1 cup raisins	1 teaspoon vanilla
1 cup water	1/2 teaspoon ground cloves
1 teaspoon baking soda	1 teaspoon cinnamon
1 cup mayonnaise	1/4 teaspoon cardamom
1/2 cup sugar	2 cups flour
1/2 cup brown sugar	1 cup chopped walnuts

Preheat oven to 350 degrees F. Butter 9-inch square pan and set aside.

In glass microwave-safe measuring cup, combine raisins and water. Microwave on high power until the water boils, about 2 minutes. Stir in baking soda and set aside.

In large bowl, combine mayonnaise, sugar, brown sugar, vanilla, cloves, cinnamon, and cardamom and mix well. Stir in flour alternately with the hot raisin mixture. Fold in walnuts.

Pour batter into prepared pan. Bake for 30–40 minutes or until cake springs back when lightly touched with finger. Let cool on wire rack for 30 minutes, then cut into squares to serve. *Serves 9*

• •

MACADAMIA BUNDT CAKE

Nordic Ware, which recently celebrated its sixtieth anniversary, is a Minnesota-based company that produces the Bundt pan. This pan was made famous by the Pillsbury Bake-Off in 1966 with the Tunnel of Fudge Cake. There are many gorgeous variations on the pan, including one that looks like a flower!

The pans bake cakes beautifully and never fail because the hole in the center helps heat move around the batter as it bakes. And they are self-decorating, so you don't need to worry about frosting.

2 tablespoons unsalted butter, softened	1/2 teaspoon ground ginger
1/2 cup chopped macadamia nuts	1/2 teaspoon salt
2 cups flour	1/4 teaspoon ground nutmeg
1 cup sugar	1 egg
3/4 cup brown sugar	1 cup buttermilk
1 teaspoon baking powder	2/3 cup butter, melted
1 teaspoon baking soda	1 1/2 teaspoons vanilla

Preheat oven to 350 degrees F. Using the 2 tablespoons softened unsalted butter, grease 12-cup Bundt pan. Sprinkle macadamia nuts over the butter so they stick to the sides; set aside.

In large bowl, combine flour, sugar, brown sugar, baking powder, baking soda, ginger, salt, and nutmeg and mix well.

In medium bowl, combine egg with buttermilk, melted butter, and vanilla and beat until smooth. Add to dry ingredients and beat until smooth.

Pour batter into prepared pan. Bake for 50–60 minutes or until toothpick inserted in center comes out clean. Let cake cool in pan for 5 minutes, then turn out onto wire rack to cool. *Serves 12*

* *

CHOCOLATE CHIP–DATE CAKE

Dates add wonderful richness to this simple cake. Do not use the pre-chopped dates you can buy in the grocery store: they are coated with sugar and too dry for the recipe. Buy whole dates and snip or chop them yourself, dipping the scissors or knife occasionally into hot water to make the process easier.

1 cup chopped dates	$1^3/4$ cups flour
1 teaspoon baking soda	$1/4$ teaspoon salt
$1^1/2$ cups boiling water	$3/4$ teaspoon baking soda
$1/2$ cup butter, softened	1 cup semisweet chocolate chips
$1/2$ cup sugar	$1/2$ cup sugar
$1/2$ cup brown sugar	$1/2$ cup chopped walnuts
2 eggs	

Preheat oven to 350 degrees F. Spray 13 x 9-inch pan with nonstick baking spray containing flour and set aside.

In small bowl, combine dates and baking soda. Pour boiling water over; stir to combine, then let cool for 30 minutes.

In large bowl, combine butter with $1/2$ cup sugar and brown sugar and beat well. Add eggs, one at a time, beating well after each addition. Stir flour, salt, and $3/4$ teaspoon baking soda into butter mixture until combined. Add date mixture and beat for 1 minute.

Pour batter into prepared pan. In small bowl, combine chocolate chips, $1/2$ cup sugar, and walnuts. Sprinkle evenly over batter.

Bake for 30–40 minutes or until cake springs back when lightly touched in center and starts to pull away from sides of pan. Let cool completely, then cut into squares to serve. *Serves 16*

* *

STRAWBERRY CLOUD CAKE

If you have a little girl in your family, this pretty cake would be wonderful for her birthday party. Tint the frosting pink too and spell out her name in pink and white candies.

1 (10-ounce) package frozen strawberries, thawed	4 eggs
1 (18-ounce) package white cake mix	1/2 cup vegetable oil
	1 cup heavy whipping cream
1 (3-ounce) package strawberry gelatin	3 tablespoons powdered sugar
	1/2 teaspoon vanilla

Preheat oven to 350 degrees F. Spray 13 x 9-inch pan with nonstick baking spray containing flour and set aside.

Drain strawberries, reserving juice. Chop strawberries into fine pieces and set aside. Add enough water to the reserved juice to equal $3/4$ cup, if necessary.

Combine cake mix, gelatin, and eggs in large mixing bowl. Beat for 2 minutes with mixer. Add oil and reserved strawberry juice mixture and beat for 2 minutes more. Batter will be quite thin.

Fold in the strawberries. Pour batter into prepared pan. Bake for 30–40 minutes or until top of cake springs back when lightly touched with finger. Cool completely on wire rack.

In small bowl, combine cream with powdered sugar and vanilla and beat until stiff peaks form. Frost cooled cake and store, covered, in refrigerator. *Serves 12*

Joyce and Howard Viken at one of the many Farm-City Day events during the 1960s.
(Courtesy of the Pavek Museum)

BANANA-PECAN BRUNCH CAKE

This is a great snack cake that can also be served as a coffee cake for brunch. For the best flavor, make sure that the bananas are really ripe—the skins should be about half yellow and half black.

$1/2$ cup butter, softened	2 cups flour
$1/2$ cup sugar	1 teaspoon baking powder
$1/2$ cup brown sugar	1 teaspoon baking soda
2 eggs	$1/4$ teaspoon salt
1 cup mashed bananas	$1/2$ cup chopped pecans
1 teaspoon vanilla	$1/4$ cup sugar
$1/2$ cup sour cream	$1/2$ teaspoon cinnamon

Preheat oven to 350 degrees F. Spray 9-inch square cake pan with nonstick baking spray containing flour and set aside.

In large bowl, combine butter with $1/2$ cup sugar and brown sugar and beat until fluffy. Add eggs, one at a time, beating well after each addition. Add banana, vanilla, and sour cream and mix well; set aside.

Sift together flour, baking powder, baking soda, and salt. Add to butter mixture and stir just until combined.

In small bowl, combine pecans with $1/4$ cup sugar and cinnamon; mix well. Sprinkle half of the pecan mixture into the prepared pan. Spoon half of batter over the pecan mixture, then top with rest of pecan mixture. Spoon remaining batter over all.

Bake for 35–45 minutes or until cake springs back when lightly touched in center. Serve warm. *Serves 9*

PINEAPPLE CROWN CAKE

Pineapple upside-down cake baked in a Bundt pan! This gorgeous cake could also be served as a coffee cake, especially for a holiday brunch. Be sure to remove it from the pan just as the recipe states; don't let it cool too long or it may stick.

1 (20-ounce) can crushed pineapple in syrup	1 (16-ounce) box pound-cake mix
$1/3$ cup brown sugar	2 eggs
3 tablespoons butter, melted	1 teaspoon grated lemon zest
	1 teaspoon vanilla

Preheat oven to 325 degrees F. Grease 12-cup Bundt pan with solid shortening and set aside.

Drain pineapple thoroughly, reserving the syrup. In a small bowl, combine 3 tablespoons reserved pineapple syrup, brown sugar, melted butter, and $1/2$ cup of the drained pineapple and mix well. Spoon into prepared pan and set aside.

In large bowl, combine pound-cake mix, eggs, lemon zest, vanilla, and $1/2$ cup reserved pineapple syrup; beat until combined. Then beat at medium speed for 3 minutes. Stir in remaining drained pineapple.

Pour batter over mixture in pan. Bake for 55–65 minutes or until cake is deep golden brown. Remove from oven and let stand for 5 minutes, then invert onto serving plate and let cool. *Serves 12*

• •

HOLIDAY CRANBERRY BUNDT CAKE

There are many, many ways to dress up a cake mix. This recipe uses cranberries, nuts, and cream cheese to add color, flavor, and richness to a lemon cake mix. It's delicious!

1 (3-ounce) package cream cheese, softened	$1^1/4$ cups ground fresh cranberries
1 (18-ounce) package yellow cake mix	$1/2$ cup chopped walnuts
$3/4$ cup milk	$1/4$ cup sugar
4 eggs	$1/2$ teaspoon ground mace
	2 tablespoons powdered sugar

Preheat oven to 350 degrees F. Spray 12-cup Bundt pan with nonstick baking spray containing flour and set aside.

In large mixing bowl, combine cream cheese with cake mix and milk. Beat on medium speed for 2 minutes. Then add the eggs and beat for another 2 minutes.

In small bowl, combine cranberries, walnuts, sugar, and mace and mix well. Fold into batter. Spoon batter into prepared pan.

Bake for 60–70 minutes until cake is deep golden brown and cake starts to pull away from sides of pan. Let cake cool in pan for 5 minutes, then invert onto wire rack to cool completely. Sprinkle with powdered sugar. *Serves 10–12*

• •

CHOCOLATE PEANUT CAKE

Small cakes are ideal for smaller families and are easy to make for kids learning how to bake. You can whip this cake up for dinner at the last minute; it's delicious served warm.

$1/3$ cup butter, softened	1 teaspoon baking soda
1 cup sugar	1 cup buttermilk
1 egg	1 cup chopped peanuts
1 teaspoon vanilla	1 cup semisweet-chocolate chips
$1^1/2$ cups flour	$1/2$ cup milk-chocolate chips

Preheat oven to 350 degrees F. Spray 9-inch square baking pan with non-stick baking spray containing flour and set aside.

In medium bowl, combine butter and sugar and beat until fluffy. Add egg and vanilla and beat until creamy.

In small bowl, combine flour and baking soda. Add alternately with buttermilk to egg mixture, beginning and ending with dry ingredients. Stir in peanuts.

Spoon batter into prepared pan. Bake for 25–35 minutes or until cake springs back when lightly touched. Remove cake from oven and immediately sprinkle with the semisweet- and milk-chocolate chips. Cover with foil for 5 minutes, then spread melted chips evenly over the cake. *Serves 9*

COCONUT BUNDT CAKE

Coconut cream pudding is the secret ingredient in this rich and moist cake. It doesn't need any frosting because the top is crusted with a coconut and pecan mixture.

1 (18-ounce) package yellow cake mix	4 eggs
1 (3-ounce) package instant coconut pudding mix	1/2 cup shredded coconut
3/4 cup vegetable oil	1/4 cup sugar
3/4 cup orange juice	2 teaspoons cinnamon
	1/2 cup chopped pecans

Preheat oven to 350 degrees F. Spray 12-cup Bundt pan with nonstick baking spray containing flour and set aside.

In large bowl, combine cake mix, pudding mix, oil, orange juice, and eggs. Beat until combined, then beat for 4 minutes on medium speed.

In small bowl, combine coconut, sugar, cinnamon, and pecans and mix well. Sprinkle half of this mixture in the prepared pan. Spoon half of the cake batter over, then sprinkle with remaining coconut mixture. Top with the rest of the batter.

Bake for 45–55 minutes or until cake springs back when lightly touched with finger. Invert onto cooling rack and cool completely. *Serves 12*

CREAM-FILLED CHOCOLATE CUPCAKES

These luscious cupcakes can be served as-is, or you can frost them with your favorite chocolate frosting. They're perfect to take to your child's homeroom for a birthday party.

3 cups flour
1 cup sugar
1 cup brown sugar
$1/3$ cup cocoa powder
2 teaspoons baking soda
$1/2$ teaspoon salt
1 cup water
1 cup chocolate milk
$2/3$ cup vegetable oil

2 tablespoons vinegar
2 teaspoons vanilla
1 (8-ounce) package cream
   cheese, softened
1 egg
$1/3$ cup sugar
$1/8$ teaspoon salt
$1 1/4$ cups miniature semisweet
   chocolate chips

Preheat oven to 350 degrees F. Line 36 muffin cups with paper liners and set aside.

In large bowl, combine flour, 1 cup sugar, brown sugar, cocoa powder, baking soda, and $1/2$ teaspoon salt and mix well with wire whisk.

Stir in water, chocolate milk, oil, vinegar, and vanilla and mix until batter is smooth. It will be a thin batter. Set aside.

For filling, in medium bowl, combine cream cheese, egg, $1/3$ cup sugar, $1/8$ teaspoon salt and beat until fluffy. Stir in chocolate chips.

Fill muffin cups $1/2$ full with the chocolate batter, then drop a teaspoon of the cream cheese filling on top.

Bake for 25–35 minutes or until cupcakes are puffy and top springs back when touched lightly with finger. Cool completely on wire racks. Dust with powdered sugar or frost before serving. *Yields 36 cupcakes*

• •

OATMEAL-RAISIN SNACK CAKE

Snack cakes are quick to make and are meant to be served unfrosted. This one is sturdy and tender, perfect for tucking into lunchboxes or serving as an after-school snack.

$1/2$ cup quick-cooking oatmeal
$1/2$ cup boiling water
$3/4$ cup milk
$1/2$ cup butter, softened
$1/4$ cup sugar
1 cup brown sugar
2 eggs
1 teaspoon vanilla

$1 1/4$ cups flour
$1/2$ teaspoon salt
$1/2$ teaspoon baking powder
$1/2$ teaspoon baking soda
$1/2$ teaspoon cinnamon
$1/4$ teaspoon cloves
$1/2$ cup raisins
$1/2$ cup chopped walnuts

199

Preheat oven to 350 degrees F. Spray 9-inch square baking pan with non-stick baking spray containing flour; set aside.

In small bowl, combine oatmeal and boiling water; stir to mix. Stir in milk and set aside.

In large bowl, beat butter with sugar and brown sugar until light and fluffy. Stir in eggs and vanilla and mix well.

Sift together flour, salt, baking powder, baking soda, cinnamon, and cloves. Add alternately with oatmeal mixture to the butter mixture. Stir in raisins and walnuts.

Spread batter in prepared pan. Bake for 50–60 minutes or until toothpick inserted in center of cake comes out clean. Sprinkle with powdered sugar and serve warm. *Serves 9*

Rhubarb Cake

Even though rhubarb is technically a vegetable, legally it's a fruit, just like the tomato is technically a fruit but legally a vegetable! At any rate, this vegetable/fruit is one of the first to appear in Minnesota's gardens in the spring. It has to be cooked with a lot of sugar, so this cake is one of the best ways to use it.

1^1/$_2$ cups brown sugar	1 teaspoon baking soda
^{1}/$_2$ cup butter, softened	1 cup buttermilk
1 egg	2 cups thinly sliced rhubarb
1 teaspoon vanilla	^{1}/$_3$ cup brown sugar
2 cups flour	1 teaspoon cinnamon
1 teaspoon cinnamon	^{1}/$_2$ cup chopped walnuts
^{1}/$_8$ teaspoon cardamom	

Preheat oven to 350 degrees F. Spray 13 x 9-inch baking pan with non-stick baking spray containing flour and set aside.

In large bowl, combine 1^1/$_2$ cups brown sugar and butter and beat until creamy. Beat in egg and vanilla.

Sift together the flour, 1 teaspoon cinnamon, cardamom, and baking soda. Add alternately with buttermilk to the butter mixture. Then fold in the rhubarb.

Spoon batter into prepared pan. In small bowl, combine ^{1}/$_3$ cup brown sugar, 1 teaspoon cinnamon, and the walnuts. Sprinkle over the batter.

Bake the cake for 30–40 minutes or until cake springs back when lightly touched with a finger. Let cool for 1 hour, then serve with ice cream. Also can be served as a coffee cake. *Serves 10–12*

PEANUT BUNDT CAKE

Peanut butter makes this cake smooth and velvety, with a fabulous flavor. Dates add chewiness, and chocolate chips add, well, chocolate! Your kids will love this cake.

1 tablespoon unsalted butter	1/2 cup vegetable oil
1/2 cup finely chopped peanuts	1 1/4 cups water
1 (18-ounce) package yellow cake mix	4 eggs
	1 cup crunchy peanut butter
1 (3-ounce) package instant vanilla pudding mix	1/2 cup finely chopped dates
	1 cup semisweet chocolate chips

Preheat oven to 350 degrees F. Using the unsalted butter, generously grease 12-cup Bundt pan. Sprinkle the pan with peanuts so they stick to the bottom and sides; set aside.

In a large bowl, combine cake mix, pudding mix, oil, water, and eggs. Beat on low speed until moistened, then beat on medium speed for 4 minutes. Beat in the peanut butter.

Pour one-third of the batter into the prepared pan. Sprinkle with half the dates and half the chocolate chips. Top with another one-third of the batter, then sprinkle with remaining dates and chocolate chips. Spoon and spread remaining batter on top.

Bake for 50–60 minutes or until the cake is deep golden brown and begins to pull away from sides of pan. Cool in pan for 5 minutes, then turn out onto wire rack to finish cooling. You can frost this cake with a thin peanut butter icing, or sprinkle it with powdered sugar. *Serves 12*

HONEY QUEEN'S HONEY APPLESAUCE CAKE

Yes, there really is a Honey Queen! Wisconsin is one of several states that have beekeeping industries; they crown Honey Queens (like the Minnesota Princess Kay of the Milky Way who has her image sculpted in butter at the state fair every year). I don't know which Honey Queen claimed this recipe, but it's delicious.

1/2 cup butter, softened	1/8 teaspoon nutmeg
3/4 cup honey	1/4 teaspoon salt
2 cups flour	1 teaspoon baking soda
1/4 teaspoon cloves	1 cup applesauce
1/2 teaspoon cinnamon	1 cup raisins

Preheat oven to 350 degrees F. Grease an 8-inch square baking pan with solid shortening and set aside.

In large bowl, cream butter until light and fluffy; gradually add honey, mixing until combined. Sift flour, spices, salt, and baking soda into the mixture and stir until smooth.

Add applesauce and raisins and beat until combined. Spoon and spread batter into prepared pan.

Bake for 40–50 minutes or until cake is golden brown and a toothpick inserted in center comes out clean. Let cool on wire rack; sprinkle with powdered sugar and serve with warmed honey, if desired. *Serves 9*

Joyce poses with a copy of her first cookbook. "We sold it at the WCCO booth at the state fair," Joyce recalls. "It sold twenty-five thousand copies!"

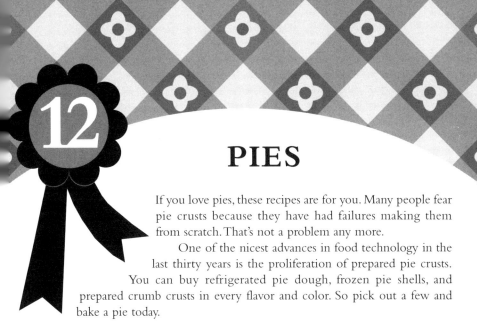

PIES

If you love pies, these recipes are for you. Many people fear pie crusts because they have had failures making them from scratch. That's not a problem any more.

One of the nicest advances in food technology in the last thirty years is the proliferation of prepared pie crusts. You can buy refrigerated pie dough, frozen pie shells, and prepared crumb crusts in every flavor and color. So pick out a few and bake a pie today.

●●●

CRANBERRY VELVET PIE

This excellent pie is perfect for the holidays. Garnish it with chocolate whipped cream, made by combining $1/2$ cup heavy whipping cream with 1 tablespoon of cocoa powder and 2 tablespoons powdered sugar; beat until stiff.

    1$1/2$ cups chocolate-cookie crumbs
    $1/2$ cup finely chopped walnuts
    $1/2$ cup butter, melted
    1 (8-ounce) package cream cheese, softened
    3 tablespoons sugar
    1 cup heavy whipping cream
    2 tablespoons powdered sugar
    1 teaspoon vanilla
    1 (16-ounce) can whole-berry cranberry sauce
    1 (8-ounce) bar dark chocolate, finely chopped

In small bowl, combine crumbs with walnuts and butter; stir to combine. Press firmly into bottom and up sides of 9-inch pie plate; set aside.

In large bowl, beat cream cheese with sugar until light and fluffy. In small bowl, beat cream with powdered sugar and vanilla until stiff peaks form. Fold whipped cream into cream cheese mixture. Fold in cranberry sauce and chopped chocolate. Pile into the pie crust, cover, and freeze until firm.

To serve, remove from freezer 15 minutes before slicing to make cutting easier. Garnish with chocolate whipped cream as described in introduction.
Serves 8

LEMON CHIFFON ICE CREAM PIE

Ice cream pies are wonderful to have on hand during the summer months, especially when unexpected company drops in. Keep a few of these pies in the freezer, and you'll be ready for anything!

Pasteurized egg whites can take longer to whip to stiff peaks than regular egg whites. If they aren't becoming stiff, add a pinch of cream of tartar; the acidity will help them whip.

3 cups vanilla ice cream, slightly softened	1/4 cup lemon juice
	1/2 teaspoon grated lemon zest
1 egg	2 pasteurized egg whites
2 egg yolks	1 cup heavy whipping cream
1/2 cup sugar	2 tablespoons powdered sugar
1/4 teaspoon salt	

Spread the ice cream onto bottom and up sides of 8-inch pie plate so it resembles a crust. Freeze until firm, about 2–3 hours.

Meanwhile, in medium saucepan, combine egg and egg yolks and beat until light. Gradually add sugar and salt and beat until thick. Add lemon juice and zest.

Cook this mixture over low heat, stirring constantly with a wire whisk, until it bubbles and thickens. Then remove from heat and chill in refrigerator until cold, about 2–3 hours.

When ice cream shell is firm and lemon mixture is cold, beat egg whites in small bowl until stiff. With same beaters, in another small bowl beat cream with powdered sugar until stiff.

Fold egg whites and cream into lemon mixture. Spoon into the ice cream shell, cover, and freeze until firm, 4–6 hours. *Serves 8*

• •

PEAR-CHEESE PIE

In September, ripe pears are at their peak. Pears contain cells called "stone cells" that give them a slightly gritty texture, but they are juicy and sweet when at their best. This simple pie is a wonderful way to serve them.

1 (3-ounce) package cream cheese, softened	1 tablespoon powdered sugar
	1 cup miniature marshmallows
1/2 cup sugar	3 pears, peeled and thinly sliced
1 teaspoon vanilla	1 (9-inch) graham cracker crust
1/2 cup heavy whipping cream	3 tablespoons brown sugar

In medium bowl, combine cream cheese with sugar and vanilla; beat until fluffy. In small bowl, beat cream with powdered sugar until stiff peaks form. Fold into cream cheese mixture along with marshmallows.

Arrange the pears in the crust. Sprinkle with the brown sugar. Spoon cream cheese mixture over the pears, completely covering them.

Chill the pie for 6–8 hours or overnight. Cut into wedges to serve. *Serves 8*

• •

APPLE-GINGERSNAP PIE

Apples and spices were made for each other. You can buy very good quality gingersnaps these days, right in the cookie and cracker aisle. This excellent pie is a nice twist on the traditional French apple pie.

5 apples	1 tablespoon flour
2 tablespoons lemon juice	$1/2$ teaspoon cinnamon
$3/4$ cup finely crushed gingersnap crumbs	$1/4$ teaspoon salt
	1 (9-inch) pie crust, unbaked
$1/4$ cup sugar	$1/4$ cup butter, melted
$1/4$ cup brown sugar	$1/2$ cup maple syrup

Preheat oven to 400 degrees F. Peel and core apples and slice thinly; sprinkle with lemon juice as you work.

In medium bowl, combine gingersnap crumbs, sugar, brown sugar, flour, cinnamon, and salt and mix well.

Place half of apples into the pie crust and sprinkle with half of the gingersnap mixture. Repeat layers. Drizzle the melted butter over the pie.

Bake for 15 minutes, then reduce oven temperature to 300 degrees F and bake 20 minutes more. In small saucepan, heat maple syrup to boiling.

Remove pie from oven and carefully pour the hot syrup over the pie. Return to oven and bake 15–20 minutes longer until apples are tender. Cool at least 30 minutes, then serve warm. *Serves 6*

• •

English Toffee Pie

A frozen pie is a wonderful treat to have on hand during the hot summer months. This recipe has been updated with pasteurized eggs for food safety reasons.

1/2 cup milk	2 pasteurized egg whites
2 egg yolks	1/8 teaspoon cream of tartar
1/2 cup brown sugar	1 cup heavy whipping cream
1/4 cup cocoa powder	2 tablespoons powdered sugar
1/8 teaspoon salt	1 teaspoon vanilla
1 teaspoon vanilla	1 (9-inch) graham cracker pie crust
1 cup crushed chocolate-covered toffee candy, divided	

In heavy saucepan, combine milk, egg yolks, brown sugar, cocoa powder, and salt and mix well with wire whisk. Cook over low heat, stirring constantly, until mixture thickens and coats the back of a spoon. Dip a spoon into the mixture and draw your finger down the back of it. If the mixture is thick enough to leave a trail, it's done. Stir in 1 teaspoon vanilla.

Cool this mixture in the refrigerator until very cold, stirring occasionally. When mixture is cold, stir in 1/2 cup of the crushed toffee; set aside.

In small bowl, beat egg whites with cream of tartar until stiff peaks form. In another small bowl, combine whipping cream, powdered sugar, and 1 teaspoon vanilla and beat until stiff peaks form.

Fold egg whites and whipped cream mixture into egg yolk mixture. Pour into the pie crust and sprinkle with remaining 1/2 cup crushed toffee. Freeze until firm. Let stand at room temperature for 10 minutes before serving for easy cutting. *Serves 8–10*

Strawberry Marshmallow Pie

This wonderful pie has one of the easiest pie crusts around. The crunchy, spicy crust contrasts beautifully with the soft, sweet, and tart filling. You could also make it with fresh raspberries.

1 1/2 cups finely crushed corn-flake crumbs	1/4 cup whole milk
1/4 cup sugar	2 teaspoons lemon juice
1/2 teaspoon cinnamon	1 cup heavy whipping cream
1/4 teaspoon nutmeg	2 tablespoons powdered sugar
1/2 cup butter, melted	1 teaspoon vanilla
18 large marshmallows	2 pints strawberries

Preheat oven to 350 degrees F. In medium bowl, combine corn-flake crumbs, sugar, cinnamon, and nutmeg and mix well. Add melted butter; stir until crumbs are coated. Press into 9-inch pie plate. Bake for 4–7 minutes or until crust is set. Cool completely.

In large microwave-safe bowl, combine marshmallows and milk. Microwave on high power for 1 minute, then remove and stir. Continue microwaving on high power for 1-minute intervals, stirring in between each interval, until mixture is smooth. Stir in lemon juice, cover, and chill until set.

In small bowl, beat cream with powdered sugar and vanilla until stiff peaks form. Using same beaters, beat marshmallow mixture until smooth. Fold the two mixtures together.

Hull, wash, and slice strawberries. Fold 3 cups of the strawberries into the marshmallow mixture and spoon into pie shell. Cover and chill for 4 hours before serving. Garnish with more sliced strawberries and serve. *Serves 8*

• •

FRESH RASPBERRY PIE

You can buy raspberries every month of the year now. Back in the 1970s, that wasn't the case. Even with this most precious fruit available every month of the year, this luscious pie is quite the treat, with a creamy filling swirled with fresh raspberries and tart raspberry jam.

1$1/2$ cups graham-cracker crumbs	2 tablespoons powdered sugar
$1/3$ cup butter, melted	1 teaspoon vanilla
$1/2$ cup chopped coconut	3 cups fresh raspberries, divided
24 large marshmallows	$1/3$ cup seedless raspberry jam
$1/2$ cup milk	$1/3$ cup dark chocolate shavings
1 cup heavy whipping cream	

Preheat oven to 350 degrees F. In medium bowl, combine crumbs, butter, and coconut and mix well. Press into bottom and up sides of 9-inch pie plate. Bake for 10–12 minutes or until crust is set and coconut is lightly browned. Cool completely.

In microwave-safe bowl, combine marshmallows and milk. Microwave on high for 1 minute, then remove and stir. Continue microwaving at 1-minute intervals, stirring after each, until marshmallows are melted and mixture is smooth. Set aside.

In small bowl, combine cream, powdered sugar, and vanilla and beat until stiff peaks form. Fold whipped cream into marshmallow mixture. Carefully fold in 2 cups raspberries, then add jam and fold together just to marble. Pour into cooled pie crust.

Arrange remaining raspberries and chocolate shavings on top of pie. Chill for 3–4 hours before serving. *Serves 8*

RICH CHOCOLATE PECAN PIE

Pecan pie is, of course, traditional for Thanksgiving. Add chocolate to this classic recipe, and you have a real winner. The chocolate whipped cream that tops each serving is just gilding on the lily. Enjoy!

$1/2$ cup butter
1 teaspoon vanilla
1 cup brown sugar
3 eggs
$1/4$ cup flour
$1/2$ cup cocoa powder
$1/2$ teaspoon salt
$3/4$ cup dark corn syrup

$3/4$ cup light cream
$1^1/2$ cups small pecan halves
$1^1/2$ cup miniature semisweet
   chocolate chips
1 (9-inch) pie crust, unbaked
1 cup heavy whipping cream
2 tablespoons cocoa powder
3 tablespoons powdered sugar

Preheat oven to 450 degrees F. In large bowl, combine butter, vanilla, and brown sugar and beat until fluffy. Add eggs, one at a time, beating well after each addition.

The WCCO booth, pictured here in 1963, was a popular stop at the Minnesota State Fair.

In small bowl, combine flour, $1/2$ cup cocoa powder and salt. Add to butter mixture and blend until combined. Stir in corn syrup and light cream using a wire whisk. Stir in pecan halves and chocolate chips.

Pour mixture into unbaked pie crust. Bake for 10 minutes, then reduce oven temperature to 325 degrees F and bake for 40–50 minutes longer until filling is almost set in center. Cool completely.

To serve, combine heavy whipping cream, cocoa powder, and powdered sugar and beat until soft peaks form. Cut pie into wedges and top each with some of the whipped cream. *Serves 8*

• •

PECAN CRUMBLE PUMPKIN PIE

The original recipe used pie crust sticks for the crust and the streusel, but Pillsbury doesn't make them anymore. So purchase refrigerated pie crust dough and use one for the bottom, then make a simple streusel for the topping. This is an excellent pie for Thanksgiving dinner.

1 refrigerated pie crust	$1/2$ teaspoon nutmeg
$1/3$ cup chopped pecans	$1/2$ teaspoon ginger
1 (16-ounce) can solid-pack	$1/4$ teaspoon cardamom
pumpkin	$1/2$ cup flour
1 (14-ounce) can sweetened	$1/2$ teaspoon cinnamon
condensed milk	$1/2$ cup brown sugar
1 egg	$1/2$ cup chopped pecans
$1/4$ teaspoon salt	1 teaspoon grated orange zest
$1/2$ teaspoon cinnamon	$1/3$ cup butter, softened

Preheat oven to 375 degrees F. Line 9-inch pie plate with the refrigerated pie crust, crimp edges, and sprinkle bottom with $1/3$ cup chopped pecans; gently press in. Place in freezer until ready to use.

In large bowl, place pumpkin. Gradually add sweetened condensed milk, beating with hand mixer. Beat in egg, salt, $1/2$ teaspoon cinnamon, nutmeg, ginger, and cardamom and mix well; set aside.

In medium bowl, combine flour, $1/2$ teaspoon cinnamon, brown sugar, $1/2$ cup chopped pecans, and orange zest and mix well. Cut in butter until crumbly.

Pour pumpkin mixture into pie shell and spread evenly. Top with pecan mixture. Bake for 50–55 minutes or until streusel topping is golden brown and pie is just set. You may need to cover pie with foil if topping browns too quickly. Cool completely and serve. *Serves 8*

• •

You would think that something as popular as Joyce Lamont's recipes would merit some clerical help, but it didn't. "I'd type them up myself," she says, "and make hundreds of mimeographed copies." (Courtesy of the Pavek Museum)

Avocado Lime Pie

This most unusual pie combines avocados with pineapple, cream cheese, and lime gelatin. It sounds strange but is really delicious and perfect for a dessert buffet.

1 (8-ounce) can crushed pineapple	1 (8-ounce) package cream
2 tablespoons lime juice	cheese, softened
1 (3-ounce) package lime gelatin	1/3 cup powdered sugar
1/4 teaspoon salt	1/2 cup heavy whipping cream
1 large ripe avocado	1 (9-inch) graham cracker crust

Drain pineapple, reserving juice. Place lime juice and reserved pineapple juice in a 2-cup microwave-safe glass measuring cup. Add enough water to make 1 cup if necessary. Microwave on high power for 2–3 minutes or until mixture is boiling.

Place gelatin and salt in a small bowl and add boiling liquid; stir until gelatin mixture dissolves. Chill this mixture until slightly thickened, about 45 minutes.

Peel avocado, remove pit, and dice. In large bowl, combine half of the avocado cubes with the softened cream cheese and powdered sugar; beat until creamy. Fold in drained pineapple and remaining avocado cubes.

In small bowl, whip cream until stiff. Fold into pineapple mixture along with the chilled gelatin mixture. Pour into graham cracker crust. Chill until firm at least 4 hours. *Serves 8*

....

Strawberry Sundae Pie

This wonderful pie can be made in so many variations, depending on your taste and your health concerns. Use vanilla swirl sorbet instead of the ice cream if you'd like to reduce fat. Layer vanilla and chocolate ice cream, or combine strawberry ice cream with chocolate. Have fun!

1 cup vanilla-wafer crumbs	3 cups vanilla ice cream
3/4 cup wheat germ	2 cups strawberry halves
1/3 cup sugar	1/3 cup sugar
1/3 cup butter, melted	1/2 cup canned pineapple tidbits, drained
3 cups strawberry sorbet	1 tablespoon lemon juice

Preheat oven to 325 degrees F. In medium bowl, combine crumbs, wheat germ, and sugar and mix well. Add butter and mix until crumbs are coated. Press firmly into bottom and up sides of 10-inch pie plate.

Bake crust for 4–6 minutes or until crust is just set. Cool completely, then place in freezer to chill.

Let sorbet and ice cream stand at room temperature for 10–15 minutes to soften. Layer in the chilled pie crust. Cover with plastic wrap and freeze until firm.

Make strawberry topping by combining strawberry halves, sugar, pineapple tidbits, and lemon juice in a medium bowl; stir until sugar dissolves. Refrigerate this mixture until serving time.

To serve, let pie stand at room temperature for 10–15 minutes to soften slightly. Cut into wedges and top with strawberry mixture. *Serves 8*

• •

Peach Cream Pie

I can never get enough fresh peaches when they are in season in August. And there are so many ways to use them. This decadent pie is so delicious and has an unusual presentation.

1 (9-inch) pie crust	2 tablespoons lemon juice
3/4 cup sugar	1 (3-ounce) package cream
2 tablespoons cornstarch	cheese, softened
1/4 teaspoon salt	1/3 cup powdered sugar
1 ripe peach, peeled and chopped	1 teaspoon vanilla
1/2 cup peach nectar	4 cups peeled, sliced peaches

Bake the pie crust according to recipe or package directions and cool completely.

In medium saucepan, combine sugar, cornstarch, and salt and mix with wire whisk. In food processor, puree chopped peach until smooth. Add to sugar mixture along with peach nectar and lemon juice.

Bring this mixture to a boil over high heat; reduce heat to medium and cook and stir until mixture is thick and clear. Cool for 20 minutes, then chill in refrigerator until cold.

In small bowl, combine cream cheese, powdered sugar, and vanilla and beat until fluffy. Spread mixture on bottom and up sides of baked and cooked pie crust.

Spoon sliced peaches over the cream cheese mixture. Pour the cooled cornstarch mixture over the peaches. Cover and chill for at least 4 hours. *Serves 8*

• •

SOUR CREAM APPLE PIE

This pie just sounds rich! It's a nice twist on the traditional apple pie. Make it in the fall when apples are plentiful and inexpensive and kids come home hungry from school and after-school activities.

1 egg	2 cups peeled, chopped tart apples
1 cup sour cream	1 (9-inch) pie crust, unbaked
1/2 cup sugar	3 tablespoons butter, melted
1/4 cup brown sugar	1/3 cup brown sugar
2 tablespoons flour	1/3 cup flour
1 teaspoon vanilla	1/2 cup chopped walnuts
1/4 teaspoon salt	

Preheat oven to 400 degrees F. In large bowl, combine egg with sour cream, sugar, and $^1/4$ cup brown sugar and beat until smooth. Add 2 tablespoons flour, vanilla, and salt and mix until combined, then stir in apples.

Pour mixture into pie crust. Bake for 25 minutes.

Meanwhile, in small bowl, combine melted butter with $^1/3$ cup brown sugar and $^1/3$ cup flour until crumbly. Stir in walnuts. Sprinkle over pie, then return pie to oven and bake for another 20–25 minutes or until topping is bubbly and pie crust is deep golden brown. Cool for at least one hour, then serve. *Serves 8*

···

CHOCOLATE BANANA TARTS

Convenience foods make these little pies quick and easy. Your kids will like to make them; you could substitute refrigerated packaged pudding for the cooked pudding for a no-heat recipe.

1 (3.9-ounce) package chocolate pudding mix (not instant)	2 tablespoons powdered sugar
	1/2 teaspoon vanilla
2 cups chocolate milk	3 bananas, sliced
1/4 teaspoon cinnamon	8–12 graham cracker tart shells
1 cup heavy whipping cream	

In medium saucepan, combine pudding mix, chocolate milk, and cinnamon. Cook and stir over medium-low heat until it boils. Remove from heat, cover, and let cool for 20 minutes. Chill until pudding is cold.

In small bowl, combine cream with powdered sugar and vanilla; beat until stiff peaks form. Fold half of the whipped cream into the pudding. Fold in sliced bananas.

Spoon mixture into tart shells and top with rest of the whipped cream. Cover and chill for 4 hours before serving. *Serves 8–12*

CRANBERRY CRUNCH PIE

This crunchy and tart pie is really fabulous served with a scoop of vanilla ice cream. Definitely include it in your holiday menus this year. And you don't need a pie crust; the crumbly sweet oatmeal mixture serves as the crust and the topping.

1 (16-ounce) can whole-berry cranberry sauce	1 cup brown sugar
1 teaspoon lemon juice	1 cup quick-cooking oatmeal
1/2 cup flour	1/2 cup chopped walnuts
	1/2 cup butter, melted

Preheat oven to 325 degrees F. Open the can of cranberry sauce and place it in a small bowl. Using a fork, break up the sauce into small pieces and stir in lemon juice. Set aside.

In medium bowl, combine flour, brown sugar, oatmeal, and nuts and mix well. Add melted butter; stir until crumbs form.

Press half of crumb mixture into the bottom and up sides of 9-inch pie pan. Top with cranberry mixture, then sprinkle rest of crumb mixture on top. Bake for 40–50 minutes or until crumb mixture is golden brown. Cool for at least 45 minutes, then serve warm. *Serves 8*

• •

CHOCOLATE CHIP EGGNOG PIE

The only thing that could make eggnog pie better is to add chocolate! This recipe doesn't use actual chocolate chips but grated semisweet chocolate, which isn't quite as sweet.

1 (9-inch) pie crust	3 ounces semisweet chocolate, grated, divided
1 (0.25-ounce) package unflavored gelatin	1 cup heavy whipping cream
2 cups eggnog, divided	2 tablespoons powdered sugar

Bake and cool pie crust; set aside. In medium saucepan, combine gelatin with 1 cup of the eggnog; let stand for 5 minutes. Stir in 2/3 of grated chocolate.

Cook this mixture over low heat, stirring constantly, until gelatin dissolves and chocolate melts. Remove from heat and add remaining 1 cup eggnog. Chill in refrigerator until it begins to set, about 1 hour.

In small bowl, beat cream with powdered sugar until stiff peaks form. Fold into eggnog mixture along with the remaining 1/3 of the grated chocolate. Pile into pie shell and chill until firm, at least 4 hours. *Serves 8*

• •

APPLE CIDER PIE

Now this is another unusual recipe! Did you know that chilled gelatin can be whipped until it's fluffy and double in volume? This pie has a wonderful flavor and texture; everyone will ask for the recipe.

1 (9-inch) pie crust	2 large apples
1 1/2 cups apple cider, divided	1 cup heavy whipping cream
2 tablespoons red cinnamon candies	1 tablespoon powdered sugar
1 (3-ounce) package lemon gelatin	1 teaspoon vanilla

Bake pie crust until light golden brown; cool completely.

In medium saucepan, combine 3/4 cup of the cider with candies; heat until the candies melt. Remove from heat and stir in the gelatin until it dissolves and mixture is clear and smooth.

Add remaining 3/4 cup apple cider and stir. Refrigerate mixture until it is very thick, 2–3 hours. Remove from the refrigerator and beat with mixer until mixture is thick, fluffy, and doubled in volume.

Peel the apples and grate; immediately fold into gelatin mixture. In small bowl, combine cream with powdered sugar and vanilla and beat until stiff. Fold whipped cream into the apple mixture. Spoon filling into pie shell, then chill for at least 6 hours until set. *Serves 6–8*

• •

CHOCOLATE BROWNIE PIE

A brownie in a pie crust! This excellent recipe is decadent and fudgy. Serve it with vanilla ice cream or sweetened whipped cream after a dinner party.

1 (9-inch) pie crust, unbaked	3 tablespoons dark corn syrup
1 cup milk chocolate chips	1 cup sugar
3 (1-ounce) squares unsweetened chocolate, chopped	1/2 cup brown sugar
1/2 cup butter	1/4 teaspoon salt
4 eggs	1 teaspoon vanilla

Preheat oven to 350 degrees F. Sprinkle milk chocolate chips into the unbaked pie crust and set aside.

In small microwave-safe bowl, combine chocolate with butter. Microwave on 50-percent power for 2 minutes, then remove and stir. Continue microwaving for 30-second intervals on 50-percent power, stirring between each interval, until chocolate is melted and mixture is smooth. Set aside.

In large bowl, beat 4 eggs until light and fluffy. Slowly beat in corn syrup, sugar, brown sugar, salt, and vanilla until thick. Beat in the cooled chocolate and pour into pie crust.

217

Bake for 25–30 minutes or until top is crusty and filling is set around the edges but still jiggly in the center. Do not overbake. Let pie cool completely on wire rack, then cut into wedges to serve. *Serves 8–10*

••

APPLE-CHEESE FLAN PIE

Flan is a Spanish dessert that consists of a very smooth custard baked with a caramel syrup. This pie uses those textures and flavors and adds apples and cheese for a fabulous dessert.

1 egg	$1/2$ cup shredded sharp
$1/3$ cup sugar	Cheddar cheese
$1/4$ cup flour	4 medium apples
$1/2$ cup heavy whipping cream	2 teaspoons lemon juice
1 teaspoon vanilla	$1/3$ cup brown sugar
1 (9-inch) pie crust, unbaked	1 teaspoon cinnamon

Preheat oven to 400 degrees F. In small bowl, combine egg with sugar; beat until light and lemon colored. Stir in flour, cream, and vanilla and beat well. Pour this mixture into unbaked pie crust and sprinkle with Cheddar cheese; set aside.

Peel apples and cut into quarters; sprinkle with lemon juice. Cut each quarter into thirds. Arrange apples in a sunburst pattern over the cheese layer in the pie.

In small bowl, combine brown sugar with cinnamon; sprinkle evenly over apples. Bake for 35–45 minutes or until pie crust is deep golden brown and apple slices are tender and glazed. Cool completely, then cut into wedges. Store in refrigerator. *Serves 6*

••

CHOCOLATE OATMEAL PIE

Oatmeal takes the place of nuts in this chewy, chocolaty pie. It has to be chilled before serving, so make sure you bake it ahead of time.

3 eggs	$1/4$ cup butter, melted
$3/4$ cup brown sugar	1 teaspoon vanilla
$2/3$ cup dark corn syrup	$3/4$ cup rolled oats
2 tablespoons flour	1 cup semisweet chocolate chips
$1/4$ cup cocoa powder	1 (9-inch) pie crust, unbaked

Preheat oven to 350 degrees F. In large bowl, beat eggs until they are foamy. Gradually add brown sugar, beating until mixture is thick.

Beat in corn syrup, flour, cocoa powder, melted butter, and vanilla and mix well. Stir in oats and chocolate chips.

Pour filling into the pie crust. Bake for 40–50 minutes or until center of pie is just barely set. Cool on wire rack for 1 hour, then cover and chill in refrigerator for at least 4 hours before serving. Serve with sweetened whipped cream. *Serves 8*

••

QUICK PINEAPPLE–CREAM CHEESE PIE

This is a wonderful pie for beginning cooks. All you have to do is make a graham cracker crust and fill it with a simple beaten mixture. There's no way to fail—and it tastes wonderful too!

15 graham cracker squares	$1/4$ cup powdered sugar
$1/3$ cup finely chopped walnuts	1 cup heavy whipping cream
6 tablespoons butter, melted	1 tablespoon powdered sugar
1 (8-ounce) package cream cheese, softened	1 (20-ounce) can crushed pineapple, drained

Finely crush the graham crackers by placing them in a plastic food storage bag and using a rolling pin. Combine in medium bowl with the walnuts, then add the melted butter. Press into bottom and up sides of 9-inch pie plate; refrigerate.

In large bowl, beat the cream cheese and $1/4$ cup powdered sugar until light and fluffy. In small bowl, beat cream with 1 tablespoon powdered sugar until stiff. Add the whipped cream to the cream cheese mixture and beat just until blended. Add the well-drained pineapple.

Spoon mixture into the pie crust; cover and refrigerate for at least 4 hours until filling is set. Cut into wedges to serve. *Serves 6–8*

••

DESSERTS

Like most Americans, I have a sweet tooth! Besides my mother's beef stew, dessert was always my favorite part of dinner. But when I was growing up, sweets weren't as prevalent as they are today: they were saved for special occasions.

Still, many people think that dinner just isn't complete without dessert. Cooks and bakers feel the same way: making dessert is the fun part of cooking. And if you include lots of fresh fruit in your desserts, you don't need to feel as guilty!

These recipes use the best of Minnesota's summer produce and will satisfy your sweet tooth. Others will provide comfort and solace during the long, cold winter. Let's bake!

MELON MELBA PARFAIT

When fresh cantaloupe and honeydew melons are on sale in July, this is the perfect dessert for a sweet end to an outdoor barbecue. To toast almonds, spread on a baking sheet and bake at 350 degrees F for 4–6 minutes until fragrant.

1 (10-ounce) package frozen raspberries, thawed	2 tablespoons water
1/2 cup currant jelly	1/8 teaspoon almond flavoring
1/4 cup sugar	6 cups melon balls
1 tablespoon lemon juice	2 cups prepared French vanilla pudding (from mix)
2 teaspoons cornstarch	1/2 cup chopped toasted almonds

In large saucepan, combine raspberries with currant jelly, sugar, and lemon juice. Cook over medium heat until mixture comes to a boil and sugar dissolves. In a small bowl, dissolve cornstarch in water and add to raspberry mixture. Cook and stir over low heat until mixture thickens, 2–3 minutes.

Remove from heat. Strain sauce to remove the seeds, then stir in almond flavoring. Cover and chill.

Layer melon balls and pudding in chilled stemmed glasses; drizzle the raspberry sauce over each layer. When glasses are full, drizzle with remaining raspberry sauce and sprinkle with toasted almonds. Refrigerate for up to 8 hours, or serve immediately. *Serves 6–8*

Sour Cream Dessert Ring

This beautiful dessert was the specialty of one of WCCO's farm hostesses, Mrs. Harold Bremer from Lake City, Minnesota. Farm-City Week was celebrated every year by Presidential proclamation, and we were there.

3/4 cup butter	1 teaspoon baking powder
1 1/2 cups sugar	2 cups sifted cake flour
2 eggs	1/2 cup chopped pecans
1 cup sour cream	2 tablespoons brown sugar
1 teaspoon vanilla	1 teaspoon instant cocoa mix
1/4 teaspoon salt	1 teaspoon cinnamon

Preheat oven to 350 degrees F. Grease and flour a 9-inch tube pan and set aside.

In large bowl, combine butter and sugar and beat until light and fluffy. Add eggs and beat again. Fold in sour cream and vanilla.

Sift together salt, baking powder, and cake flour and fold into butter mixture. In small bowl, combine nuts, brown sugar, cocoa mix, and cinnamon.

Spoon half of the batter into prepared tube pan and sprinkle with half of the nut mixture. Repeat layers. Bake for 50–60 minutes or until toothpick inserted in center comes out clean. Cool in pan for 10 minutes before removing. Serve warm. *Serves 12*

Coconut Bread Pudding

Old-fashioned bread puddings are pure comfort food. When topped with a sweet meringue, this pudding is transformed into an elegant dessert you will be proud to serve at the fanciest dinner parties. Try it for the holidays!

3 cups milk	2 egg yolks
1 cup coconut milk	1/2 cup sugar
1 1/2 cups soft white bread crumbs	1 cup flaked coconut, divided
2 tablespoons butter	1/2 teaspoon grated lemon zest
1/4 teaspoon salt	2 egg whites
2 1/2 teaspoons vanilla	1 teaspoon lemon juice
1 egg	1/4 cup sugar

Preheat oven to 325 degrees F. In large saucepan, heat milk and coconut milk just until steam rises. In large bowl, combine bread crumbs and 1 cup of hot milk mixture, mashing well. Add remaining milk mixture, butter, salt, and vanilla.

In small bowl, beat 1 egg and 2 egg yolks, then blend in $1/2$ cup sugar. Add to bread crumb mixture along with $3/4$ cup coconut and lemon zest.

Turn mixture into greased $1^1/2$-quart casserole. Set into another pan and add hot water to depth of 1 inch. Bake at 325 degrees F for $1^1/2$ hours.

When time is almost up, beat egg whites, lemon juice, and $1/4$ cup sugar in clean small bowl until stiff peaks form and sugar is dissolved.

Remove pudding from oven and top with meringue, spreading to edges and making peaks with back of spoon. Sprinkle with remaining $1/4$ cup coconut. Return to oven, increase heat to 425 degrees F, and bake for 10–15 minutes or until meringue and coconut are lightly browned. Cool for 30 minutes, then serve. Store leftovers in the refrigerator. *Serves 6*

• •

RHUBARB CRISP

Rhubarb is the first fresh produce to appear in the spring. This comforting and homey dish is a wonderful way to prepare it. Serve with vanilla ice cream or plain heavy whipping cream poured over warm pieces just out of the oven.

1 cup flour	4 cups chopped rhubarb
1 cup quick-cooking oats	1 cup sugar
1 cup brown sugar	$1/4$ cup flour
1 cup chopped walnuts	1 teaspoon cinnamon
$1/2$ teaspoon baking powder	$1/2$ cup orange juice
$1/2$ cup butter, melted	

Preheat oven to 350 degrees F. In medium bowl, combine 1 cup flour, oats, brown sugar, walnuts, and baking powder and mix well. Pour melted butter over and mix until crumbly; set aside.

In large bowl, combine rhubarb, sugar, $1/4$ cup flour, and cinnamon and mix well. Drizzle orange juice over rhubarb mixture and toss to coat.

Spray 8-inch square glass baking dish with nonstick baking spray containing flour. Arrange rhubarb mixture in dish and top with oat mixture.

Bake for 35–45 minutes or until topping is golden brown and rhubarb is tender. Serve warm or cold. *Serves 6–8*

• •

CARAMEL-APPLE BREAD PUDDING

Bread pudding is the ultimate comfort food. And this recipe, which combines creamy, smooth caramel with tart apples and tender bread, is the best!

The University of Minnesota is famous for its horticulture department. They have developed many varieties of apples over the years, including the Haralson, which is excellent for cooking, and Honeycrisp, introduced in 1991. If you have a chance, make a day trip to the Minnesota Landscape Arboretum, in Chanhassen, to visit the gorgeous gardens maintained by the university staff.

$1/2$ of a 14-ounce bag caramels, unwrapped

3 cups whole milk, divided

$2^{1}/2$ cups cubed raisin swirl bread

2 eggs

$1/4$ teaspoon salt

2 teaspoons vanilla

$1/4$ cup butter, melted

2 cups peeled, diced Haralson or Granny Smith apples

1 cup raisins

1 cup slightly crushed granola

Preheat oven to 325 degrees F. In microwave-safe large bowl, place caramels and $1/4$ cup of milk. Microwave on 50-percent power for 2 minutes, then remove and stir. Continue microwaving at 50-percent power for 1-minute intervals, stirring after each interval, until caramels are melted and mixture is smooth.

Slowly, using wire whisk, stir in remaining milk until smooth. Add bread to caramel mixture.

In small bowl, combine eggs, salt, vanilla, and melted butter and beat to combine. Add to caramel mixture along with apples and raisins and stir until combined.

Butter $1^{1}/2$-quart casserole. Pour caramel mixture into casserole; sprinkle top with granola. Place casserole in large roasting pan. Place in oven. Pour water into roasting pan so it comes up 1 inch on sides of casserole.

Bake for 65–75 minutes or until pudding is set and top begins to brown. Cool for about 20 minutes, then serve in bowls, topped with a commercial caramel sauce or ice cream. *Serves 8*

Blueberry Ice

This recipe is a forerunner of the tremendously popular granitas that are all the rage today. It's so easy to make and has the most wonderful color and flavor. Serve it with some toasted angel food cake for a nonfat dessert.

1 (16-ounce) can blueberry
  pie filling
1 (6-ounce) can frozen
  lemonade concentrate

1 cup cold water
1 tablespoon lemon juice
$1/3$ cup sugar
1 cup frozen loose-pack blueberries

In large bowl, place pie filling; beat until blueberries are mashed. Stir in remaining ingredients, stirring until sugar is dissolved.

Pour into 2-quart glass baking dish and freeze until slushy, about 1 hour. Stir thoroughly, then return to freezer and freeze until firm.

To serve, let stand at room temperature for 10–15 minutes until slightly softened, then scoop into serving bowls. Or you can run a fork over the solidly frozen mixture to create a granita-like texture, then spoon into serving bowls. *Serves 8–10*

• •

Strawberry Meringue Squares

Minnesotans love summer, with its heat, sunshine, blue lakes, and fresh produce. We relish the fresh fruits and vegetables our state produces and honor the best of the best at the Minnesota State Fair every August.

Strawberries have a short season, but when they're ripe, there's nothing better. Have you ever picked fresh strawberries from a pick-your-own farm? They are simply the essence of summer. Strawberries that you purchase in the supermarket taste nothing like berries right off the vine. Eat them out of hand and save some to use in this gorgeous recipe.

$1 1/2$ cups crushed vanilla
  wafer cookies
$1/4$ cup butter, melted
4 egg whites
$1/8$ teaspoon cream of tartar
$1/2$ cup sugar

1 teaspoon vanilla
2 cups sliced strawberries
3 tablespoons sugar
1 cup heavy whipping cream
3 tablespoons cocoa powder
3 tablespoons powdered sugar

Preheat oven to 350 degrees F. In medium bowl, combine cookie crumbs and melted butter. Press into the bottom of 8-inch square glass baking dish.

In large bowl, combine egg whites and cream of tartar; beat until soft peaks form. Gradually beat in $1/2$ cup sugar until stiff peaks form. Add vanilla and beat. Spoon and spread meringue over crumbs in pan. Bake for 14–18 minutes or until meringue is light golden brown. Let cool (meringue will settle when cool).

While meringue is cooling, combine strawberries with 3 tablespoons sugar in small bowl and gently mix. Refrigerate.

When ready to serve, combine cream with cocoa powder and powdered sugar in medium bowl. Beat until stiff peaks form. Spread cream mixture over meringue. Cut dessert into squares and top each square with a generous spoonful of the strawberry mixture. *Serves 9*

∙∙

PEACH PUDDING CAKE

Pudding cakes are an old-fashioned type of dessert made by baking together a cake batter and a flavored sauce. They're delicious served warm from the oven, topped with ice cream or Hard Sauce.

Make Hard Sauce by beating together $1/2$ cup softened butter with $1^{1}/2$ cups powdered sugar, 1 teaspoon vanilla, and 1–2 tablespoons cream or rum. The sauce will melt into the dessert as you eat it.

The cake mix for this recipe is made by Jiffy, a classic company that has never advertised. They've always depended on word-of-mouth advertising for their products, a rarity in today's marketplace.

$3/4$ cup sugar	1 teaspoon vanilla
2 teaspoons cornstarch	1 (9-ounce) package yellow cake mix
$3/4$ cup peach nectar	$3/4$ cup finely chopped dates
1 tablespoon lemon juice	$1/3$ cup milk
3 peaches, peeled and chopped	$3/4$ cup chopped pecans
1 tablespoon butter	

Preheat oven to 325 degrees F. In medium saucepan, combine sugar, cornstarch, peach nectar, and lemon juice and mix well. Add peaches. Cook over medium heat, stirring constantly, until mixture thickens and just comes to a boil. Remove from heat and stir in butter and vanilla. Pour into 8-inch square glass baking dish and set aside.

In medium bowl, combine cake mix, dates, milk, and pecans and mix until combined. Drop batter by tablespoons over the peach mixture. Bake for 45–55 minutes or until cake is set and golden brown. Let stand for 15–20 minutes, then serve. *Serves 6–8*

∙∙

UNBAKED FRUITCAKE

This fruitcake is a bit sweeter and lighter than most. It also takes less time to make since it isn't baked. You could use any type of dried or candied fruit in this recipe. This is one fruitcake you can confidently give to family and friends for Christmas; it won't be "regifted"!

1 (16-ounce) package honey graham crackers	2 cups whole pecans
1 (8-ounce) package raisins	1 cup whole Brazil nuts
1 (8-ounce) package whole dates, chopped	1 cup whole salted cashews
	2/3 cup milk
1 cup dried cranberries	1/4 cup butter
1 cup dried blueberries	1 (16-ounce) package marshmallows
1 1/2 cups mixed candied fruit	1 cup miniature marshmallows

Butter 6 miniature foil loaf pans (about 6 x 4 inches) and set aside. Finely crush graham crackers and combine in large bowl with raisins, dates, cranberries, blueberries, candied fruit, pecans, Brazil nuts, and cashews; mix with hands until blended.

In medium microwave-safe bowl, combine milk and butter; microwave on high until butter is melted and mixture is hot, 1–2 minutes. Stir in both kinds of marshmallows. Microwave on 50-percent power for 1–2 minutes or until marshmallows melt. Stir until smooth.

Stir marshmallow mixture into graham cracker mixture. Mix well with clean hands. Wet hands and pack mixture into prepared pans. Cover and chill for 24 hours.

To serve, remove fruitcake from pans and slice very thinly with a sharp knife. You can store the fruitcakes in refrigerator for about a week or freeze, well wrapped, for longer storage. *Yields 6 fruitcakes; each serves 10–12*

• •

CHOCOLATE-MINT PARFAITS

These delicious frozen parfaits will delight kids and adults alike! If you'd like, you could tint the marshmallow mint mixture with some red or green food coloring. This is another make-ahead dessert perfect for entertaining.

1 (7-ounce) jar marshmallow crème	1 1/2 quarts chocolate ice cream
1/4 teaspoon peppermint extract	24 chocolate-peppermint layered candies, chopped
1 tablespoon heavy whipping cream	

In small bowl, combine marshmallow crème, peppermint extract, and cream and mix well.

Soften the chocolate ice cream slightly. Fold in the chopped candies.

Layer marshmallow crème mixture with ice cream mixture in 8 parfait glasses, beginning and ending with ice cream mixture. Cover and freeze until frozen solid.

To serve, let stand in refrigerator for 15 minutes before serving to soften slightly. Garnish with more of the chocolate candies. *Serves 8*

••

STRAWBERRIES IN ORANGE CREAM

When strawberries are at their peak, serve with this delicious and simple orange sauce. The topping of pistachio nuts adds color and crunch to this excellent dessert.

3 cups strawberries	$1/2$ cup orange juice
2 tablespoons sugar	1 cup heavy whipping cream
$1/2$ cup sugar	1 tablespoon powdered sugar
2 teaspoons grated orange zest	$1/2$ cup chopped pistachios

Hull strawberries and cut in half lengthwise. Place in serving bowl, sprinkle with 2 tablespoons sugar, and refrigerate.

In small saucepan, combine $1/2$ cup sugar, orange zest, and orange juice. Bring to a boil, stirring frequently. Then reduce heat to low and let mixture simmer for 10 minutes to reduce syrup. Chill until cold.

In small bowl, combine cream and powdered sugar; beat until stiff peaks form. Fold orange syrup into cream.

Divide strawberries among 6 chilled sherbet dishes and top with orange cream. Sprinkle with pistachios. *Serves 6*

••

LEMON MILK SHERBET

You can make sherbets and ice cream without an ice cream maker. Just follow the instructions for freezing and beating the sherbet mixture carefully. This refreshing sherbet isn't like anything you can buy in the grocery store!

2 pasteurized egg whites	2 cups whole milk
$1/8$ teaspoon cream of tartar	1 teaspoon grated lemon zest
$1/4$ cup sugar	$2/3$ cup lemon juice
1 cup light corn syrup	

In large bowl, combine egg whites with cream of tartar and beat until soft peaks form. Gradually add sugar, a tablespoon at a time, beating well after each addition. Beat until stiff peaks form.

Gradually add light corn syrup, then add milk. Slowly stir in lemon zest and lemon juice.

Pour this mixture into freezer trays (ice-cube trays with the dividers removed or 9 x 5-inch loaf pans), making sure the mixture is only about an inch deep.

Cover and freezer until a layer 1-inch wide is frozen around the edges of the trays. Pour mixture into large bowl, scraping the sides of the trays, and beat with electric beater until smooth but not completely melted.

Return to trays, cover, and freeze until firm. *Yields about 4 cups*

This beautiful cake was part of the fiftieth-anniversary celebration of Joyce's first time on the air.

PEACH COBBLER

In the late summer and early fall, peaches are at their peak and are inexpensive. Buy a crate and eat peaches out of hand, fold them into chicken and salmon salads, and make lots of peach desserts.

Cobblers are made by pouring a simple cake batter over fresh fruit, then baking until the fruit juices bubble and the batter is puffed and golden brown. Serve with heavy whipping cream poured over each serving.

1/2 cup butter	2 teaspoons baking powder
2 cups peeled, sliced peaches	1/2 teaspoon salt
1/4 cup sugar	1/2 teaspoon nutmeg
1 cup flour	1 cup whole milk
1/2 cup sugar	1 teaspoon vanilla
1/2 cup brown sugar	

Preheat oven to 350 degrees F. Place butter in 1-quart casserole and place in oven for 5–8 minutes or until butter melts. Remove casserole from oven and arrange peaches in butter. Sprinkle with 1/4 cup sugar and set aside.

In medium bowl, combine flour, 1/2 cup sugar, brown sugar, baking powder, salt, and nutmeg and mix well. Add milk and vanilla and stir just until a batter forms.

Pour batter over peaches in casserole. Bake for 25–35 minutes or until cobbler is golden brown and peach juices are bubbling. Let cool for 15–20 minutes, then serve. *Serves 4–6*

• •

BANANA–GREEN GRAPE DESSERT

Bananas and green grapes are available all year round. They combine in this unusual and refreshing dessert that's perfect for a potluck dinner.

1 (10-ounce) box vanilla wafers	2 teaspoons vanilla
2 pasteurized egg whites	3 bananas
1/8 teaspoon cream of tartar	2 tablespoons lemon juice
3 tablespoons sugar	2 cups green grapes
2 pasteurized egg yolks	1 pint heavy whipping cream
1 1/4 cups powdered sugar	2 tablespoons powdered sugar
1/2 cup butter, softened	

Crush vanilla wafers. Place 2/3 in the bottom of a 13 x 9-inch glass baking dish and set aside.

In small bowl, combine egg whites with cream of tartar and beat until soft peaks form. Gradually add 3 tablespoons sugar, beating until stiff peaks form; set aside.

In large bowl, combine egg yolks with $1^1/4$ cups powdered sugar and beat until light yellow and thick. Beat in softened butter and vanilla. Fold egg whites into egg yolks mixture and spread over crumbs in baking dish.

Peel and slice bananas; sprinkle with lemon juice and toss to coat. Place a layer of banana slices over the egg mixture. Cut grapes in half and place, cut side down, on top of bananas.

Then whip the cream with 2 tablespoons powdered sugar and pile on top of grapes. Sprinkle with remaining crumbs.

Cover and chill for at least 8 hours before serving. Cut into squares to serve. *Serves 12*

CRANBERRY-PECAN DESSERT

This is a cross between a pie and a cake, perfect for a quick dessert during the holidays. Serve it warm from the oven with Hard Sauce (see Peach Pudding Cake, page 226) or butter pecan ice cream.

3 cups cranberries	$1/2$ cup sugar
$3/4$ cup sugar	$1/4$ cup brown sugar
$1/2$ cup chopped pecans	$3/4$ cup flour
2 eggs	$3/4$ cup butter, melted

Preheat oven to 325 degrees F. Grease a 10-inch pie plate with solid shortening. Combine cranberries, $3/4$ cup sugar, and pecans in the pie plate; mix well and spread evenly in the pie plate; set aside.

In medium bowl, beat the eggs until light and lemon colored. Gradually add sugar and brown sugar, beating constantly. Then beat in flour and butter until batter is smooth. Pour batter over cranberry mixture in pie plate, smoothing the top.

Bake for 35–45 minutes until crust is golden brown. Serve warm. *Serves 6*

APPLE MACAROON

Macaroons are crisp cookies filled with coconut or chopped almonds. The topping for this simple dessert resembles a macaroon when baked, providing the perfect contrast to tender, sweet-tart apples. This is a great treat to serve hungry kids when they come home from school.

6 Granny Smith apples	1/2 cup sugar
2 tablespoons lemon juice	3/4 cup flour
1/2 cup brown sugar	1/8 teaspoon salt
1/2 teaspoon cinnamon	1/3 cup butter
1/4 teaspoon nutmeg	1/2 cup chopped walnuts
1/8 teaspoon cardamom	1 cup coconut

Preheat oven to 350 degrees F. Peel and core apples and slice 1/8-inch thick; sprinkle with lemon juice as you work. In buttered 1 1/2-quart casserole, combine apples with brown sugar, cinnamon, nutmeg, and cardamom and toss; set aside.

In medium bowl, combine sugar, flour, and salt and mix well. Cut in butter until crumbs form, then stir in walnuts and coconut. Sprinkle over apples in casserole.

Bake for 35–45 minutes or until apples are tender and crust is browned. Let cool for 20 minutes, then serve. *Serves 6*

• •

FROZEN BUTTER MINT SQUARES

Butter mints are also known as after-dinner mints; they're the non-chocolate, rectangular, colored sugar mints that melt in your mouth. As they melt, you can taste the butter flavor. They're delicious in this old-fashioned recipe.

1 (13-ounce) can crushed pineapple, undrained
1 (3-ounce) package strawberry gelatin
1 (10-ounce) package miniature marshmallows
1 cup graham-cracker crumbs
1/3 cup butter, melted
1 cup heavy whipping cream
2 tablespoons powdered sugar
1 (4-ounce) package soft butter mints, crushed

In large bowl, combine pineapple with its juice, gelatin, and marshmallows; mix to combine. Cover bowl and chill in refrigerator overnight.

The next day, combine crumbs and butter in small bowl; mix to coat and press into 9-inch square pan.

In another small bowl, combine cream and powdered sugar; beat until stiff peaks form. Fold into pineapple mixture along with crushed mints.

Spoon mixture over crumbs, smooth the top, and freeze for at least 4 hours before serving. *Serves 9*

••

CANTALOUPE ICE CREAM

Well, this is a flavor of ice cream you'll never see in the grocery store! Apparently Ben & Jerry's have perfected their recipe for this flavor but can't make it in large batches. So you should definitely make your own at home.

1 cup diced cantaloupe	1/8 teaspoon cinnamon
1/2 cup light cream	Pinch salt
2 tablespoons honey	1/2 cup heavy whipping cream
1 teaspoon lemon juice	1 tablespoon powdered sugar
1/8 teaspoon nutmeg	

In blender or food processor, combine cantaloupe with light cream, honey, lemon juice, nutmeg, cinnamon, and salt. Blend or process until smooth.

Pour into shallow casserole dish and freeze until mixture is mushy. In small bowl, combine whipping cream with powdered sugar and beat until stiff peaks form.

Add cantaloupe mixture to cream and beat until smooth, then pour back into casserole and freeze until firm, stirring occasionally. *Serves 4*

HARVEST HOUSE CHEESECAKE

Harvest House cafeteria was an old-fashioned restaurant chain that was prevalent in shopping malls in the 1950s and 1960s. They were sometimes found in Woolworth stores (these names take me back!). This wonderful dessert is from that restaurant.

Make sure the evaporated milk is very well chilled. Refrigerate it for at least 24 hours, then freeze for 1 hour; then it will whip into soft peaks. Your family will love this old-fashioned dessert.

2 cups graham-cracker crumbs	1 (8-ounce) package cream
1/2 cup butter, melted	cheese, softened
1 tablespoon powdered sugar	1 1/4 cups sugar
1 (3-ounce) package lemon gelatin	1 teaspoon vanilla
1/2 cup boiling water	1 (13-ounce) can well-chilled
1/2 cup cold water	evaporated milk

In medium bowl, combine crumbs with butter and powdered sugar and mix well. Reserve 1/4 cup of this mixture. Press remaining in bottom and up sides of 9-inch baking pan.

In small bowl, combine gelatin with boiling water and stir until gelatin is completely dissolved. Add cold water and mix well; set aside.

In medium bowl, beat cream cheese until soft and fluffy. Gradually beat in sugar, then beat in vanilla.

In large bowl, whip cold evaporated milk until soft peaks form. Stir in gelatin mixture, then beat in cream cheese mixture just until combined. Do not overmix.

Pour into graham cracker shell and top with reserved crumbs. Cover and chill for at least 6 hours before serving. *Serves 6–8*

••

CHOCOLATE MOUSSE LOAF

Mousses are usually served in individual cups. This one is a bit stiffer, so it can be sliced and served. Top it with some whipped cream and a drizzle of chocolate sauce.

1 (0.25-ounce) package	3 pasteurized egg yolks
unflavored gelatin	1 teaspoon rum flavoring
2 cups milk, divided	3 pasteurized egg whites
3/4 cup sugar	1/4 teaspoon cream of tartar
3 (1-ounce) squares unsweetened	1 cup heavy whipping cream
chocolate, chopped	1 tablespoon powdered sugar

Grease 9 x 5-inch loaf pan with unsalted butter and set aside. In small bowl, combine gelatin with $1/2$ cup of milk and set aside.

In large saucepan, combine remaining $1^1/2$ cups milk, sugar, and chopped chocolate. Cook and stir over low heat until chocolate melts and mixture is smooth. Remove from heat and stir in softened gelatin mixture; stir until gelatin dissolves completely.

Beat in egg yolks and rum flavoring. Cover and chill until mixture sets.

Meanwhile, in small bowl, beat the egg whites with cream of tartar until stiff peaks form. In another small bowl, beat cream with powdered sugar until stiff peaks form.

Fold egg whites and cream into chocolate mixture. Pour into prepared loaf pan. Refrigerate until firm, at least 6 hours. Unmold onto serving plate, then slice and serve with whipped cream and shaved chocolate or chocolate sauce. *Serves 8*

• •

NECTARINE BREAD PUDDING

When nectarines are ripe and sweet in the late summer months, there's nothing better. Except this recipe! Serve this elegant dessert in stemmed goblets with some sour cream.

4 slices bread	$1/4$ teaspoon salt
2 tablespoons butter, softened	1 teaspoon vanilla
2 cups sliced nectarines	2 cups milk
3 eggs	3 tablespoons brown sugar
$1/3$ cup sugar	2 tablespoons butter, softened

Preheat oven to 350 degrees F. Butter $1^1/2$-quart shallow baking dish.

Spread bread with softened butter on both sides, cut bread into cubes, then place on cookie sheet. Toast bread in the oven, turning occasionally with a spatula, until golden brown, 10–15 minutes.

Place half of toasted bread cubes in the prepared baking dish. Top with half of the nectarine slices. Repeat layers.

In medium bowl, beat eggs with sugar, salt, and vanilla until smooth. In medium saucepan, heat milk over medium heat until steam rises and tiny bubbles form around the edges. Gradually add scalded milk to egg mixture, beating until combined. Pour mixture slowly into baking dish over nectarines and bread cubes.

Bake for 35–40 minutes or until custard is set. Remove pudding from oven and turn oven to broil.

Meanwhile, in small bowl, combine brown sugar with 2 tablespoons butter. Sprinkle on top of the pudding. Broil pudding for 2–4 minutes or until topping bubbles. Let cool for 1 hour, then serve pudding with Hard Sauce (see Peach Pudding Cake, page 226) or vanilla ice cream. *Serves 6*

Peach Graham Cracker Dessert

Fresh peaches are another great treat in late summer. Try finding some at the farmers' market and eat them any way you can: out of hand, sliced on top of ice cream, and in this fabulous dessert.

6 peaches	1/4 cup milk
1/2 cup sugar	1/4 teaspoon salt
1/2 teaspoon cinnamon	16 graham cracker squares
1/4 cup butter, softened	1 teaspoon baking powder
1/2 cup sugar	1 teaspoon vanilla
1 egg yolk	1 egg white

Preheat oven to 350 degrees F. Peel peaches and cut in half. Remove pit and place peaches, cut side up, in a shallow baking pan. Sprinkle with 1/2 cup sugar and 1/2 teaspoon cinnamon.

In medium bowl, combine butter with 1/2 cup sugar and beat until fluffy. Add egg yolk, milk, and salt and beat well.

Crush graham crackers into fine crumbs. Fold into egg yolk mixture along with baking powder and vanilla. Beat egg white until stiff and fold into graham cracker mixture.

Pour batter over peaches in baking pan. Bake for 20–30 minutes or until batter is puffed and light golden brown. Serve hot or cold, with vanilla ice cream or heavy whipping cream. *Serves 6*

• •

Strawberry-Pineapple Sherbet

Any ice cream or sherbet made at home is going to be special. This recipe, with the fresh fruit combined with a divinity-like base, is really delicious. Make some with freshly picked strawberries, and you'll dream about this dessert during the winter.

You must use a candy thermometer to make this dessert. Watch the syrup carefully; when it reaches 230 degrees, it will seem to just hover there, then it will suddenly shoot up to soft-ball stage. The egg whites don't need to be pasteurized in this recipe because the hot syrup brings them up to a safe temperature.

3 cups strawberries	1/2 teaspoon salt
2 tablespoons lemon juice	1 (8-ounce) can crushed
2/3 cup water	pineapple, drained
1 tablespoon light corn syrup	1/2 cup coconut
1 1/2 cups sugar	1/4 cup heavy whipping cream
2 egg whites	1 tablespoon powdered sugar

Remove hulls from strawberries, rinse, and cut into pieces. Puree in blender or food processor until smooth. Stir in lemon juice and set aside.

In medium saucepan, combine water, corn syrup, and sugar. Bring to a boil over high heat, stirring frequently, then cover pan to let steam wash down the sides of the pan. Remove cover, reduce heat, and simmer without stirring until syrup reaches the soft-ball stage, 236 degrees F.

When the sugar syrup reaches 230 degrees F, in a medium bowl, combine egg whites with salt. Beat until stiff peaks form.

When the syrup reaches soft-ball stage, slowly pour it over the egg whites, beating at high speed with mixer until the mixture resembles meringue. At low speed, blend in strawberry puree, drained pineapple, and coconut.

In a small bowl, combine cream with powdered sugar and beat until stiff peaks form. Fold into strawberry mixture.

Pour mixture into freezer container and freeze until the mixture is slushy. Empty into a large bowl and beat until fluffy and light, then return to freezer container and freeze until firm. *Serves 6*

••

SWEDISH APPLE PUDDING

The Upper Midwest was settled by Germans and Scandinavians, all of whom, it seems, were good cooks! This classic and very simple recipe is delicious for the holidays. Serve it warm from the oven with Hard Sauce (see Peach Pudding Cake, page 226).

40 graham cracker squares	3 cups applesauce, divided
$1/2$ cup butter	1 teaspoon cinnamon, divided
$1/3$ cup brown sugar	

Preheat oven to 350 degrees F. Crush graham crackers to make fine crumbs. Melt butter in large skillet over medium heat. Add the crumbs; cook and stir for 5 minutes to toast the crumbs until they absorb the butter. Remove from heat and stir in sugar until blended.

Spread one third of the crumbs into 9-inch square baking pan. Spoon $1^1/2$ cups of applesauce over the crumbs and sprinkle with half the cinnamon; top with $1/3$ of the crumbs. Repeat layers, ending with crumbs.

Bake for 40–50 minutes or until pudding is set. Serve warm, with Hard Sauce, whipped cream, or vanilla ice cream. *Serves 6–8*

••

HOUSEHOLD HINTS

I collected household hints for years, even though they were not included in the monthly recipe mailings. Sometimes these hints were read on the air. They range from recipe variations to a Christmas tree preservative to uses for dried herbs!

USES FOR ALUMINUM FOIL

• When you are baking cookies in quantity and have just one or two cookie sheets, place sheets of foil on the counter and drop cookies on them. When the first batch is done, remove the cookies to a wire rack to cool and slide a sheet of foil with cookie dough onto the sheet.

• If you have a pan with a wooden knob or handle and have to use it in the oven, cover with a double thickness of heavy-duty aluminum foil.

• Put a sheet of foil under the pie pan in the oven when baking a fruit pie.

• To loosen a cake from the pan, before you add the batter, put a strip of foil across the pan bottom, with one end extending up the side like a tab. Most cakes stick in the center, so all you have to do is pull the foil tab and the cake will come out easily.

• If you have lots of ice cream in the freezer, wrap containers completely in foil to protect the flavor.

• When a mirror is scratched, fit a piece of foil over the mark on the back of the mirror and cover with a coat of plain shellac. When the shellac is dry, the scratch will disappear.

• Put heavy-duty foil under the ironing-board cover. The heat from the iron will be reflected and ironing will go twice as fast.

• Before putting slipcovers on your furniture, put sheets of foil over the arms to keep soil from going through the covers into the upholstery.

··

Opening a Stubborn Jar

There are a few tools now available for opening jars. These are available at household supply stores, grocery stores, and hardware stores. But if you don't have one on hand, try these tricks.

• Turn the kitchen faucet to hot and run water over just the jar lid. This will help the metal expand, and the lid should twist right off. If it doesn't come off the first time, try rinsing it some more.

• You can also try tapping the container, upside down, gently on the kitchen counter. Sometimes this will break the seal, and the jar will open.

• Finally, put on a rubber glove and twist the lid. This can help you get a better grip. Try this after you've tried the other two steps.

··

Drying Gourds

If you grow gourds, they should stay on the vine until fully ripe. Do not pick until after the first frost.

When you bring the gourds home, wash in hot, soapy water and rinse in clear water that has a bit of bleach included. Place on several layers of newspaper in a warm, dry place for 1 week to let the shell harden. Turn the gourds every day.

Then wipe them again and dry thoroughly. Place in a warm, dry, dark place, turning occasionally, for about a month.

Rub down gourds with very fine steel wool; do not use sandpaper. You can apply a water wax and polish them to a shine. Or you can use a water varnish to heighten the natural color.

··

Formula for Preserving Christmas Trees

Make sure that pets and children do not have access to this mixture.

With a saw, remove the bottom inch of tree trunk. Crush the fibers at the cut with hammer blows. Stand the tree in a holder. Pour in this solution: 4 teaspoons bleach, 2 cups light corn syrup, and 1 gallon hot water along with $1/4$ cup horticultural iron (known as Green Garde), mixed well.

Homemade Finger Paint

Finger painting isn't as popular as it once was, but it's fun for everyone. Here's how to make your own finger paint.

In medium saucepan, combine $1/2$ cup cornstarch and $3/4$ cup water. In small bowl, combine 1 envelope unflavored gelatin and $1/4$ cup water. Add 2 cups hot water to cornstarch mixture and cook over medium heat, stirring with wire whisk, until it boils and turns clear. Remove from heat and add gelatin mixture. Add $1/2$ cup pure Ivory soap flakes and stir until dissolved.

Let the mixture cool completely, then divide into 5–6 portions and put into jars. Add food coloring to desired intensity.

To finger paint, dampen paper, then add some finger paint. Use your thumb and fingers to make patterns, and make details with fingertips. Use your masterpiece to wrap gifts or make place cards.

Uses for Denatured Alcohol

• After dusting mirrors, go over them with a soft cloth dampened with denatured alcohol.

• Wash a new paint brush in denatured alcohol before dipping it into a can of shellac. The shellac will be easier to apply and the brush easier to clean.

• Remove mildew from pages of books by rubbing the stains gently with a soft cloth dipped in the alcohol.

• Keep ivory piano keys white by polishing them once a week with a soft cloth dipped in the alcohol.

THINGS TO DO WITH MAYONNAISE

Blue Cheese Dip: In small bowl, combine $1/4$ pound blue cheese, 1 (3-ounce) package soft cream cheese, $1/2$ cup mayonnaise, 1 clove crushed garlic, and $1/4$ cup heavy whipping cream. Chill one hour, then serve with chips and crackers.

Sauce Verte: To $1^1/2$ cups mayonnaise, add $1/4$ cup well-drained frozen chopped spinach, $1/4$ cup chopped watercress, $1/4$ cup chopped parsley, $1/2$ teaspoon salt, $1/8$ teaspoon pepper, 1 tablespoon buttermilk. Serve with poached salmon or fish.

Green Velvet Soup: Prepare green-pea soup according to package directions. Add $1/4$ cup mayonnaise, 1 tablespoon lemon juice, $1/2$ teaspoon dried dill weed, and chill until serving time.

GLAZES FOR BAKED HAM

Ham should be glazed during the last half hour of baking. Score the fat and insert whole cloves at the intersections of the scored lines.

• Pour a jar of apricot glaze over the ham.

• Combine 1 cup orange marmalade, $1/2$ cup brown sugar, and 3 tablespoons of orange juice and use this as a glaze.

• Mix 1 cup red currant jelly with 1 tablespoon prepared mustard and $1/2$ teaspoon ground cloves.

• This glaze should be applied before the ham is baked: Sprinkle 1 teaspoon ground cloves on the ham. Sprinkle contents of 3-ounce package of raspberry gelatin over the ham and pour honey over this. Cover ham tightly and bake for $1^1/2$ hours at 350 degrees F, then open the foil and bake 20–30 minutes longer so the glaze browns.

Using Herbs

Basil: Herb has a clove-like flavor, good in tomato dishes. Add dried basil to any canned soup or add to butter and serve on fish.

Bay leaf: Pungent, slightly bitter flavor. One leaf is strong enough to flavor an average dish. Try putting a leaf in the cooking water when simmering vegetables.

Chervil: Mild parsley-like flavor. Good with fish and poultry; sprinkle a little over the meat before cooking.

Dill weed: Best known as a seasoning for pickles. Good for sweet vegetables like peas and green beans.

Marjoram: Aromatic, like oregano but sweeter. Good in stuffings, stews, and in scrambled eggs.

Mint: Good as a seasoning for roast lamb. Also delicious sprinkled in with peas or carrots as they cook. Adds a fresh flavor to pasta salads.

Oregano: Peppery and spicy, this herb pairs well with tomatoes. Also add it to seafood salads and garlic bread.

Rosemary: This herb has a sweet and piney scent. The dried leaves should be used in soups or stews and finely crushed or minced. Add to chicken, pork, and lamb dishes. Try minced fresh rosemary in baking powder biscuits.

Sage: Traditionally used in turkey stuffings, sage has a soft, woodsy flavor and aroma. Add a pinch to your meat loaf recipe or add to the water when cooking great Northern or lima beans.

Savory: Savory is aromatic with a piquant flavor. Add it to mixed green salads, green vegetables, and greens or lentils.

Tarragon: This herb has a licorice-like flavor that is mildly sweet. It's delicious with fish and chicken and adds a fresh flavor to salad dressings.

Thyme: Thyme is warm and pungent with a lemony undertone. Use it on fish, in soups and chowders, in tomato sauce, and in scrambled eggs.

ALL-PURPOSE HAMBURGER MIX

This mix can be used in many ways. Keep several batches in the freezer to make any of these recipes at a moment's notice.

Basic Mix: Fry 4 chopped onions, 2 cups chopped celery tops, and 4 cloves garlic in $1/4$ cup oil. Add 4 pounds hamburger and cook until lightly browned. Add 1 teaspoon salt, $1/2$ teaspoon pepper, and 2 12-ounce bottles ketchup. Simmer for 20 minutes, then freeze in 5 1-pint freezer containers.

You can let the mix sit in the refrigerator overnight to thaw or thaw it in the microwave oven. Each of the following recipes uses 1 pint.

Sloppy Joes: Heat the Basic Mix in a saucepan. Pour over split, toasted hamburger buns.

Chili con Carne: Heat Basic Mix with 1 15-ounce can drained red kidney beans and $1/2$ cup chili sauce; season to taste with chili powder.

Noodle Casserole: Heat Basic Mix in a skillet. Add 8 ounces cooked noodles and a 10-ounce package of cooked frozen mixed vegetables. Sprinkle $1/2$ cup shredded cheese over the top, cover, and heat until cheese melts, 3–4 minutes. Serve from skillet.

Spaghetti: Heat Basic Mix in a skillet. Add $1/2$ teaspoon dried Italian seasoning and 1 8-ounce can tomato sauce. Cook $1/2$ pound spaghetti pasta and stir into mix. Top with grated Parmesan cheese.

Tamale Pie: Thaw Basic Mix. In a 2-quart casserole, combine the mix, 1 (16-ounce) can creamed corn, 1 chopped green bell pepper, 1 tablespoon chili powder, 1 (14.5-ounce) can diced tomatoes, and $1/2$ cup olives. Stir $1/2$ cup cornmeal with 1 cup milk and stir into meat mixture to marble. Bake at 375 degrees F for 1 hour.

Rice Casserole: Heat Basic Mix in a skillet. Add 2 cups cooked rice, 1 cup frozen corn, and $1/2$ teaspoon dried thyme leaves. Simmer until flavors are blended and food is hot.

Pizza: In large bowl, combine 1 package of dry yeast with $3/4$ cup warm water. Add $2 1/2$ cups biscuit mix. Knead 20 times on a floured surface. Divide into 4 parts, roll each into a 10-inch circle. Place on baking sheets.

Combine 1 cup tomato sauce and 1 pint of the thawed Basic Mix; spread over the pizzas. Top each pizza with $1/2$ teaspoon oregano and slices of pepperoni. Top with shredded Mozzarella and Monterey Jack cheese. Bake at 425 degrees F for 15-25 minutes until crust is deep golden brown and cheese has melted and is brown. *Yields 4 pizzas*

EQUIVALENTS

This is a handy list! Use it when you need to know how much quantity is in fruits and other foods and when you run out of an ingredient.

Apples
1 cup sliced = 1 medium
1 pound = 3 medium

Bread crumbs
3 slices oven-dried bread = 1 cup dry bread crumbs
1 slice fresh bread = $3/4$ cup soft bread crumbs

Cheese
$1/4$ pound shredded = 1 cup

Dates
8-ounce package = $1^1/4$ cups chopped

Flour
1 pound = 4 cups

Gelatin
1 envelope unflavored = 1 tablespoon

Graham crackers
15 crackers = 1 cup fine crumbs

Lemon
1 medium = 3 tablespoons juice
1 medium = 1 tablespoon grated zest

Nuts
$4^1/2$ ounces = 1 cup chopped

Rice
1 cup uncooked white rice = 3 cups cooked
1 cup uncooked brown rice = $3^1/2$ cups cooked
1 cup uncooked wild rice = $3^1/2$ cups cooked

Sugar
1 pound granulated = $2^1/2$ cups
1 pound brown = $2^1/4$ cups
1 pound powdered = 4 cups

SUBSTITUTIONS

Lacking This	Substitute This
1 tsp. allspice	$1/2$ tsp. cinnamon + $1/8$ tsp. cloves
1 tsp. pumpkin pie spice	$1/2$ tsp. cinnamon + $1/4$ tsp. ginger + $1/8$ tsp. nutmeg + $1/8$ tsp. cloves
Chow mein noodles	Canned potato sticks
1 cup tomato juice	$1/2$ cup tomato sauce + $1/2$ cup water
$1/2$ cup tartar sauce	6 Tbsp. mayonnaise + 2 Tbsp. pickle relish
$1/2$ cup ketchup	$1/2$ cup tomato sauce + 2 Tbsp. sugar + 1 Tbsp. vinegar + $1/8$ tsp. cloves
$2/3$ cup honey	$1/3$ cup water + 1 cup sugar
$1^1/2$ cups light corn syrup	1 cup sugar + $1/2$ cup water
1 ounce baking chocolate	3 Tbsp. cocoa powder + 1 Tbsp. butter
1 cup buttermilk	1 cup milk + 1 Tbsp. vinegar
1 tsp. baking powder	1 tsp. cream of tartar + 1 tsp. baking soda
1 Tbsp. cornstarch	2 Tbsp. flour

COOKING SHORTCUTS USING CONVENIENCE FOODS

In the 1960s and 1970s, convenience foods started dominating the aisle in supermarkets and grocery stores. These are some easy recipes using those foods.

Italian Marinated Shrimp: Combine 2 cups cooked shrimp in a bowl with a cup of thinly sliced onions. Prepare a package of Italian salad dressing mix and pour over shrimp. Serve with cocktail picks as an appetizer.

Golden Buck: Combine 1 ($10^3/4$-ounce) can condensed cheese soup with $1/2$ cup beer and a dash of cayenne pepper. In a heavy saucepan, beat 2 egg yolks with 2 tablespoons heavy whipping cream and $1/2$ teaspoon Worcestershire sauce. Add cheese soup mixture and cook over medium heat until thick. To serve, spoon over toasted English muffins.

Soup aux Poisson: Combine 3 ($10^3/4$-ounce) cans condensed cream of tomato soup with $1^1/2$ soup cans milk. Add one 6-ounce can crab, one 8-ounce can minced clams, 1 9-ounce can chopped shrimp, and $1/4$ teaspoon garlic powder. Bring to a boil, stirring constantly. Serve with grated Parmesan cheese.

Sour Cream Peach Pie: Put a bakery peach pie in the oven to heat through, then carefully remove top crust. In small bowl, combine 1 cup sour cream, 1 pasteurized egg, 2 tablespoons sugar, 1 teaspoon vanilla, and a pinch of salt. Spoon onto hot filling. Sprinkle with crumbled macaroon cookies and dust with cinnamon.

Strawberry Tarts: Whip some heavy whipping cream with 1–2 tablespoons of powdered sugar and place in prepared graham cracker tartlets. Top with sliced strawberries. Melt $1/2$ cup currant jelly and pour over the berries. Chill before serving.

MONTHS TO SHOP FOR BARGAINS

January: Fur coats, Christmas items, winter clothes, towels, linens, and bedding. Air conditioners, baby furniture, bicycles, books, bridal gowns, carpeting, power tools, musical instruments.

February: Sleds and snowsuits for children, overcoats, next year's Valentines. Air conditioners, dishwashers, furniture, new houses, luggage, outdoor furniture, power tools, major appliances.

March: Television sets, stereo equipment, ski equipment. China, silverware, home improvement items, small appliances, television sets.

April: In after-Easter sales, good buys in women's and men's spring suits and coats, women's hats. Garden equipment and supplies, hi-fi equipment.

May: Garden tools, camping equipment, boats and boating supplies. Books, winter and spring clothing.

June: Winter and spring clothing for men, women, and children. Carpeting, sporting goods, white goods.

July: Final sales of spring clothing. Vacations in winter hot spots like the Caribbean, Florida, or Mexico. Furnaces, heating fuels.

August: Summer clothes for the family. New cars, costume jewelry, major appliances.

September: New cars: Dealers need to make room for new cars this month. Supermarkets often have buys on canned and processed foods to make room for the new packs. Books, television sets.

October: Summer camping merchandise, lawn and garden furniture. Bridal gowns, summer styles. Cabins, fishing equipment, television sets.

November: Look for a good buy in a new home, priced for sale before winter arrives. Used cars, fishing supplies.

December: After Christmas sales. Fruit cakes, candied fruit, Christmas cards, ornaments, and wrappings. Boats, new and used, new houses.

· ·

VITAMINS AND PRESCRIPTION DRUGS

• Vitamin tablets and liquid have expiration dates; follow them to the letter.

• Get rid of prescription drugs as soon as you recover from the ailment. Follow dosage instructions carefully.

• Store all drugs and medications in a cool, dark, dry place, away from sunlight and heat sources. Keep out of the reach of children.

• Some drugstore products will keep indefinitely: petroleum jelly, rubbing alcohol, mercurochrome, and boric acid.

· ·

THE CLASSIC RULE OF FOURTEEN

A famous Parisian designer published this classic Rule of Fourteen to help ladies in the 1950s and 1960s be sure they were not overdressed. No woman should wear a costume, daytime, or street outfit comprised of more than fourteen elements. Here are the counts for different items. When you dress, add them up, making sure that the total stays at fourteen or fewer.

POINTS	ITEM OF APPAREL
1	Solid color dress
2	Figured dress
1	Contrasting flowers
1	Belt attached to dress
1	Contrasting buttons
1	Stockings
1	Plain shoes, heel and toe in
2	Plain shoes, heel or toe out
1	Bows or buckles on shoes
1	Purse, all one color
2	Purse, contrasting trim
1	Hat
1	Each color on hat
1	Veiling on hat
1	Earrings
1	Bracelet on one arm
1	Necklace
1	Ornamental pin or brooch
1	Watch
1	Engagement and wedding rings
1	Additional rings (for each one)
1	Gloves, plain
2	Gloves, with fancy decoration
1	Wrap, jacket, or coat
5	Rhinestones, sequins, fringe, metallic cloth

FIRST-AID KIT

A well-stocked first-aid kit should include the following:

- Adhesive bandages
- Antiseptic
- Sterile gauze pads
- Absorbent compress dressings
- Surgical cotton
- Space blanket
- Breathing barrier
- Aspirin and pain relievers
- Rubbing alcohol

- Cotton swabs
- Adhesive tape
- Instant cold compress
- Antiseptic wipes
- Scissors
- Tweezers
- Nonlatex gloves
- First-aid instruction booklet

AWARENESS OF POISONOUS PLANTS

Here is a list of common poisonous plants. Keep in your pantry along with the number for your local poison control center.

Hyacinth, Narcissus, Daffodil: Bulbs may cause nausea and vomiting and can be fatal if ingested.

Oleander: Leaves and branches are extremely poisonous.

Poinsettia: Leaves may cause digestive upset; sap may cause skin irritation.

Dieffenbachia and Elephant Ear: All parts can cause intense burning and irritation of the mouth and tongue.

Caster bean: Seeds are fatal. One or two of the seeds can cause death in adults.

Mistletoe: Berries are fatal.

Larkspur: Young plants and seeds can cause digestive problems, may be fatal.

Monkshood: Fleshy roots cause digestive problems, may be fatal.

Lily of the Valley: Leaves and flowers cause irregular heartbeat and pulse.

Iris: Underground stems cause severe but not necessarily serious digestive problems.

Foxglove: Leaves are one of the sources of the heart drug digitalis. It can cause dangerous irregular heartbeat, may be fatal.

Bleeding heart: Foliage and roots may be poisonous in large amounts.

Joyce's fame with recipes was almost an accident. "Some grocery stores sent out a publicity release featuring that week's 'good buys.' I thought this might be useful information, so I put it on the air. It was an immediate success."

Rhubarb: Leaves are poisonous and can be fatal.

Wisteria: Seeds and pods can cause mild to severe digestive upset, especially in children.

Oaks: Acorns affect kidneys gradually, with symptoms appearing days or weeks later.

Buttercups: All parts have irritant juices that injure the digestive system.

Yew: Berries and foliage can be fatal when ingested. Death is sudden without symptoms. Foliage more toxic than berries.

Black locust: Bark, sprouts, foliage are poisonous. Children have suffered nausea and weakness after chewing bark and seeds.

NATURAL INSECTICIDES

- Chives and garlic planted near roses will protect them against aphids and black spots.

- Nasturtiums planted near beans protect against Mexican bean beetles. Plant near broccoli for protection against aphids and plant near melons, cucumbers, and squash to protect against cucumber beetles and squash bugs.

- Companion planting will also help protect against bugs and disease. Plant beans with strawberries, tomatoes with asparagus, savory with beans, and basil with tomatoes.

Joyce Lamont in the early days, and today. "When I look back on my career, it feels like I won a million dollars in the lottery!" she says.

INDEX